Virginia Hamilton

Twayne's United States Authors Series

Ruth MacDonald, Editor

Bay Path College

TUSAS 630

VIRGINIA HAMILTON.
Photo by Carlo Ontal. Used by permission.

Virginia Hamilton

Nina Mikkelsen

Twayne Publishers • New York
Maxwell Macmillan Canada • Toronto
Maxwell Macmillan International • New York Oxford Singapore Sydney

Virginia Hamilton
Nina Mikkelsen

Twayne Publishers   Maxwell Macmillan Canada, Inc.
Macmillan Publishing Company   1200 Eglinton Avenue East
866 Third Avenue   Suite 200
New York, New York 10022   Don Mills, Ontario M3C 3N1

Library of Congress Cataloging-in-Publication Data

Mikkelsen, Nina.
    Virginia Hamilton / Nina Mikkelsen.
        p. cm.— (Twayne's United States authors series; TUSAS 630)
    Includes bibliographical references and index.
    ISBN 0-8057-4010-4 (alk. paper)
    1. Hamilton, Virginia—Criticism and interpretation. 2. Children's literature,
American—History and criticism. 3. African-Americans in literature. I. Title.
II. Series.
PS3558.A444Z78 1994
813'.54—dc20   94-621
                                                                        CIP

10 9 8 7 6 5 4 3 2 1

Printed in the United States of America.

Contents

Preface   vii
Acknowledgments   ix
Chronology   xi

Chapter One
Childhood and Beyond   1

Chapter Two
In the Beginning: Realistic Fiction   10

Chapter Three
Fiction of Psychic Realism   41

Chapter Four
Fiction of Contemporary Realism for Young Adults   69

Chapter Five
For Younger Readers: Fiction of Historic and
    Hometown Interest   88

Chapter Six
Biographies and Folklore Collections: Liberation
    Literature   115

Chapter Seven
For All Ages: Historical Folk Fantasy   125

Chapter Eight
Virginia Hamilton as Writer   143

Notes and References   153
Selected Bibliography   161
Index   167

Preface

In the past 26 years, as she was publishing 30 books for children, Virginia Hamilton has received nearly every possible honor for her writing, the most recent being the Hans Christian Andersen Award, considered by many as the Nobel Prize of children's literature, for the entire body of her work.

A scholar of folklore and a writer who has produced a notable example of almost every genre for children—realistic fiction, fantasy, historical fiction, biography, legend, myth, folk tale, and picturebook—she has also produced many well-crafted essays focusing on her life and her work. And she often lectures for audiences at home and abroad in the fields of education, library science, and children's literature.

The breadth of her vision for children and the artistic depth of her books has not gone unnoticed by critics, reviewers, editors, and fellow writers. Her ability to create multifaceted characters, engaging plots, thought-provoking language patterns, and authentic and strikingly imaginative portraits of black experience, has won the respect of readers of all ages. And the plentiful paperback editions of her books reveal that this award-winning work is not simply collecting dust on library shelves. Hamilton has maintained a wide readership, while never lowering her writing standards merely to attain popularity. Her books have continued to be both subtle and obscure enough to be taught and written about, accessible enough to be read, read widely enough to be popular, but not so popular they are considered unworthy of serious study.

Thus this first book-length study of Virginia Hamilton recognizes a writer who has broadened the knowledge of readers about the African-American cultural experience specifically and deepened the understanding of readers about human strengths and conflicts generally. Above all her books have revealed a great deal about the human condition of childhood, and of adulthood as it frames and embraces childhood, and this study of her work is designed to extend our awareness of the special talents she brings to readers.

Chapter 1 presents a biographical portrait of Virginia Hamilton as a child growing up in a large, extended, rural, midwestern, African-American storytelling family, in which the nurturing of narrative produced both a wealth of material she could later draw on in story after story and a vibrant imagination to weave these materials through her fiction.

Chapters 2–7 examine the books by genre and, to some extent, by chronological order of their publication, beginning with realistic fiction, then proceeding to fiction of psychic realism, young adult fiction, realistic fiction for younger readers, biographies, folklore collections, and fantasy.

Chapter 8 describes the unique qualities of Virginia Hamilton that set her apart from many other contemporary children's writers: her narrative process, her personal knowledge of parallel cultures and her strong commitment to multicultural concerns, her narrative creativity and diversity, as well as her vision of children as survivors in the everyday struggle for personal and cultural diversity.

Because Hamilton is such a prolific and inventive storyteller and because she utilizes stories in so many ways in her books, I have focused on the various purposes of stories and storytelling in the books, especially the way she reveals characters sharing stories and thinking in terms of stories, in order to move the main story forward, slow it down, or stop the action completely at times, for a number of reasons.

Stories thread themselves so often through the main tapestry of these books that, it seems to me, if we examine them in terms of the many-storied final design, or the way stories work in these books, we begin to see more about Virginia Hamilton the person, the writer, the artist, and the wordkeeper of ethnic heritage. We also see why this way of writing (writing through storytelling) produces such richly textured, deeply layered fiction, or in terms of the thesis here, produces the secret of Hamilton's success.

The family and community stories that weave through Hamilton's life is the subject of the first chapter of this book. How she tells stories and how stories function in the context of the literature she produces, as well as the cultural "lessons" these stories hold for children and young adults, become the subject of the remainder of the book.

Acknowledgments

The dust jacket illustration in Chapter 2 by Symeon Shimin is from *Zeely*, by Virginia Hamilton. Copyright © 1967 by Macmillan Publishing Company. Reproduced by permission of the publisher.

The dust jacket illustration in Chapter 3 by Leo and Diane Dillon is taken from *Sweet Whispers, Brother Rush*, by Virginia Hamilton. Copyright © 1982 by the Putnam Publishing Group. Reproduced by permission of the publisher.

The dust jacket and frontispiece photographs of Virginia Hamilton are the work of Carlo Ontal, New York City.

Additional photographs have been contributed by Virginia Hamilton. I would like to thank the following people for their generous help with this book. Virginia Hamilton and Arnold Adoff for being so encouraging from the beginning; Arnold for setting the project in motion by organizing and scheduling the interview, and Virginia for contributing so much of her time and knowledge in letters, notes, conversations, and phone calls, for reading preliminary drafts of the manuscript and responding with additional information and generous remarks, and for providing photos and copies of unpublished materials. the Twayne editors: Ruth MacDonald for her insightful commentary and valuable suggestions for the manuscript, Barbara Sutton for her meticulous scrutiny of the final draft, and Mark Zadrozny for his clear directions and helpful advice in preparing the book for publication. And my family: my children, Vincent and Mark, for their responses to *The Magical Adventures of Pretty Pearl*, at ages 13 and 11; my son Mark for typing this manuscript with care and concern for the smallest detail; and my husband, Vin, for his constant interest and support and for converting me at last to the computer.

Chronology

1936   Virginia Esther Hamilton born 12 March in Yellow Springs, Ohio, the fifth child and third daughter of Kenneth James and Etta Belle Perry Hamilton.

1953–1956   Wins full scholarship to Antioch College, Yellow Springs, Ohio.

1956–1958   Studies at Ohio State University, majoring in literature.

1959   Studies fiction writing at the New School for Social Research.

1960   Marries Arnold Adoff, writer and teacher, in New York City.

1963   Daughter, Leigh, born, New York City.

1967   Son, Jaime, born, New York City. *Zeely* published, named ALA Notable Book, wins Nancy Block Award.

1968   *The House of Dies Drear* published, wins Edgar Allan Poe Award for Best Juvenile Mystery, named ALA Notable Book and *School Library Journal*'s "Best of the Best."

1969   *The Time-Ago Tales of Jahdu* published. Adoff family moves back to Yellow Springs, Ohio.

1971   *The Planet of Junior Brown* published, named John Newbery Honor Book and *School Library Journal* "Best of the Best," wins Lewis Carroll Shelf Award.

1972   *W. E .B. Du Bois* published.

1973   *Time-Ago Lost: More Tales of Jahdu* published.

1974   *M. C. Higgins the Great* published, wins John Newbery Medal, National Book Award, Lewis Carroll Shelf Award, *Boston Globe–Horn Book* Award, and Peace Prize of Germany; named *New York Times* Outstanding Children's Book of the Year, Hans Christian Andersen Honor Book, *School Library Journal*'s "Best of the Best," and ALA Notable Book. *Paul Robeson* published.

1976   *Arilla Sun Down* published, named ALA Notable Book.

1979   Hamilton is delegate to Second International Conference
            of Writers for Children and Youth, Moscow.

1980–1981   The Justice trilogy—*Justice and Her Brothers, Dustland*,
            and *The Gathering*—published, named ALA Notable
            Book.

1982   *Sweet Whispers, Brother Rush* published, wins Coretta
            Scott King Award, *Boston Globe–Horn Book* Award,
            IBBY Honor Book Citation, and American Book
            Award; named John Newbery Honor Book; nominat-
            ed for ALA Best Book for Young Adults, ALA
            Notable Book, *Booklist*'s Best of the 1980s, *Booklist*'s
            Editor's Choice, Library of Congress Best Book for
            Children, NCTE Teacher's Choice, and Notable Trade
            Book in the Field of Social Studies.

1983   *The Magical Adventures of Pretty Pearl* published, named
            ALA Best Book for Young Adults, ALA Notable Book,
            Coretta Scott King Honor Book, Notable Children's
            Trade Book in the Field of Language Arts, and
            Notable Children's Trade Book in the Field of Social
            Studies.*Willie Bea and the Time the Martians Landed*
            published, named ALA Notable Book.

1984   *A Little Love* published, named ALA Best Book for
            Young Adults, *Booklist*'s Editor's Choice, and *Horn Book*
            Fanfare Honor Book; wins Coretta Scott King Award.
            The Virginia Hamilton Lecture in Children's Literature
            is established at Kent State University.

1985   *The People Could Fly* published, wins Coretta Scott King
            Award and *School Library Journal* Best Book of the Year
            Award; named ALA Notable Book, *Booklist*'s Editor's
            Choice, *Horn Book* Fanfare Honor Book, NCTE Teacher's
            Choice, *New York Times* Best Illustrated Book, and
            Notable Children's Trade Book in Social Studies.*Junius
            over Far* published.

1987   *The Mystery of Drear House* and *A White Romance* pub-
            lished.

1988   *Anthony Burns: The Defeat and Triumph of a Fugitive Slave*
            published, wins *Boston Globe–Horn Book* Award and
            Jane Addams Award; named Coretta Scott King

Honor Book, ALA Best Book for Young Adults, ALA Notable Book, *Horn Book* Fanfare Honor Book, IRA Teacher's Choice, Notable Children's Trade Book in the Field of Social Studies, and *School Library Journal*'s Best Book of the Year. *In the Beginning* published, named American Bookseller's "Pick of the Lists," ALA Best Book for Young Adults, ALA Notable Book, *Horn Book* Fanfare Selection, *Learning Magazine*'s "Winners across the Curriculum," National Science Teachers Outstanding Science Trade Book for Children, Newbery Honor Book, Notable Children's Trade Book in the Field of Social Studies, *Parents Magazine*'s Best Book of the Year, *Time Magazine*'s One of the Twelve Best Books for Young Readers, 1988; wins Lewis Carroll Shelf Award.

1989   *The Bells of Christmas* published, named ALA Notable Book, *Booklist*'s Editor's Choice, and Coretta Scott King Honor Book. Hamilton is named distinguished visiting professor, Graduate School of Education, Ohio State University.

1990   Receives honorary D.Litt., Bank Street College. *Cousins* published, named ALA Notable Book, *Booklist*'s Editor's Choice, New York Public Library's 100 Titles for Reading and Sharing, and Notable Children's Trade Book in the Field of Social Studies. *The Dark Way* published.

1991   Hamilton receives the Catholic Literary Association's Regina Medal. *The All Jahdu Storybook* published.

1992   Hamilton wins Hans Christian Andersen Award for Writing, given biennially by the International Board on Books for Young People, and lectures at the Royal Biblioteche, Copenhagen. *Drylongso* published.

1993   Hamilton delivers May Hill Arbuthnot Honor Lecture, Richmond, Virginia. *Many Thousand Gone* published, selected for Book-of-the-Month Club. *Plain City* published. Hamilton speaks at Pacific Rim Conference, Kyoto, Japan.

1994   Receives honorary degree, Doctor of Humane Letters, Ohio State University.

Grandpa Levi Perry and Grandma Rhetta Perry.

Parents Kenneth and Etta Belle in 1958.

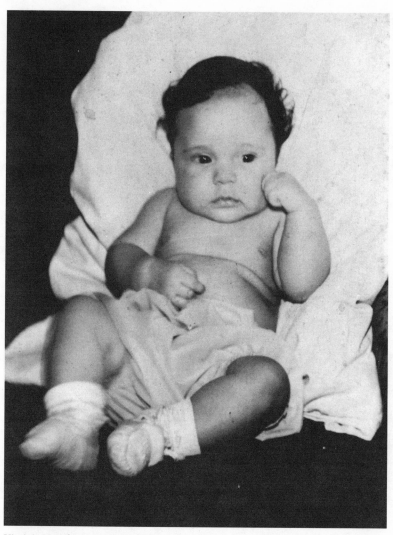

Virginia Hamilton at six months.

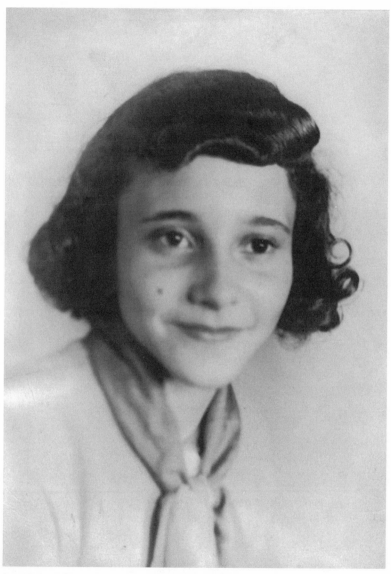

Age 12, in 1948.

Virginia (*center*) with sisters Barbara (*left*) and Nina on the porch of their Yellow Springs home.

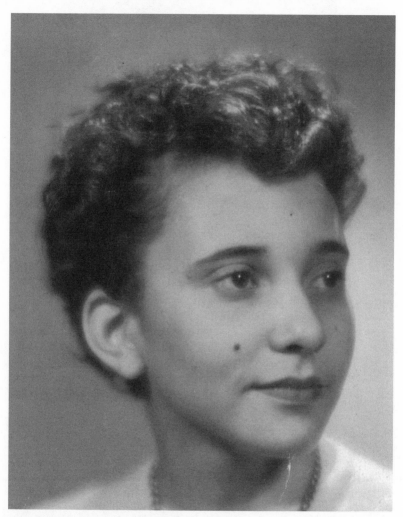

High school graduation, age 18.

Hamilton and her future husband, Arnold Adoff, 1958.

With daughter Leigh, 1963.

Virginia, Jaime (age two), Leigh (age six), and Arnold in Yellow Springs, ca. 1969–70.

Virginia and Arnold at Culebra Island, Puerto Rico, ca. 1985.

Children Jaime and Leigh, December 1991.

At a book signing in 1989.

Chapter One
Childhood and Beyond

It is surely no secret to readers of Virginia Hamilton that her writing talent rises on the foundation of family storytelling. As Hamilton tells it, "My father was a storyteller. He wrote poetry too. And he also ran a newspaper with another man before it folded. He was a musician, a classical mandolinist. And if you think of music and composition as a kind of storytelling too, I think that traditionally that kind of composing or that creativity was in the family. Plus the fact that storytelling was a very vital part of my family."[1]

Many writers come from storytelling families, yet they do not turn out to be Virginia Hamilton, of course. But Hamilton's family was not just any storytelling family. It was an American family with deep roots in the African-American storytelling tradition. Hamilton continues,

> My mother's family and the whole black community, in a sense, told stories; that was the way of relating, whether it was about other people, or part vicious or not. Most of it was gentle storytelling within the family. But I can remember there were itinerant storytellers coming around to the churches to do the Creation and there was one gentleman who did all the parts and we would be mesmerized for the three hours it took him to do that. It was just incredible. We'd never seen anything like it. And of course there was the minister and his stories of the Bible. It's a very traditional kind of thing in that era of black families.

Of course many writers come from African-American families yet still do not use storytelling in their work to the extent and in the highly inventive ways Hamilton does. Hamilton's family was not just any African-American family, however. Hers was also a midwestern family, and the special storytelling "personality" of this particular family seems to have arisen from location, the place in America where the Perry and the Adams families had settled and thrived and where Hamilton grew up calling home. "I grew up in Southern Ohio, in Yellow Springs," says Hamilton. "Black people there are black and Indian, black and other things; and the influences I grew up with were farm, populace, black church, radical, FDR New Deal; all so general so many times, yet so specifically clannish Perry clan: eccentric, very different, very standoffish, very proud. They didn't want to be like anybody."

Hamilton is a storyteller, she declares, because of the informal way she learned from her mother and her relatives talking to pass the time, to transmit information, to entertain, to picture family members as characters of stories, or to sort them out through stories, in this rural, farming locale: "The Perrys are interesting talkers. They began as farmers who had been fugitives from injustice. Acquiring land and homes, place and time, was to them the final payment in the cause of freedom. After long days, a long history in the fields, they talked their way into new states of mind. They could appreciate a good story in the companionship of one another, not only as entertainment but as a way to mark their progress. Stories, talking, grew and changed into a kind of folk history of timely incidents."[2]

When "true memory might lapse," Hamilton adds, "creativity" would "come into play. It was the same creativity and versatility that had helped the first African survive on the American continent" ("ASR," 637). This condition—an intriguing "gray" area bridging fact and fiction—she describes as "rememory," an "exquisitely-textured recollection, real or imagined, which is otherwise indescribable" ("ASR," 634). Anything from the "astonishing lies" of a storytelling uncle to her mother's story of the day an uncle was killed and ivy fell from the neighbor's house can become a "rememory" ("ASR," 637), a pivotal psychic center from which so many of her stories come spinning centrifugally forward.

For Hamilton, "rememory" occurs when memory of one's own life or of someone else's life heard about through stories is revised (memory is fitted through the lens of imagination) or when new knowledge is combined with existing knowledge, dreams, beliefs, or superstitions. "I came from a family of daydreamers," she says. "No one interfered with anyone else's daydreams. . . . We were always permitted our dreams."[3]

Hamilton's father, she says, was the one with the "Knowledge"[4] in her home. A man some years older than her mother when they married, he brought extensive experience of the world, as well as wide and deep knowledge of the family's ethnic heritage. (And he was very likely the inspiration for Willie Bea's father in *Willie Bea and the Time the Martians Landed*, a man who also married into an Ohio farming family with little of the farming knowledge that his wife's relatives had.)

Kenneth Hamilton was a business school graduate who could only obtain work as a janitor at the turn of the century in Iowa—a humiliating experience for a bright, young man with dreams. He threw the mop and bucket that was handed him "the length of the establishment," Hamilton writes, "never to return. Soon after, he left his home as well, to become a restless wanderer ranging the length and breadth of the North American continent, seeking but never quite finding that for which he searched" (*PR*, xv).

Hamilton's father went on to become a porter on the Canadian Pacific Railroad at one point and a newspaperman at another. Later he would marry her mother, Etta Belle Perry, when she traveled to Canada to visit her sister, Bessie, the wife of one of Kenneth's friends. A very adventuresome woman, Etta Belle had actually jumped out a window at her home in Yellow Springs and run away some years before this because, in Virginia's words, "her father was very strict and she could date only ministers, AME [African Methodist Episcopal] at that, not Baptists. Methodists! She didn't like it, so she went to Detroit and worked and finally ended up in Canada where she met my father at a ball. He was a great ballroom dancer, an extraordinary dancer. He came dancing in to 'Bye, Bye, Blackbird.' She saw him and said that was the man for her." Kenneth and Etta Belle moved back to Ohio when their first child, Nina, was born. "She [Etta Belle] wanted to go home," says Virginia. "And he wanted to go to a big city like Cleveland. But it was the depression, and he never got away."

Kenneth used his experiences as a waiter and porter to become a food service manager for Antioch College in Yellow Springs, eventually earning faculty status and the friendship and respect of thousands of students, faculty members, and alumni for his abilities as a teacher and manager. In several novels Virginia has drawn on the knowledge she obtained about food service jobs, when she worked for her father in the college dining hall, alongside her brother.

Kenneth Hamilton subscribed to the *New Yorker* and the NAACP magazine, *The Crisis*, edited by W. E. B. Du Bois, the prominent educator who had married a cousin of Kenneth's. Virginia remembers as a child seeing "many coverless, musty periodicals stacked about"[5] in her home and discovering a picture of the Watutsi people in one of her father's magazines. From this picture her interest in Africa and ultimately her first book, *Zeely*, emerged. She also remembers her father's collection of Conan Doyle's books and how from them she learned how the best mysteries were plotted. Without them, she says, she probably never would have written *The House of Dies Drear* ("FN," 5).

A child of older parents, Virginia was the youngest of five children (three girls and two boys), with a mother in her forties and a father in his fifties at her birth, and she profited by their maturity and attention. "I was very spoiled when I was young," she recalls, "the apple of my father's eye, and I never had to do anything except play with my cousins [who were more her own age than her older siblings], and yet a lot was expected of me. The two things kind of worked hand in hand. I was a very good student all through school."

Of course there are many youngest children who are well-schooled by doting, adventuresome, older parents, even parents filled with the gift of cultural storytelling, and they still do not become the Virginia Hamiltons of this world. We must look deeper to discover the secret of this writer's success. Hamilton has told the story of Grandpa Levi Perry, who at 77 often took her walking with him, and how his hand had been burned shut from a fire in the mill where he worked:

> And from the time that his life and mine coincided, his hand was a fist with burn scars hidden in the tightly shut palm. I would lace my fingers over his closed fist, and he would lift me up and up, swing me around and around—to my enormous delight. Ever after, the raised black fist became for me both myth and history, and they were mine. Grandpaw Perry was John Henry and High John de Conquer. He was power—the fugitive, the self-made, the closed fist in which I knew there was kept magic. Oh, but the rememory! ("ASR," 637–38)

Virginia's grandfather arrived as a fugitive slave in Jamestown, Ohio, around 1857 at the age of five. He had traveled on the Underground Railroad from the state of Virginia (hence the author's first name) with his mother, who seems to have disappeared back into the Underground movement at that point.[6] Says Hamilton, "To this day she remains nameless. . . . She—well, her name might have been Sarah, as it was in that fiction, *M. C. Higgins the Great*."[7]

Levi Perry married into the Adams clan of Yellow Springs, another family of freed slaves, but of Indian heritage as well (Etta Belle's mother, Rhetta, was part Cherokee). And the names of Perry, Levi, Adams, Belle, and Rhetta/Lorhetta are woven through Hamilton's books. Levi was crucially important for linking Africa and America together in the chain of stories his daughter Etta Belle would hear and pass down to Virginia and her brothers and sisters.

"The first story," says Virginia, "is of course the story of Grandpa Perry running from slavery, and the fact that he said every year he sat those ten children down and said, 'Listen children, I want to tell you this story of when I ran away from slavery, so slavery will never happen to you.' And this was the original story as far as I'm concerned. That was the beginning of the family culture and after that, storytelling must have been in that family from early on, because everyone told stories."

Of course many people with an important cultural reason to write still do not devote their lives to such a worthy cause, nor do they ultimately choose to focus their attention on the world of childhood and their own childhood memories in their writing, as Virginia Hamilton has done. Even among those who do, there are few who do so with the striking abilities of this writer. How did it all begin for her, this life of a children's book writer? And what happened—beyond the beginning—to produce the writer she has become today—ususual, prolific, mysterious, and wise?

Hamilton does not remember telling stories of her own as a child, but she does remember writing from a very early age and winning prizes in school for reading the most books. "I'm running home," she writes in a lilting passage from an essay about her childhood, the seed of a children's book of its own. "I am quite young, I am happy, for I've won a prize for having read the most books during the year. The prize is a good-sized, shiny book with the colorful cover parading three yellow ducks. It was my first award and more glorious for being what it was—a new book, which was never easy to come by in my childhood. Ever after, I have been an ardent reader, not only of books but of most anything—old match covers, catalogs, whatever falls into my hands" (*PR*, x).

She has theorized that she writes children's books for the "sheer joy" of evoking memories of her childhood, which was "particularly fine," and she does not remember, as a child, ever wanting to be anything else but a child (*PR*, xi). In the summer, childhood on her family's land in Yellow Springs meant being on her own all day long to entertain herself by roaming the countryside like M. C. in *M. C. Higgins the Great*. Her father's farm and the neighboring land of her mother's family resembled more, however, the farmland of Uncle Ross in *Zeely*, since her family raised hogs just as Zeely's father did.

In the winter, childhood meant school, and this was not an altogether unpleasant experience either. She remembers teachers who were strict but fair and who allowed her to write creatively, praised her for doing so, and who may also be credited for contributing to her later success: "They also indulged me as I was such a good student, and when you're encouraged to do something, you continue to do it."

School in the 1940s, however, had its bleaker moments for the African-American child. As Hamilton wrote in 1968, a year after the publication of *Zeely*,

> We had no Negro teachers. And the closest we came to any understanding of our history through schooling was a muddle of capitalized words: Missouri Compromise; Underground Railroad; Harriet Beecher Stowe; Uncle Tom; Topsy—I shall never forget Topsy; and Liza on the ice. And we sang "Ole Black Joe" (in dialect) quite a lot. My teachers had a strong regard for poor Black Joe, I assume, for we sang the song most every morning. We Negro children were made uncomfortable by the song. We would fidget through it, not even looking out of the window or at the songbook or at one another. Each day, we grew smaller within ourselves. It was as though our teacher had a compunction to remind us we were different, that we were minor folk not as good as others. ("FN," 3)

Yet Hamilton was also very inner directed, seldom worrying about what others were doing, simply wishing to be the best. "If our white classmates were proper, then we were more so," Hamilton had written. "If they were bright, we felt we had to be smarter, and often we were smarter and we were proud of ourselves for showing that we were as good as they were. But oh, how terrible for children to always have to think this way. What an awful toll it took of our spontaneity" ("FN," 5).

Today Hamilton remembers being a leader. "I always wanted to be better than anyone else, but it was really because I wanted to lead. I wanted to shine. I don't know why that happens, maybe because I was left alone to do it. Nobody ever said, 'You can't do this!' I remember one time telling my older sister that I was going to be a famous writer someday; and of all the responses she could have given, she said, 'Oh goody, then I'll be famous too!'"

Writing in a "famous" sense would eventually materialize for Virginia, after much self-discipline and creative focus. Formal instruction began when she enrolled as a writing major at Antioch College in her hometown. Later she attended Ohio State University in nearby Columbus as a literature major. In high school she had written a play that her classmates performed for a senior assembly.[8] In college she wrote short stories, and eventually the college life of writing flowed out into "real" writing in New York. "I left Yellow Springs," Hamilton recalls, "to seek my fortune in the big city. College [Antioch] and crisscrossing the country on co-op jobs led me naturally back to New York. Moreover, Yellow

Springs, I knew, was a dead end for me. And boring. No men. Just cousins!"

Her co-op work also led to moonlighting jobs related to her musical talents. She sang in nightclubs in Brooklyn and at Manhattan's St. Nicholas Ballroom; she was also a guitarist for a dance group. And these experiences would later enable her to create two musical mothers for her fiction, Banina in *M. C. Higgins the Great* and Bluezy Sims, Buhlaire's mother in *Plain City*, a roadhouse singer.

Writing continued to be a driving force for her once she moved to the East. She worked part time at an engineering firm as a cost accountant, something she taught herself to do. And the other part of the day she stayed home and wrote, a rather "solitary existence," she explains. "I often went for days without talking to anyone. . . . I hid myself within columns of figures and made no friends."[9] Eventually she decided it was time to "step into the flow of the city," moving from the Village uptown, "closer to my people and still near the Hudson River. I could spend days writing and get nowhere. But if I went down to the river to sit awhile, I could come back home feeling as though I had partaken of a healing potion. . . . My writing grew better as I grew older inside. I came to understand that the river's flow was the flow of freedom inside us all ("PA," 238).

In the fall of 1958 Hamilton met her future husband, the teacher and writer Arnold Adoff. As he remembers it, "I was a young poet and Virginia was working on her first novel. We were both interested in jazz; I was working as a manager for a jazz musician, Charles Mingus. We met at a Christmas party for him."[10] Both Arnold and Virginia were attending the New School for Social Research where many working artists and writers taught periodically. Arnold was studying poetry; Virginia studied fiction writing with Hiram Haydn, a founder of Atheneum when he was executive editor at Random House. She and Arnold would go to the New School together, Virginia remembers, Arnold having lent her the money for the course with Haydn. "Hmm," she adds. "I don't remember ever paying him back."

She had not published any novels at this time. But a classmate at the New School convinced her that one of her college short stories might make a good children's book. She had never really considered what a children's book was, nor had she ever really thought of becoming a writer specifically for children, but with the help of an editor, she was soon on her way. "I started out with Dick Jackson," she remembers. "He was my first editor on *Zeely*. And we were living in the South of France, and Dick wrote me marvelous letters that would say, 'between this line and that line is a chapter. Think about it, Virginia.' And I would sit down and think about it. And I learned how to write from him."

After living for 10 years in New York, and for a time in Europe, as she worked on her first books and settled into marriage and motherhood, Virginia returned with her husband and two children to Yellow Springs to live, having never come to terms, she says, with the "noise and the fact that it [New York] wasn't green."[11] It was years before she realized that the Hudson was not the river that had really nourished her; it was instead the Ohio ("PA," 239). "My commitment to family in my books," says Hamilton, "has its foundation in my background and the intimate and shared places of the home town and the home town's parade of life. Home town would seem to be the emotional landscape for my own spiritual growth, even when the home town folks pick themselves up and move to somewhere else."[12]

The Adoffs purchased two acres of the Hamilton family land to build their home in Yellow Springs at this time—a house that turned out to be "massive, made of redwood and glass, and has no windows, only sliding glass doors and clerestory light."[13] ("I live in a glass house," quips Virginia.) And they have all lived happily ever after there, Leigh and Jaime growing up on the land that gave Virginia her heritage and so many of her stories, and Virginia and Arnold producing the books that have not only supported the family but have resulted in a "Newbery" swimming pool too.

For Virginia, life in Ohio has been interrupted occasionally over the years with trips back to New York to consult with editors, to visit friends and family, and now to visit the children. (Taking up where their mother left off with her singing, Leigh and Jaime have returned to New York to pursue musical careers.) And recently she accepted a distinguished visiting professorship, with Arnold, at Queens College, in the teaching of writing, followed by another stint at teaching, this time at Ohio State University. There have also been frequent trips to vacation homes in Puerto Rico and Florida. "Arnold and I and our children seem to be wanderers," says Virginia. "Restless, always seeking something, we live in several places. But the Ohio land is our base, that rich dark countryside . . . a lush and green place, country and safe. It is where I go when I need quiet and rest, and where I write most" ("PS," 675).

In addition to providing a sanctuary for writing, returning to Yellow Springs and making her adult life there has kept her close to the extended family and community "family" that feeds her creative energy, her sense of history, and her deeply felt convictions about preserving the earth's resources. Living in the Ohio village of her ancestors, on the farm land of her family home, so close to nature—on what she calls a "sweep of hopescape" ("HBJ")—she has often found herself creating characters who live in more than one dimension of time.[14] And this ability or talent for storying human lives, in the context of home, heritage, and personal and ancestral rememories, is what sets her apart from many writers and provides a thematic resonance clearly her own.

Living in Yellow Springs also provided her a way to live near and care for an aging parent, her mother, Etta Belle, who died in 1990 at the age of 97. As the youngest child, Virginia became the one to assume this care. And as the child with the writer's listening ear, she was the one to hear and record more of her mother's remembered stories during her mother's last years—stories she in turn would record about Levi Perry, the fugitive slave, for her folk tale collection, *The People Could Fly*. She was also the one to remember her mother's nursing home experiences and to translate them, in "rememory," into her novel *Cousins*. "I think a lot of my books resolve things in my life, like my mother's passing and the guilt of having to put her in a nursing home—and all kinds of things," Hamilton says.

Cousins is a story about coming to terms with death and life—whether one is 11, like Cammy, the child protagonist, or 94, like Gram Tut. Written by the youngest child in a large, midwestern, African-American family founded by a fugitive slave who told the first story and left it all to his children—and their children—to keep the stories going, this novel, her seventeenth and in many ways her finest, shows that Virginia Hamilton has more than fulfilled the promise of her earliest years—a time we will begin examining in some detail now.

Chapter Two

In the Beginning: Realistic Fiction

Virginia Hamilton burst onto the literary scene in 1967 with a book entitled *Zeely*. Two equally distinctive novels followed it—*The Planet of Junior Brown*, in 1971, and *M. C. Higgins the Great*, in 1974. A look at these books today tells us a great deal about then and now in the children's book world, as well as about Hamilton's unique talent. At a time when most books about black children were written by white authors about issues of racial prejudice and school desegregation, or about interracial friendship in which color was not a relevant factor in the story (and the black child's ethnic experiences could therefore be sidestepped), Hamilton tried something new.

Following in the footsteps of Arna Bontemps and his spirited and authentic black child characters of the 1930s,[1] Hamilton in the late 1960s and early 1970s told stories of black children discovering, from one another and from black adults, the beauty and mystery of their African-American heritage and a great deal about pride, courage, and self-esteem. Whereas white writers at this time were driven to show equality in terms of similarity, Hamilton dared to say that children could be equal and still be different (Mikkelsen, 20).

Zeely

Zeely is now a quarter of a century old and still going strong, and it is difficult to underestimate—or to overstate—the importance it had in its own day for encouraging other black writers to speak for the black child. A decade after the publication of the book, Hamilton had been joined on the children's book stage by such talented black authors as John Steptoe, June Jordan, Lucille Clifton, Tom and Muriel Feelings, Eloise Greenfield, Sharon Bell Mathis, and Mildred Taylor.

The importance of *Zeely* today, however, rests not only with its innovative thrust at the time of publication but with its ability to take on, in successive decades, the "tune" of other times. The cheerful, colorful cover picture by Jerry Pinkney for the first Aladdin paperback edition of 1986,[2] compared with the original solemn, sepia illustrations by Symeon Shimin for the original hardcover edition,[3] reveals how the book has adapted to a different era, or how a different era is calling forth a new and equally important meaning for the story—the true mark of a classic.

Pinkney produces a three-dimensional blending of various strands of black heritage in America. In the background is a small snapshot of an American farmhouse, superimposed on which is an old, frayed magazine photo of a young African woman. Then, as if stepping out of both pictures, two children stand in the foreground, arms entwined, suitcase in hand, ready to begin their travels through the story to learn more about their African-American heritage and how they as individuals are developing within it.

Shimin shows two children staring fixedly—almost inwardly, or as if they are standing before a museum portrait—at a cultural ancestor, a tall black woman striding quickly by in a long, swirling African dress. It is fortunate that Shimin's illustrations have been retained in the paperback edition, evoking the era in which the book was created and envisioning more clearly the historical associations that emerge as the story unfolds.

At its core *Zeely* is a female initiation story, but the protagonist, Elizabeth (or Geeder, as she calls herself for a great portion of the book), is also an African-American child; therefore her story becomes an initiation story of the black female experience. In the late 1960s, however, when the book was first published, a nation in the throes of a civil rights movement and a black population concerned with building a stronger sense of self-esteem in its people felt the need for a "black is beautiful" statement. And Hamilton turned this theme into a rich tapestry of individual—and ethnic—experience for readers in any era.

At her uncle's farm in the country for the summer, 11-year-old Elizabeth has been left in charge of her younger brother, John. Relishing her freedom, she sets out with great imaginative zeal to make this time special. It is not long before beautiful and stately Zeely Tayber, the daughter of a hog farmer living nearby, inspires Geeder to imagine she has seen a Watutsi queen. Later Zeely must help Elizabeth see things in more realistic terms, and not surprisingly, she does it through stories that Elizabeth hears, then retells and reshapes as she moves through her summer experience, growing into a young adult, African-American female.

Dust jacket illustration by Symeon Shimin. From Zelly, by Virginia Hamilton (New York: Macmillan, 1967.) Copyright © 1967 by Macmillan Publishing Company. Reproduced by permission of the publisher.

Inner and Outer Storytelling

Story, then, is the vehicle Hamilton uses to transport the heroine in her cross-cultural journey through this stage of the growth process. As she has said, stories taught her about her family history and traditions, as well as what the world was like—what her family's values were and what her social order was (how people lived and what was expected of them). "Our lives are stories," says Hamilton. "That's how we relate to one another."

Since Hamilton first began writing books, stories have been a way of action for her characters to define their worlds, just as, conversely, their actions have become a way of storying their lives. In *Zeely* the stories Elizabeth hears—and tells—begin to teach her more about her family history, as well as what the world is like—what her own values will be and what she will ultimately expect of herself and others.

Within the main thread of story (Elizabeth's trip to the farm with her brother, their encounter with Zeely, and the friendship she forms with Zeely) are approximately 16 internal stories, or narrative embeddings in which characters tell stories to one another or to themselves as dreams, daydreams, and fantasized or remembered stream-of-consciousness musings. Such fictional stories-within-the-story become a close, or "continued," replication of life itself, or a quality that fiction shares with life. As Barbara Hardy has asserted, "We dream in narrative, daydream in narrative, remember, anticipate, hope, despair, believe, doubt, plan, revise, criticize, construct, gossip, learn, hate, and love by narrative. In order really to live, we make up stories about ourselves and others, about the personal as well as the social past and future. . . . [W]e come to know each other by telling, untelling, believing, and disbelieving stories about each other's pasts, futures, and identities. . . . We tell stories in order to escape from the stubbornness of identity."[4]

One characteristic of most novels, adds Hardy, "is the sheer number of narratives they contain" (Hardy, 16). And the importance of such embedded narratives for readers, especially critical readers, is that the author can utilize internal narrative as artistic scaffolding for the outer story. Some writers, as Hardy shows, are more clearly in control of this relationship between internal storying (stories the characters tell among—or within—themselves) and the "story" of the novel itself (Hardy, 20) than others.

Some authors, in other words, gain greater command of their craft from utilizing "inner" stories. The result is stronger revelation of character—degree of insight, curiosity, sensitivity, critical inquiry, power of observation, or, in the case of children's literature, growth of the child character, as revealed by the character's own storytelling process. The author can also deepen the literary context (aspects of theme, conflict, background details or setting, and plot pattern) through the use of internal stories, for characters, individually or collectively, often tell themselves or one another stories in order to puzzle out the outer story, or the total story "picture." Narrative is, as David Lodge asserts, "one of the fundamental human tools for making sense of the world."[5]

In the case of *Zeely,* we see that Elizabeth's storying begins at the very beginning, on the train to Uncle Ross's farm, when she chooses new names for her brother and herself. He will be called Toeboy, because at the farm he can go without shoes if he wishes (the name actually originated from the nickname of a childhood friend of Hamilton's, she says), and she has renamed herself Geeder, because "horses answer to 'Gee'" (*Zeely,* 9). Both names signal to the reader that Elizabeth is weaving a story out of the new "world" into which she has stepped—as well as that she is an imaginative, dramatic, and assertive child who wishes to explore a new identity. We tell stories, says James Britton, in order to inhabit more lives than the one we have, to extend our experiences, or to come to terms with "undigested experience"[6] in our attempts to explore a variety of social roles.

When the stars appear Geeder watches for "night travellers"—an imaginary concept or half-remembered phrase that she uses to frighten her younger brother. By day she imagines Zeely walking up to her in the farm pump room to ask for a drink of water. Geeder and Zeely do finally encounter one another in daytime reality, and it is Geeder's fantasy that is instrumental in bringing this about. Because storying has given Geeder the idea that she and Zeely could be friends, or that Zeely may need her friendship (she manages through story to alter her own perception of reality), she can take action on the basis of her imaginings. In this new imagined role of friend, she decides to help Zeely save an ailing sow one day when Zeely's father begins to strike it as they are driving the hogs to market.

The hogs, in their oppressed, crowded, prodded condition, produce historical associations with slavery here, especially since Geeder has, in her storying, renamed the nearby town "Crystal" and the road leading to it "Leadback" road (*Zeely,* 24). The town actually becomes at this point a "story" in itself, when she says she can stand on the road leading to the town and see the "beginning, the middle and the end of it, just the way you can see through a piece of glass" (*Zeely*, 24), and she can hear what the people there are saying. The town Crystal, she also decides, has a crack in it. Thus the term "Leadback" suggests that America is "fractured" by its history of slavery and that remembering the past can lead us back to see and know better this fault.

In addition, although Hamilton had not encountered Zora Neale Hurston's work at this time, she nevertheless utilized the sow in very much the same way that Hurston utilized the mule in *Their Eyes Were Watching God*, to suggest black, female oppression generally. ("De nigger woman is de mule uh de world,"[7] says Hurston's Janie.) Janie's sympathy for the mule's mistreatment at the hands of the black men in her Florida town of Eatonville is similar to Zeely's empathy for the sow that is being mistreated by her father. And creating the striken animal not only as a lowly pig but also as female enables Hamilton to imply the position of black females in the human power structure (black or white) and to render a female (Zeely) with the power this time to liberate the animal—and herself. Here as Zeely struggles with Nat Tayber, her father (and, by extension, the patriarchal cultural oppressor), she stares at him; then she speaks softly, finally freeing the pole that he uses to prod the pig. (Physical resistance to male oppressors must be balanced with firm mental action or resolve.)

Geeder's fantasies continue to grow when she discovers the picture of a tall, Watutsi noblewoman in an old discarded magazine in Uncle Ross's shed and decides that Zeely is an African queen who has come to Crystal from the South, from the Florida town of Tallahassee. Uncle Ross explains the resemblance as ancestral traits (native or cultural resemblance). His "story" of the picture juxtaposed with Geeder's reveals that Geeder is clearly misreading the "facts" that surround her, but she is unable to see his realistic perspective at this time. Instead her story continues to build. She imagines that she and Zeely are sisters, that Zeely talks to no one but her, that she saves Zeely's life at another point, and that Zeely then makes *her* the queen. Storying, or taking over Zeely's life through imagined stories, eventually helps her attain vicarious power and importance, when she takes over Zeely's life through imagined stories, especially when she tells these stories to her friends, who actually believe them.

Later Uncle Ross tells Geeder stories of her own family and the care that family members through the generations have given to the old oak table in his house—a true story that shows her another way to examine life, one rooted in real experiences and real family strengths or empowering qualities. Geeder's real world continues to break away from the imaginary one when she hears Uncle Ross singing old slave and prisoner songs one night and telling of "night travellers" as those who wished to "walk tall" and "run free" (*Zeely*, 83). "It is the free spirit in any of us breaking loose" (*Zeely*, 83), he explains to Toeboy, who has been caught up in Geeder's storytelling too.

Hamilton has defined the term "night traveller" elsewhere as the "persecuted moving and searching for a better place" ("PA," 239). And when Zeely later tells Geeder that she has actually traveled to the Midwest from Canada, rather than from the South, we see Zeely's courage and responsible actions as related to the risk-taking free spirits of Underground Railroad days, and the "lesson" Hamilton is teaching (the danger of fantasizing—or romanticizing—slavery days or the South, since the truly free spirited had to escape slavery by becoming "night travellers").

When Uncle Ross describes the night as dark as the slave's skin, Geeder suddenly wonders if Zeely Tayber and the night traveler are "the same thing" (*Zeely*, 86), a notion that Uncle Ross finds credible, since Zeely is over six feet tall, "thin and deeply dark as a pole of Ceylon ebony" (*Zeely*, 31), and she does walk the road each night "with extra feed to check on the hogs" (*Zeely*, 86). No human is truly free, he implies, if any creature is still oppressed. It remains only for Zeely to meet Geeder and explain herself through stories of her own who she really is and how important it is to know who you are, rather than live a life of illusions about yourself—or others.

The stories Zeely tells juxtapose reality and fiction once again. The first is a creation story about a woman who, at the beginning of time, was waiting for a message to tell her who she was and what she was to do. She eventually learned that she was destined for a tall man with no language who was waiting for her just as she was waiting for his message so that she could send him a message of her own: that she was waiting to teach him a language, to help him to be unafraid, and to laugh with pleasure at his happiness when he at last emerged at his destination. The story teaches what it means to love and be loved. The second story, drawn from Zeely's real experiences, concerns an old woman mistaking Zeely for the night because of her color and Zeely's later understanding that she could become the night (or more than herself) because someone had seen her as more than she was. The story teaches what it means to love and respect oneself.

As Zeely tells and explains her stories, Geeder learns more about how and why stories are told—as the gift of one friend to another, or the gift of friendship—and wisdom. As Harold Rosen has asserted, stories "become a way in which the storyteller appraises his life experiences."[8] Even Zeely's gestures, Geeder notices, contribute to the emergent meaning-making of her stories. Fantasy and reality, inner and outer knowledge, come together as last for Geeder, to complete the quest of the child in search of self and place, the female child in search of her passage to adulthood, and the African-American child in search of her cultural identity.

Back at her uncle's farm, Geeder tells Uncle Ross and Toeboy about her magical time in the forest, and this last action of storying enables her to believe it all happened and helps to establish it in her mind as fact. Reflecting on her experience, Geeder, now Elizabeth once more, talks to learn or to ascertain for herself who Zeely really "is." No one thinks of Zeely as smelling of hogs, she asserts, even though Zeely sees herself in this way. It is what is inside when you swim in a dark lake (courage) or when you walk down a dark road to feed the hogs (caring) that makes you a queen, she declares.

Through stories—those she has told and those she has heard—Elizabeth has learned that reshaping the world through her imagination has risks and dangers if she loses her sense of balance and proportion, but if her storymaking grows out of the social context of her own family, culture, and place, she will be able to see better how she fits into the large scheme of things.

Functions of Stories

Myles McDowell has defined a good children's book as one that makes complex experience available to its readers (in contrast to the adult book, which "draws attention to the inescapable complexity of experience").[9] The good children's book, he adds, provides new knowledge for the child reader, builds the unknown into the known, and stretches the child's existing self-knowledge, when the child's growing understanding is based on "confrontations with the details and truth of experience, not just an emotional reaction to it" (McDowell, 153).

Hamilton often makes complex experience available to the reader by creating an unreliable narrator, or one who for the greater part of the book is misreading the signs or the picture of her setting (reacting more from emotion than from the details of what really "is") as we see in the stories the narrator tells. And all the while the protagonist and other characters in the story are creating a plot picture with their stories, the stories are, in turn, presenting varying possibilities that help to complete or fill in the missing pieces of the life picture or puzzle of the story world. Therefore stories that characters tell to one another often "speak" to one another, in what M. M. Bakhtin calls the "dialogic" function of language or speech itself,[10] to foster interplay of ideas. Stories stimulate social interaction among the characters who share, comment on, and develop one another's perceptions, as when Geeder and Uncle Ross each view Zeely through a different lens (hers of fantasy, his of realism).

But other important functions of stories occur here too. Stories are a healthy "training ground" for the unconscious. Geeder invents a life for Zeely, the opposite of her own situation. Later she acts in the way she has imagined, to come to terms with her narrative illusions. Stories thus serve to help Geeder grow into an important dimension of awareness. Strengthened and sustained by Zeely's stories, Geeder begins viewing life through a more realistic lens. Zeely's creation story—about the girl who believes herself to be descended from royalty—shows Geeder that the real role of royalty is one of responsibility and sacrifice (Zeely's self-appointed task of caring for the pigs each night as she walks the dark road). The stories of both Zeely and Uncle Ross are also useful for showing the way stories work to store and transmit social memories, family history, and cultural or ethnic knowledge. As Rosen has noted, stories are a means of "learning what as a collectivity we really are . . . no stories, no community."[11]

Finally, Hamilton uses stories here to help the child protagonist organize the world or define the self and the world through stories, since by talking or storying in order to *learn* and to "repair" the fragmented picture of our world, we construct through corroborating with others "what we feel and believe about the world" (Britton, 106), a basic social need. Geeder's ideas are "checked and calibrated" (Britton, 106) when Zeely corrects her faulty assumptions and teaches her through storytelling another way to see; afterward Geeder tests this new learning by sharing it with her uncle and brother.

In encouraging Geeder to shape her own meaning "at the point of utterance" (Britton, 141), Uncle Ross reveals himself to be an effective educator, in Britton's terms. He simply leans forward with Toeboy to listen without judgment as Elizabeth tells of her time with Zeely. An effective educator herself, when she provides for readers this important "lesson" in how children grow into self-knowledge, Hamilton reveals what authorial "teaching" at its best can be. And we might consider the cultural learning that occurs when gifted writers like Hamilton, in their efforts to make complex experience available to children, help them to "read" better their personal and social worlds. As Hamilton has written, "One of the marks of an exceptional story is the feeling that there is much more to it than the obvious pleasure of reading it. One learns something one has not known before from the story. The reader is startled by what is there to be learned. The situations presented are astonishing in that they reveal characters, ideas, that had never been dreamed of by the reader before."[12]

Certainly a novelist of ideas, Hamilton provides with *Zeely* a great many ways for readers to grow in cultural knowledge. We learn about identity perception as connected to storytelling (or how, why, and when we tell stories). We learn about the kinds of stories we tell in our everyday lives (fantasy stories, factual stories, creation stories), as well as the time and need of each for individual growth and cultural meaning. We learn more about African and African-American folklore and history from the talk stories about night travelers. We learn more about choices for female roles from Zeely's stories. Women can wait for their destiny, as did the woman in the creation story, or women can take the initiative, as Zeely does when her father strikes the sow. And at times both choices may exist within the same female mind, since Zeely is both "creating" her stories and "living" her life stories.

All in all, stories in *Zeely* take Geeder and child readers more deeply into what Louise Rosenblatt calls an "aesthetic" mode or "stance," whereby "consciousness [is] activated and ideas, sensations, feelings and images" of past experience are synthesized into something new.[13] Just as Geeder tries on roles, imagines outcomes, and experiences growth in social understanding and knowledge of her cultural condition from listening to Zeely's stories and from constructing stories of her own, children can journey through the book alongside her, trying on roles, imagining, and growing with her, as a "lived-through process of experience" (Rosenblatt, 35).

In all the books she wrote after *Zeely*, Hamilton would continue to show characters telling stories in order to attain personal, social, and cultural knowledge. At the same time she would, with each book, explore areas of cultural experience in the main stories of these books that were new to her own canon and often just as new for the canon of children's literature generally. The plight of the dispossessed, or homelessness, is suddenly on all of our minds these days and is just as suddenly cropping up in children's books, including Hamilton's 1993 novel, *Plain City*. But she was also discussing this subject in *The Planet of Junior Brown* over 20

years before, and in many ways that book is today as much at home in
today's world as it was then—perhaps a sign that in two decades
America has made very little progress in resolving societal inequities.

The Planet of Junior Brown

The idea for *The Planet of Junior Brown* began during the time when
Hamilton was still living in New York. Sitting in the park one day with
her young daughter, Leigh, she began watching a boy "on the hook"
(skipping school) who was eventually to become the character of Buddy
Clark. Soon, however, a friend for Buddy named Junior Brown also
began unfolding in her mind, and she had to start the book over again
(Ross, 210), a fortunate change of events actually. In revising the book
she created a unique shaping pattern for the story and a nearly perfect
symmetry for her focus—one that keeps Junior and Buddy balanced del-
icately throughout the story as dual protagonists.

"Essentially the book is Buddy's," Hamilton has said. "The dénoue-
ment comes with Buddy Clark. And Junior Brown does not get better in
this book; it's Buddy Clark that does. So it really was his book, I think"
(Ross, 210). Hamilton's uncertainty on the point of Buddy as protagonist occurs in another and more recent interview as well: "For many
chapters I had no Junior Brown, which seems odd now because he's the,
in a sense, the main character. Really Buddy Clark is the main character
in that book."[14] Hamilton's hesitancy to proclaim Buddy her sole protagonist may result form what she and readers both know about the
book—that Junior steals the show. He may not get better psychological-
ly before the book ends, but sick or well, he remains one of her most
fully realized characters—comically tragic, tragically funny, and wiser,
even at his most irrational moments, than anyone around him—not a
small achievement for an author in the eariest days of her writing.

Narrative Focus and Structure

The Planet of Junior Brown, like *Zeely* and the soon-to-follow *M. C.
Higgins the Great*, is a realistic novel of a different kind. Surrealistic might
be a better description of what Hamilton was creating with each of these
books. *Zeely*, not only because of her height but also because of her
determination and spirit, was bigger than life. And the teenage black
male protagonists of *Planet* and *M. C.*, in their behavior and perceptions,
reveal infinite, symbolic possibilities of what life might become with

"minds at liberty." Or they suggest "emotional truths,"[15] as Hamilton has said, rather than ordinary life as we know it. Junior Brown in his circumference (he is disastrously overweight), as well as in his musical talent and intellectual sensibility, is also "bigger" than life. Buddy Clark, his homeless friend, is similarly "bigger" in his emotional maturity, his intellectual gifts for leadership and survival, and in his ability to sense or perceive knowledge, hidden or unseen, by others.

Yet *The Planet of Junior Brown* is also grounded in Hamilton's prophetic abilities. "This was a time," says Hamilton, "before any of our sensibilities were focused on the homeless. In fact, there wasn't the large number of homeless at the time. But writers are observers. I lived in New York, and I must have had an inkling of something because I wrote about kids organized in 'planets,' homeless children who lived in abandoned buildings. Halfway through the book, the *New York Times* came out with an article on the hundreds of homeless children in New York. This was all out of my head, but I must have been observing" (Nicholson).

Lessons in urban cultural learning abound in this book, the result of Hamilton's process of observation. Children reading the book absorb knowledge about (1) small group survival in the face of cultural inequities; (2) the value of balancing independence with knowledge of dependence on others (the "lesson" that Buddy learns); (3) preserving the planet by helping to preserve one another; (4) black identity in a white power structure; (5) alternative "families" as replacement for disintegrating or failed family units; (6) friendship as a powerful force for survival; (7) critical thinking and planning as preparation for social action; (8) loss of a sense of reality resulting from urban loneliness; (9) story as a way of making sense of the world through words, music, art, and scientific exploration; and (10) the courage and confidence necessary for urban survival.

Going through the "wall" is essentially what the book is about: emotional, physical, and mental survival in the modern world. "When you find yourself up against the wall long enough," says Hamilton, "you begin to calculate your endurance against the wall. You begin to know how strong you are. You are beautiful, and you think in terms of going through the wall. . . . I'm interested in human beings who have changed emotionally, who have evolved so fundamentally and extremely that they see no difficulty in going through walls. Walls are the sides of buildings, and enough buildings make cities" ("TCB," 63).

The main story follows Junior as he becomes "irrational" enough to go (literally) through the wall of an abandoned building of Buddy's city. Ironically, he must become so mentally disturbed that he can be taken through the window of a wall (by Buddy) to a dark hidden place underground, where he can recover away from societal and family meddling. Thus Hamilton reveals that "sanity" provides no yardstick for human growth and may even at times stand in the way of it. From the beginning of the story Junior is fighting the "fact" that his mother's demanding personality is crowding out everything else in his mind or entering his thoughts as a schizophrenic voice.

Speaking of this aspect of the book and Junior's later decision to leave home and join Buddy as a homeless wanderer, Hamilton says that when life becomes "totally unaccceptable to [an] individual . . . he leaves it and goes to nothing. From nothing he begins again, sometimes in a radically different style. He may move himself away only mentally or mentally and physically; but by whatever method he chooses he will escape in order to renew, to become himself" ("TCB," 62). Junior escapes his mother by progressing more and more deeply into mental illness.

The main story also follows Buddy Clark, a homeless survivor both blessed and burdened by his lonely freedom who long ago managed to penetrate enough urban walls to make the city his own. It is the friendship of these two unlikely survivors that is the subject of the book. Both boys serve equally as protagonists of the story, as the organizational structure reveals clearly.

The twin stories of how Junior Brown is falling swiftly into insanity and is at the same time saved by Buddy—and how Buddy is suddenly face to face with the question of his existence and how he finds meaning for his life by saving Junior—take place in a week's time, Friday to Friday, in seven chapters. As each chapter increases in number by one, the number of scenes in each chapter increases by one, beginning with one scene in chapter 1, and ending with seven scenes in chapter 7. The scenes, evenly distributed between the two boys, reveal the moments when their lives intersect and merge to form an important theme of the book: that living for others is a higher law for survival than learning to live for oneself. When the world of each boy, as he knows it, collapses, he is left to meet the moment of decision with whatever inner strength he possesses. Each boy meets the test in a way that defines him and his growing awareness of his feelings and values and that reveals the difficulty of trying to survive in an adult, urban, "white" world.

Chapter 1 has one scene, the basement room of Junior and Buddy's school, where the two boys, drop-out students, and Mr. Pool, a drop-out teacher, are viewing and discussing the model of the solar system that Buddy and Mr. Pool have made for Junior. (Pool works as a janitor at night and conducts a one-room "school" for Junior and Buddy by day because he sees them as hope-bringers for the race.) The one long scene here sets the "scene" for the entire book, introducing as it does the characters and the question of Junior's unfolding story: "Who am I?"[16] The scene also foreshadows the subject of planetary survival. Buddy and Mr. Pool tell the story of how they made the solar model so that the imaginary "lines" running from Junior's planet to the stars and the sun could intersect, thus revealing the interconnections of one human (one "planet") to another, in "gravitational equilibrium" (*PJB*, 11).

In chapter 2 Junior and Buddy travel through two scenes, on the way to Junior's Friday afternoon piano lesson. Chapter 3, with three scenes, focuses primarily on Junior, a gifted pianist who is not allowed to play his teacher's piano. The piano teacher, Miss Peebs (also mentally ill), has a delusion that "someone" does not wish the piano played. Junior, nevertheless, still returns to her home each week for his "lesson" in the desperate hope that conditions will change.

Chapter 4, in four scenes, focuses primarily on Buddy and his busy existence as a "Tomorrow Billy" (an "administrator" of homeless boys in their various "planet homes" in deserted buildings around the city). A "planet" here, in Hamilton's schema, is a school itself of sorts—a place where boys learn a way to survive despite deprivation and loss of family or other institutional support. And Hamilton creates it as a better school than the conventional one, in that here there is cooperation, communication, and learning for minds at liberty: a "joyful school" ("TCB," 64).

Chapter 5, covering a span of five days—Saturday through Wednesday in this "week" of chapters—reveals the boys together in Mr. Pool's basement and in Junior's house, where Buddy discovers Junior must also play a silent piano at home (his mother has removed the strings for her own peace and quiet). It also reveals Buddy and Junior talking to each other and playing checkers in Junior's room. Junior explains that when he plays with his father he "takes" the black—and black always wins (*PJB*, 128)—and that he cannot take the black with Buddy ("take" signifying both winning the checkers game and coping with his racial state) because he is always "red." He is fire (or angry, we see soon after), since he imagines that Buddy sees him as a Mama's boy.

He is also suppressing a great deal of anger about his mother's chronic illness and the responsibilities imposed on him by an absentee father.

Chapter 6, Thursday, has six scenes, beginning with Junior's painting a scene called "The Red Man" in his room. Later Junior and Buddy are caught in their truancy and sent to the assistant principal's office, where the reason for Buddy's drop-out status is explained: "So you get an education, Buddy wanted to tell him. So what? Half of the educated cats on the street couldn't remember the last time they had even a lousy job" (*PJB*, 154).

At this time Mr. Pool is also caught for not being around the school during the day—a sign that he must dismantle the model of the solar system. Junior at home cannot find his "Red Man" painting. Later he reasons (and we see in flashback) that his mother had destroyed the painting when she discovered that her son painted a picture of the city in all its rich and terrible inclusiveness: inch-high people of all shapes and colors "living their most private [and sexual] lives" (*PJB*, 163), another layer of the "red" metaphor. Junior's world collapses now, the last shred of his creativity having been silenced and censored. As a runaway, he heads for Mr. Pool's basement room, where he gives away his warm winter clothes to Buddy, whose own resources are very limited.

Chapter 7, Friday once again, has seven scenes. Buddy and Junior go to the next piano lesson; the "relative" supposedly prevents Junior from playing the piano (both Junior and Miss Peebs, the piano teacher, seem to see this hallucinatory figure as real now); Buddy, Junior, and the "relative" take the bus back to the school; they take a ride in Mr. Pool's car from the school to Buddy's "planet" building; Buddy helps Junior go "through" the wall of the building (the window). Then, finally, in the last scene, Buddy, Mr. Pool, and Junior are inside the "planet" (the tenement basement where Buddy trains his young friends in this "school" for the homeless survivors). The toy model of the solar system has turned into *real*.

Function of Stories

Hamilton often makes complex experience available to the reader in very subtle ways. Yet she also draws attention often—with even more subtlety—to the inescapable complexity of experience ("the best children's book," says Hamilton, "is a book for everyone"). Thus her books are at times considered too complex and obscure for children. The fact is, however, that children are often the best readers of her books, since once hooked on a book they become excellent detectives, searching for missing pieces of a story-puzzle. And the clues are always there. *Planet*, in fact, reads very much like a mystery, with internal stories functioning here almost entirely to fill in gaps of the main thread of story that serve to create puzzles and to build suspense. As Wolfgang Iser explains, "Whenever the reader bridges the gaps, communication begins. . . . Hence the structured blanks of the text stimulate the process of ideation to be performed by the reader on terms set by the text."[17]

Stories, then, in this book aid in the ideation process; the terms set by the text arise out of the intermeshing of gaps and out of the stories that help to fill these gaps. The big puzzles of *Planet* arise from Junior Brown's words and thoughts. In chapter 1, he asks, "Who am I? What can I know?" In chapter 3 he says about Miss Peebs, "She's got something in there [in her living room] who doesn't like music. A relative living there?" (*PJB*, 46), and he wonders what that "something" really is.

The gap of chapter 1 is filled at various points in the book: when Junior struggles with his growth in awareness (his notion of who he is and what he must do to be what he wishes to be), when he paints his "story" of "The Red Man," when he decides to leave home, and, finally, when he is taken into Buddy's planet basement, where the healing process of his "connectedness" to others can begin. The gap of chapter 3 is partially filled when, later in that same chapter, Junior and Miss Peebs create an interconnecting story, in dialogic terms, of the "relative" who will not allow her to play the piano. A fantasy emerges at this point for them both when Junior asks if there is someone there, and Miss Peebs, in her demented state, decides that there is (the power of suggestion).

In chapter 7, when Miss Peebs expands this fantasy into a full-fledged apparition in her living room, the gap is filled to a greater extent, for it occurs to Junior "quite suddenly what he could do to save Miss Peebs and the grand piano [for his lesson] too" (*PJB*, 179). As Hamilton has explained, "Junior Brown and Miss Peebs both live in the same isolation caused by the same conditions, and Junior instinctively knows that by saving her he may save himself" ("PA," 240).

Junior enters Miss Peeb's fantasy because he wants to help save them both. But his own problems are too great: he feels he is ugly and rejected by society; his father's long-term absences prevent him from "taking" the black (dealing with racial injustices that a white power structure imposes on black Americans); his mother usurps his life and his creativity; and he is becoming aware of his sexuality. When his mother's censorship makes him feel ashamed of his "Red Man" fantasies, the "filthy" relative appears to send him sinking into the fantasy as deeply as Miss Peebs is submerged in it.

Buddy's part in the story also brings gaps that are filled by his memories of himself as a homeless person and his memory of another homeless boy (called a "Tomorrow Billy") teaching him how to survive. He remembers the boy saying that the highest law was to live for yourself—an important gap or faulty assumption in Buddy's own reasoning, since, in actuality, Buddy is living for the other boys—and for Junior—much more than for himself (hence the name Buddy). His commitment to others, in fact, seems almost *too* amazing; Hamilton even describes him "as finely tuned a human sensation as one could imagine" ("TCB," 64). But it falls to him to be extraordinary, all adults in the story having failed in their efforts to teach, parent, or guide children. (The "squeaks" that Pool detects in his solar model represent here a microcosm of the blighted earth that causes old and young old alike to fall through the cracks of the "system.")

Buddy, the child who has lost his childhood in order to survive and who seems too adultlike to be "real," is actually the only one here who knows the world well enough (the result of his long, homeless wandering in it) to see that Junior, in his current mental state, cannot survive in the flawed system "out there." Thus Junior must not be institutionalized with strangers, Buddy decides. "They'll hit on how fat he is. . . . [W]e got to get him skinny [they will say]. . . . They'll see how black he is . . . and they'll say . . . we got to get to the white inside" (*PJB*, 188). Junior's grand size reveals he is capable of (or bursting with) *big* things; he must not be diminished or reduced to monocultural "sameness." His ethnic and individual identity must be nurtured and allowed to grow.

At last, watching Junior Brown in the deep cavernous basement of the deserted building, his mind beginning to heal in the "closeness of all of them together" (*PJB*, 210), Buddy remembers the real story that he had forgotten all these years, "or [that he had] changed with the passage of time to fit with his loneliness" (*PJB*, 210). And he tells these homeless boys all about the highest law—living for one another—and how he can teach them to do that.

Buddy looks at Mr. Pool who has joined them there to help Junior through the wall, and their eyes hold, as Junior dozing hears Buddy's words in music. The triangle that Mr. Pool spoke of at the beginning—of earth, sun, and the planet of Junior Brown—holds firm at last in "gravitational equilibrium," the orbit that Buddy and Junior together have made as survivors of urban walls.

M. C. Higgins the Great

In some ways a companion piece to *Planet*, Hamilton's next novel, *M. C. Higgins the Great* (1974), also portrays the close friendship of two teenage boys, one of whom is considered a misfit. Each book has as its protagonist a young teenage male (or males) coming to terms with adolescent emotions and with the "squeaks" of the system. In *M. C.*, however, the protagonist is rooted firmly in home and family rather than homeless and is learning to cope with the dehumanizing effects of strip mining on the Ohio mountain where he lives.

Each book has several relationships supporting the major theme of the adolescent's search for identity and his merging of self with a significant "other." Buddy and Junior are involved with three adults (Mr. Pool, Miss Peebs, and Junior's mother) and with the boys of Buddy's "planet." M. C. has ties to his family (his father, Jones, his mother, Banina, and his siblings); to his friend Ben and Ben's family; later to Lorhetta, an older teenager who is wandering through the area as a camper; and to a folklorist he calls the "dude," who has come to the mountain to record old songs before they are lost.

Narrative Focus and Creative Process

M. C. Higgins the Great has won more awards than most of Hamilton's other books and more honors than most children's authors have ever won for a single book. Critics have complained at times about various shortcomings they find in Hamilton's other early books (obscurity, occasional unconvincing or wooden characters, or implausibility of plot), but they have rarely, if ever, had the slighest complaint about this book. David Rees, the most exacting critic of Hamilton's early period, even describes this novel as "one hundred percent successful,"[18] praising it for its range and depth, its credible plot, and convincing characters.

Two changes in Hamilton's creative process may account for such positive reader response. First, Rees says landscape plays a more important role here than in Hamilton's previous books, having "moulded the character of the few people who live there" (Rees, 174). Hamilton was obviously on very firm ground here, describing the region of her own child life. Second, Hamilton has spoken of the tendency at the beginning of her writing to accentuate the physical traits of characters in order to control what a character did. She portrayed them less at times as "living" people than as emblems ("ASR," 639): she created characters surrealistically tall and ghostly, or fat, or devil-like in appearance. In *M. C.*, however, she was able to transfer this emblematic effect to an object of the landscape (M. C. *sits* on a pole rather than *looks* like a pole, as Zeely did). Race is, as a result, more subtly tied to the theme of the book here than previously. That M. C. is black has less to do with his pole sitting talent than it has to do with Hamilton having grown up black and feeling more comfortable writing about a milieu she knew well. As she has said, "I concentrate on the emotions all of us share, and I use the most comfortable milieu or vantage point from which to reveal them" ("ASR," 639).

What it means to love someone, what it means to be a family, is what Hamilton focuses on very clearly here, although family love is tied closely to other themes, such as concern for the environment, two contrasted ways of living (the communal, socialistic way of Ben's world versus the individualistic path that M. C.'s nuclear family takes), the male passage into adolescence, and generational conflict. Thus in many ways *M. C.* is a very conventional book, but it is still more intricately developed and tightly focused than either of her previous novels.

Hamilton created a rich texture for the novel by increasing both the number of details as well as the amount of dialogue. Thus she produced an old-fashioned, well-told story in which narrative greatly overshadows explanation, in contrast to the books of the Justice trilogy she would later produce, in which so many abstract concepts would need to be introduced and defined. And even though ideology is as important as character development and plot in *M. C.*, it appears to grow out of each quite naturally. Subtleties of thematic meaning are also reduced to a minimum, in contrast to *Planet*, where intricate metaphorical patterns are at times used to convey or "signify" concepts of sex, race, or political concern in the real world (as with the "black" and the "red" of Junior's checkers set), and the peeling off of so many layers of meaning involves numerous rereadings.

Here metaphors work quickly and easily to reveal more about the story world, as when Hamilton describes the dude's face as the "color of barn-dried walnuts with deep creases,"[19] and we see the person linked to the places he frequents as a folklorist. She tells us that M. C. hears the sound of rain, "like hundreds of mice running through corn" (*M. C.*, 70), and we notice his sensitivity to sound at the same time we accept more readily his father's conviction that M. C. may have "second sight." Above all her description of M. C.'s mother when she peers at the dude, "diving deep into him with her wide-set eyes like gold spoons cutting through some shaking jello" (*M. C.*, 102), helps us see clearly how searching and perceptive Banina is.

M. C. is a more straightforward, accessible book than most of Hamilton's books, and it has perhaps been rewarded (or awarded) more profusely as a result. Yet it is unconventional and innovative in very subtle and extending ways; thus the awards are especially deserved.

The book has 14 chapters and at least 33 internal stories, in contrast to *Planet*, with its seven chapters and 18 inner stories. But the number of characters telling stories remains essentially the same (five); therefore we come to know the characters better here, because they are much more fully developed. Also, each book has 28 scenes, but the scenes here, in contrast to *Planet*, never exceed three to a chapter. Therefore they too are developed in much greater detail.

In *Planet* each chapter increases the number of scenes by one until the reader has moved through a week of chapters and of scenes, the seven scenes reaching a crescendo of meaning at the end, when loose ends of story are tied up to resolve the conflicts, mysteries, or puzzles. In *M. C.* Hamilton uses details or statements to fill in the gaps of context quite unobtrusively so that the reader often continues reading without any puzzlement, only to be caught by surprise later (just as the protagonists's assumptions are also often overturned by an unexpected twist in things). The surprise causes the reader to reverse the forward motion, to go *backward* in order to see what clue or authorial signpost was missed, just as it causes the protagonist to think back to what he had not taken into consideration before.

This way of writing (or reading) places us in the realm of what Iser describes as "negation" (indicating a meaning not yet developed or established in the reader's mind)—another kind of blank or gap that arises from the "dense interweaving of perspectives. . . . The segments of the perspectives are viewed first from one, then another standpoint, so that their hidden sides are constantly being exposed" (Iser, 212). Even a "partial negation," Iser explains, "opens up new vistas" on what has previously been taken for granted.

In this novel the surrealistic 40-foot-tall pole on which M. C. sits to view and interpret his world functions primarily as a negation developing, in the light of the reader's forward and backward movement throughout the story, more of the story picture. (Why is the pole so tall?

Where did it come from? Why is it there? What does it mean to M. C. and others?) But at least two other negations are pivotal for the reader's sorting out of story clues and story meaning: the swimming "event" of M. C. and Lorhetta in chapter 9 and the dude's comment in chapter 13 that he cannot sell Banina's voice.

In the first chapter of the book, however, characters tell stories to convey the prestory: to set the scene, develop a picture of the characters, set the plot in motion, and foreshadow the story's major conflict and indicate possible solutions—very traditional or conventional roles for the interior stories of novels generally.

The major thread of story in chapter 1 involves M. C. rising, going down the mountainside to check his rabbit trap the day the book begins (the entire book takes place in one 48-hour period), then meeting his friend Ben Killburn and eliciting his stories, after which M. C. sets off for home. Inserted into these three scenes, however, are 10 internal stories. The first four are M. C.'s memories: a story being circulated at this moment about a traveling "dude" (a collector of folk songs) who M. C. suddenly decides might help his mother become a singing star; a story about his neighbors, the Killburns; a story about himself as a swimmer; and a story about the vine bridge he helped the Killburns construct several years before this.

As M. C. spies Ben, he remembers a story of the Killburns and their witchy hands and their legendary magical powers, as well as his nightmares about the spoil heap tumbling down on his side of the mountain. (Hamilton says that she based these curious mountain people on a 12-fingered, orange-haired, light-complexioned, merino family she observed in a nearby Ohio town. But traits of the Killburns—magical powers, communal or socialist living conditions, and vegetarian beliefs—were additions of her own.) Ben's stories, told to M. C., reveal additional knowledge about the Killburn family (their touch on the strip-mining cuts works to heal the mountain) and about the "dude."

Alone on his way back home, M. C. sees a girl on the path and remembers another girl he kissed in this same place once. Then he sees his pole, his prize for swimming the Ohio River, and he reminisces about the pole. All of these stories signal the main threads of story that will weave through the book: the dude who will play a great part in M. C.'s expansion of consciousness; the Killburns and their alternative way of life, which will cause him to think more independently about his own values as part of his passage to adulthood; the strip-mining cuts that are causing his fears for his family; the girl and emotional pull he feels toward her; as well as the pole itself.

The supremely tall pole—his own private and powerful vantage point for surveying the world and drawing inspiration from it—gives him the superior view of a landscape that represents his family inheritance or history. Thus it gives him his vision of how he fits into the world, because of his family's land. At the same time, in terms of the Amerind vision quest that Hamilton will later develop in *Arilla Sun Down*, the pole reveals how he fits into the life "circle of birth and growth and death and rebirth."[20]

Inner Stories and Development of Conflict

Chapter 2 reveals M. C. sitting on the pole as three memory stories emerge to lead him more deeply into the major conflict he is facing. First he imagines a story set in the future, when the spoil heap has fallen and destroyed everyone except himself. This fantasy reveals his strong connection to his family roots and foreshadows what he really wants and what he will eventually choose: not to leave the mountain despite the risk and danger of the sliding heap. The story also reveals that his adolescent need to assert himself as "ruler" of the family, or to displace his father, is stronger at this point than either his desire to help the entire family survive together or to explore the world beyond Sarah's Mountain without them.

The second story is a remembered one: that of Great-grandmother Sarah, whom he often senses as a presence climbing the mountain or hovering ghostlike around it. This story explains why he chooses unconsciously, in the previous daydream, to stay there—loyalty to his heritage. Sarah was an escaped slave who settled on this mountain, and the mountain belongs to his family now because of her courage and perseverence.

Finally, he remembers a third story, that of his little sister Macie Pearl sitting motionless waiting for him when he has gone hunting—one that emphasizes his connections to family and the mutual commitment of family members. He takes care of the younger children as his parents work; the children cooperate with him as he pursues his own "work" of hunting for the family supper. (Macie Pearl, vulnerable and caring, spirited and brash, is one of the best drawn characters here; later she will grow into Pretty Pearl, of *The Magical Adventures of Pretty Pearl*, and, still later, into Cammy of *Cousins* and Buhlaire of *Plain City*.)

The three stories all "speak" to one another in dialogic terms, to reveal the tension of home and outside world that produces the underlying conflict of the book. The first and third stories show M. C.'s adolescent need to obliterate his family in order to assert his individuality and his separation from inherited traits and values, as well as his understanding that although love of heritage binds him to the mountain, it also makes him what he is. To leave would be to obliterate himself as the first story shows, and this he does not wish to do. Yet fear of a landslide also produces his desire to flee the mountain in order to save himself.

Down the pole he comes in the second part of this chapter, to wander off to the summit of the mountain. There he has spotted the dude, who may provide a solution to the problem. If his mother can become a singing star, and if her music can take her away from this place, there is hope for wrenching everyone away and saving all their lives. (In the desire for fame, fortune, and survival he forgets family heritage.) Talking to the dude, M. C. tells the story of the strip-mining disaster, and the dude tells a story signaling his own values (you cannot leave what you love) and the reason he is there ("for me, it's worth it all to discover voices like the kind your mother is said to have" [M. C., 45]). It also foreshadows how he will handle the problem M. C. is handing him.

Chapter 3 shows M. C. later that day on the pole once again, waiting for his father and remembering a story his father has told, one that reveals his ties to the land. Chapter 4 reveals Jones home from work telling M. C. the story of Sarah and her mountain, and speaking of the "past's enormous mystery" (M. C., 72) as he explains to M. C. that "something big belongs to you" (M. C., 72). In this chapter M. C. also produces a remembered story "picture" of his mother, Banina, coming home from a far hill once on his birthday. The story is important for revealing the mother in her natural context, singing "so all the hills could hear" (M. C., 78), which is her gift back to Sarah—a scene that shows why the dude chooses not to sell her voice. It also functions as transition to the next chapter, where the memory of the strip mining and the danger of the slideheap leads M. C. to think there may be no more birthdays.

Chapter 5 brings M. C. and Ben together once more, at which time M. C. remembers a possum hunt with Ben. He is now actually "hunting" the girl he saw on the path earlier, and this story sets the tone for the sexual aggression he is beginning to feel—and show. When he finally sees her, they scuffle on the path. Afterward, when he kisses her, she flings her flashlight at him. He scrapes her back with his knife; then when they struggle, she breaks free and runs away.

Later that evening, as his mother is returning from work, she and M. C. climb the hill together and she tells him the story of the pole. She had asked Jones to remove the family gravestones that filled the yard so the children could play. Jones replaced the stones with pieces of junk he had collected (so that the dead were still remembered), the pole becoming the marker for the dead. Now for Jones the pole is much more than a pole. "My pole," M. C. says, beginning to sort it all out. "The junk in a circle. A monument" (*M. C.*, 97). Because the story reveals what the pole means to Jones, as opposed to M. C., it serves to intensify the home-world conflict that M. C. is facing. Jones will never leave the mountain now, M. C. realizes; he will never be able to leave the pole.

Such a reversal of expectations affects M. C. strongly, since from the beginning he has seen the pole as his own special property, and sharing the pole with his father is certainly not what he (or we as readers) expected. The scene pulls us *backward* through the text to fill in this gap, and the clues are there as early as chapter 1, when sitting atop the pole, on the bicycle seat he has attached to it, M. C. wonders "why he [Jones] won't ever throw away that junk" (*M. C.*, 27).

In the next chapter, which has only one scene (thereby emphasizing the importance of the action here), the dude visits M. C.'s home to hear Banina sing, and as the evening begins M. C. remembers a story of how his mother furnished their home with a special red carpet that she found in a Washington embassy when she worked there, and how she gave up her job to marry Jones and follow him to this mountain. (The devotion Banina shows for her husband in this story foreshadows her easy acceptance later that the "dude" cannot help her become a star.)

Chapter 7 tells of Banina and M. C. on their way for a swim the next morning. At this time Banina tells M. C. a story about Ben's family and how Ben's mother, Viola, once stopped the blood gushing from a child's cut simply by her touch. Thus the Killburn family is reintroduced as healers with mystical power that frightens Banina, so strong is her belief in what she has seen Viola do: "Theirs might be power for bad in some way we don't recognize—isn't the Lord supposed to have the power for good?" (*M. C.*, 118).

In the next chapter M. C. encounters Lorhetta (the female stranger on the path) outside the tent where she is camping. She tells him the story of her life back home. Then M. C.'s sisters and brothers appear, and they all go swimming—except for Lorhetta, who (we later learn) cannot swim but does not want to admit it. When she hears that M. C. can swim through an underground passage by holding his breath for a long time, she challenges him to take her with him.

Chapter 9 is the one chapter of the book with no internal story, only the story of the swimming event as the main thread of narrative, and such a memorable and dramatic story it is that Hamilton has selected it for her contribution to *The Newbery Award Reader* (a collection of short fiction by her and her Newbery peers). Hamilton's prose is exemplary for creating the horror of these long moments when M. C. discovers, in the tunnel, that Lorhetta cannot swim and that he must save them both by holding his breath and bearing the weight of her dead pressure: "Fractions of seconds were lost as he tried twisting her arm to pull her body into line. Fishes slid over his skin, tickling and sending shivers to his toes. . . . *Won't make it.* Horror, outrage stunned him. He had taken for granted the one thing he should have asked her. For the want of a question, the tunnel would be a grave for both of them" (*M. C.,* 143–44).

We are led back to the previous chapter to find the clue, and as before it is there: "He was wondering if he had forgotten something he should have remembered to ask" (*M. C.,* 138). Lorhetta later chides him for not asking her if she could swim, but he clarifies just whose error it really is. And we see that because he did not lose his head in the tunnel, he *does* deserve the title has given himself, M. C. Higgins the Great: "'*I* took it easy,' he said 'If I hadn't, you wouldn't be here, girl.'"

In the next chapter M. C. and Lorhetta have had lunch, cooked by Jones, when the Killburn men come to deliver ice. M. C. remembers his father's story about merino people—people with witchy skin—a story advancing the family superstitions that such light-skinned people are frightening. When Lorhetta argues reasonably against Jones's superstitions, M. C. sees that the boy/son in him must grow away from the man/father in order to attain his own identity—and that he does not have to leave home to grow. (The story also illustrates how prejudice, superstition, and irrational fears grow to such illogical proportions in people generally, of whatever color, as well as *within* a particular cultural or ethnic group, as is happening here.) In chapter 12, when M. C. visits the Killburn compound, he sees the circular "eye of Gawd" (*M. C.,* 199), as Ben's father describes it, an intricate cobweb vine structure connecting all the Killburn houses of the compound that enables the members of this large, extended family to travel back and forth without disturbing the plants growing in the garden below. The image connects, in dialogic terms, with the memory-story of chapter 1, when M. C. at a younger age had suggested to Ben that vines of the ravine in Kill's Mound could be used to make a lattice weave bridge, the vines exemplifying the self-reliance that vines continue to represent in the African rain forest to this day.[21]

Now he realizes that the "cobweb" of the mound had given him the idea for the bridge and that in having seen how to use the vines, he was able to give Ben's father back his idea—a mutual support system between the families that always lies dormant in the face of his parents' fears and superstitions of merino people.

Inner Stories and Indeterminacies

In chapter 13 the dude returns to say he cannot sell Banina's voice. He never sells anything much, he tells M. C.—a jarring comment that sends M. C.'s hopes plummeting and might send readers turning pages backward for the clues. As always they are there. In chapter 2 the dude had told M. C. he was a collector, but M. C. had already drawn his own conclusions (or he did not yet understand the difference between collecting and preserving folk materials and *using* folklore for commercial purposes). In chapter 3 Jones asked M. C., "You sure you got it right?" (*M. C.*, 64). In chapter 6 there was the dude's enigmatic statement, "Now I have to sort it out" (the question of what to do with Banina's singing voice) and "see what will be the best course to take" (*M. C.*, 111). But the clues end there. His words remain a permanent blank space, or what Iser, following Roman Ingarden, calls a "spot of indeterminacy" or a gap impossible to close "within the context of the work" (Iser, 171).

The dude explains to M. C. at the end of the book that he only meant to save Banina's voice before it went "the way these hills are going" (*M. C.*, 212), meaning he meant only to collect and preserve it, rather than profit from it in any way. But his earlier comment about "sorting it out" did provide a real ray of hope for M. C. Was the dude actually thinking of trying to make her a recording star? Was he caught up in the moment (for just a moment) to think of "taking" her voice with him and using it to make a record, as M. C. wanted? Or was he simply playing for time, hoping that M. C. would ultimately see the folly of his own wishes. Indeterminacies—often a mark of adult fiction as subtle and astute as that of Henry James and Toni Morrison—produce richer children's fiction and may help to account for the attraction this book has had for readers of all ages.

The largest spot of indeterminancy of the book, arises at the end when it is left unresolved whether the spoil heap finally descends on the Higgins home or if disaster is averted. Chapter 14 begins with M. C. still waiting for Lorhetta, then finally returning to her camping place to discover that she is gone but that she has left him her knife. (Constantly attempting to emasculate M. C. in order to deflect his sexually aggressive behavior, she at last offers him his manhood—in absentia.) He speaks to the knife when he finds it—a personified substitute in his thinking now for their severed relationship—and the knife answers, "in the voice of Lorhetta: 'Follow me'" (*M. C.*, 226). He follows it (carries it before him like a magical divining rod) and it leads him finally to the pole.

On the pole he asks Lorhetta why she left him the knife. "Out of kindness," she answers, in this last "story" he is imagining—and because she does not need it; she does not live on a mountain. He goes then to the mountain behind his home, to stab the earth with the knife and "talk" to Lorhetta about staying on the mountain and surviving if he can. But how, he wonders? Then "a perfect idea forms in his mind" (*M. C.*, 229). With everyone working together (another "bridge") they can make a wall between them and the spoil, in the event that it comes tumbling down. Even Sarah's stone will eventually be added to this wall—by Jones.

We lose ourselves by leaving what we are, M. C. now understands. We find and keep ourselves by understanding that we belong to the past's enormous mystery. Finally, with Ben, who molds and packs the earth with them at the end of the story, M. C., like Buddy and Junior before him, has found a way to go through the wall; in this case it is by building a wall. And Ben's character is not one to be minimized in this book, especially as it relates to this constantly shifting image of the pole.

"The juxtaposition of the pole on the mountain," says Hamilton, "indicates oppositions." As she explained in her Newbery speech,

> I began with M. C. atop a forty-foot pole, lofty, serene. Too serene, perhaps, too above it all, and so I conceived Ben Killburn, created out of darkness at the foot of the pole. Earthbound, Ben is dependable in a way M. C. is not. Ben, in turn, is constricted by Jones Higgins, M. C.'s father, a man of strength and integrity, yet superstitious and unyielding. So too is Jones illuminated by the Dude from out of nowhere, who clarifies for M. C. his father's inability to face the reality of the endangered mountain. As though in a spiral from the top of the pole, each character bears light to the next until they all form a circle revolving at the base of the pole. . .

their lives as intertwined and fragile as the thin flashing ribbons of a May dance . . . the spoil hovering above.[22]

The book ends with M. C. building his wall—or, as Hamilton emphasizes, starting to build it. Whether this wall can really stop the tons of spoil hanging in the balance, she admits, is "open to question" ("NAA," 342). What is important is that he has moved forward to *try* to do something. Yet one answer, one possible way to fill this indeterminancy, is found in M. C.'s insistence that Ben help them at the end and his realization that he will use the knife against his father if his father intervenes. "Killburn men and women could heal a bad wound by touching it" (*M. C.*, 12), as he has known from the beginning of the book; the author's signpost here is that the mystical in this case might just work.

If we believe that the Killburns have actual healing powers because of their sensitivity, their closeness the earth, and their empathetic gifts (at one point M. C. says he feels he can tell Viola anything), then we will believe that M. C. has made something of the past's enormous mystery. At least he has found a way to keep the past intact—or to protect it, nourish it, save it—when he invites Ben to lay his hands on the mountain as a way of healing the cuts. And if we believe in Ben's power, as M. C. at last appears to do, then we will believe with M. C. that they all will be saved. If not, we see at least that in taking a stand to include Ben at this point as a member of the "family" M. C. has become, in Paulo Friere's terms, an "integrated" person, one who has not merely adapted to reality but who has used the "critical capacity to make choices and to transform that reality."[23]

M. C.'s mother provides another signpost that they will be saved. She thinks that Viola has mystical power; she senses Viola's power. Banina is a rational thinker who *believes*, in other words, and this acceptance gives us some assurance that the power is there. Hearing Banina's story about the child's gushing wound may be what causes M. C. to believe in Ben's power also and to try to utilize the Killburn psychic energy to heal the mountain. Or perhaps not. He might have invited Ben to make the wall simply to seal their friendship and to signify his independent thinking about merino people now. (A true indeterminancy, as this one surely is, will ultimately remain indeterminate.)

Stories then, we see here, connect M. C.'s inner world of dreams wishes, and nightmares to an outer world of social responsibility. As he stories to learn more about himself, others, and the world, M. C. carves an answer out of the web of time and place in which he is caught.

Through stories—those he hears and those he remembers and imagines—he learns that he can make a difference; *he* can make a pattern, a design; he can produce his own solutions rather than be victimized or trapped by a ready-made pattern imposed on him by society, family, fate, or destiny.

The power of story for M. C. is that it enables him to shape and reshape his evolving ideas as it releases his thoughts for personal and social action. And that we can engage in social action or make individual choices to preserve what we value may be the most important or dominant cultural "lesson" that Hamilton presents here, especially in the area of ecological concern. M. C.'s storying becomes a way of shaping his cultural learning, or in Friere's words, a way of evoking *conscientização*, the "development of the awakening of critical awareness" (Friere, 19).

Cultural Learning and Thematic Interests

Cultural learning and the "negation" or ideational picture forming in the reader's mind work especially well together here, in that as M. C. is engaged in cultural learning—his critical awareness is developing in the same way Iser explains that negations emerge for readers. In retracing his steps to "reread" his world, his learning is characterized very much in the way that Friere describes a "critically transitive consciousness": by a deeper "interpretation of problems, by the substitution of causal principles for magical explanations, by the testing of one's findings and by openness to revision; by the attempt to avoid distortion when perceiving problems and to avoid preconceived notions when analyzing them" (Friere, 18).

From the beginning M. C. is sorting out and assimilating lessons of ecology, such as how strip mining is affecting not just the land (producing the spoil heap that hangs above his home) but also animal life, vegetation, and water resources, and we as readers are learning along with him. Flocks of wild turkeys are rarely seen here now, we discover, from listening in on his thoughts and stories of the early chapters. No deer or elk are left in the area; no trees are left standing on the outcropping; harsh acids wash down from the mining cut when it rains, contaminating the soil for the grapes growing below; the streams are changing color; vegetables are smaller than they once were. And these conditions are affecting not only M. C.'s family who hunt animals for food but also their Killburn neighbors who are vegetarians.

Communal living versus nuclear family ideals provides additional cultural lessons. Ben would never be consumed with dreams of his mother achieving stardom, even if she did sing, since in the Killburn world "all were the same, names had no great importance" (*M. C.*, 192). The men of the Killburn family do not kill animals for food or sport; Ben's father even feeds the snakes (befriends them as part of the family commune). Nuclear family ideals, as seen in the Higgins family, do not, however, preclude concern and care of the earth, or feelings of interconnectedness among living forms. Just as Viola uses her sensitivity to the human pulse and the rhythm of life to stop a child's arterial bleeding, Jones, as we see from M. C.'s story, passes down family knowledge in the story of Sarah, the fugitive slave; and for M. C., Sarah becomes a strong, living presence. Jones also is instrumental in teaching M. C. that Banina's voice, emanating from the hills that inspire her singing, can neither be uprooted nor transplanted and still thrive. The entire book, in fact, is built around M. C.'s growing understanding of the concept of folklore as a way to preserve the past and use it to understand and deal with the present (or to heal the cuts and scars that culture has imposed on nature).

What it means to be a "collector" is an idea M. C. is uncovering here, as a "negation" developing in the light of the entire story. Do we collect in order to sell something "good"? To preserve what is "good"? To *discover* what is "good"? What is the *real* meaning of "discovery?" To make a person famous or rich? To preserve something so it is not lost? To share it with other living beings for their pleasure? And what is the meaning of "good?" That which is popular or purchased readily in the commercial marketplace? Or that which is life-sustaining and nurturing to those closest to us? Banina gets back what she gives, says Jones, and this is love—something that can be neither bought nor sold but must be learned from those we love.

Banina teaches M. C. what love is from the way she accepts Jones's feelings for the pole as family "totem": "'He's Jones,' Banina said simply. 'And don't you ever forget it'" (*M. C.*, 97). M. C. ultimately begins to see that we fill the places we love with our own unique presence and to separate a person from a place may erase the "self" of that person. Watching his father cooking, he says to himself, "We leave, and how much of him will walk away too?" (*M. C.*, 164). He also sees that if Lorhetta leaves something of him will walk away too. (Loving someone means giving a part of yourself to that person to "take.")

When Lorhetta does leave, however, he learns that she leaves him a great deal more than he had before. Lorhetta's cultural lessons have helped him to see how prejudice works and how he has "inherited" his feelings about the Killburns from his father. Because of Lorhetta, he begins to see the courage and confidence he has for rural survival. From the swimming experience he learns that he did not ask the right question, but that he performed well under pressure. From her confrontational questions about the Killburns and his family's superstitious fears he sees that he must examine his untested assumptions more closely rather than accept myths or preconceived notions. Lorhetta, the Outsider, tests M. C., the Insider, and he must pass the Outsider's tests in order to keep his title; otherwise he is noncompetitive. But he does not have to leave Sarah's mountain to be competitive, he ultimately discovers. There are tasks to be met on the home front and he meets them, by the story's end, wisely and well.

Could Hamilton have produced anything more after this touchstone of excellence with its memorable characters, richly textured setting, well-orchestrated plot structure, finely tuned organizational pattern, and deep repository of cultural learning? The answer is in fact, yes: each book she wrote in the years following this one had new but equally important strengths. These three early books, however, provide the foundation for all the others.

With *Zeely, The Planet of Junior Brown*, and *M. C. Higgins the Great* the pins were in place for many of the thematic interests and lessons in cultural learning to come: family and extended family as wordkeepers for ethnic heritage; the beauty of parallel American cultures; the "misfit" syndrome of young adolescence; the mentally disabled as victims of cultural and social displacement; concern for the future of the earth and for survivors of all kinds; the earth as both threatening and protective force; story as a path to self-identity and a way for characters to fill in a fragmented world picture; choices for female roles; cross-generational families as important resources for meeting individual needs; and individual and social differences among members of particular ethnic communities.

As Hamilton continued to add one book after another to her literary repertoire, the connections—or dialogic voices—between and among books then and now continued to grow, with links emerging from book to book in themes, settings, characters, actions, and emblematic objects, as we will be noticing in the following chapters.

Chapter Three
Fiction of Psychic Realism

In the decade following publication of *M. C. Higgins the Great* Virginia Hamilton wrote eight novels, all with black, female protagonists ranging in age from 11 to 17. Five of these books—*Arilla Sun Down, Justice and Her Brothers, Dustland, The Gathering*, and *Sweet Whispers, Brother Rush*—are closely linked in several ways.

Each has child characters with clairvoyance or psychic power—as a cultural ability or gift—who either revisit scenes of early childhood or see a future cultural existence. Each protagonist struggles to achieve selfhood in the face of strong male sibling influence. Each book is unconventional and clearly innovative, in contrast to Hamilton's previous novels, since all have realistic characters who mind-travel to a mythic "space" where time is in continual flow and they can use their psychic powers for the good of themselves, others, or the world. Thus as a group these books represent Hamilton's most deeply layered texts, and they are in many ways her most richly rewarding books. They can be read and reread, with still more ideas about characters, structure, and theme surfacing, primarily because Hamilton has placed her protagonists in more than one dimension of ancestral time and cultural space.

Arilla Sun Down

In the area of temporal and spatial constructs, *Arilla Sun Down* (1976), the earliest of Hamilton's fiction of psychic realism, is very likely the most complex in style and concept, or the most difficult to comprehend on a first reading. "It was an experimental book," Hamilton explains, "written right after the Newbery, and my publishers indulged me. It's a different book." Especially different is the structural arrangement of chapters. There are three large blocks of actual time in the present, separated from one another by three smaller blocks of childhood memory—or psychic time in the past. And each block of time, past or present, is filled with embedded or "internal" stories, producing a nested or framed effect.

With time moving forward and backward for Arilla in a circular "flow" of time and space, the novel becomes a fictional exploration of Hamilton's concept of "rememory." It thus becomes "metafiction," as Patricia Waugh defines the term, in that it "explores a *theory* of fiction through the *practice* of writing fiction."[1] When Arilla attempts to remember her early childhood in order to write about it for a school assignment, suddenly stories of the past begin blooming in her mind.

Story Framing and Narrative Structure

Similar to Geeder and Buddy Clark before her, Arilla is an unreliable narrator. Says Hamilton, "The whole book is showing how one character can misread her whole environment completely" (Apseloff, 210). The nested configuration of stories is crucial for unfolding Arilla's awareness of reality (versus what she often mistakenly conceives it to be), and Hamilton's rare use of first-person narration is a perfect sleight of hand for pulling us into these false assumptions alongside Arilla.

Framing, in Bakhtinian terms, sets up an important dialogic tension of authorial intentions: "Behind the narrator's story we read a second story, the author's story; he is the one who tells us how the narrator tells stories, and tells us about the narrator himself. . . . We puzzle out the author's emphases that overlie the subject of the story, while we puzzle out the story itself and the figure of the narrator as he is revealed in the process of telling his tale."[2] Here Hamilton, the author, is in one dimension telling a story about Arilla's life, within which, Arilla, the narrator, is telling stories in order to illuminate further or explore more fully the main thread of story, the life of the main character, Arilla. In metafictional novels, says Waugh, "obvious framing devices range from stories within stories" to "characters reading about their own fictional lives" (Waugh, 30).

The concept of the frame, according to Waugh, "includes Chinese-box structures which contest the reality of each individual 'box' through a nesting of narrators," with frames involving several "levels" of "visions, dreams, hallucinatory states and pictorial representations which are finally indistinct from the apparently 'real.' . . . There is ultimately no distinction between 'framed' and 'unframed'" (Waugh, 31); there is finally or ultimately only The Story.

Story and stories merge as Arilla, the narrator/character, tells her story. And her storytelling is much more complex than we first imagine. Actually she is creating a "book" that grows out of a simple school assignment, as she tells the story of herself as a seventh grader, living in a biracial family in a small midwestern American town, and each chapter of Hamilton's book becomes a segment of this life story. At the beginning, however, all we can see is that she has returned to deeply buried memories that are surfacing now, this year of her twelfth birthday, as she struggles to discover who she is, as a separate identity from a domineering older brother.

Sledding as a young child with her father, Arilla goes crashing over a hill, and her brother, Sun, then still very young himself, rescues them with his lasso. This is the first story. But other stories are buried deeply within this one. There is the story of Arilla's mother hating Cliffville and wanting to leave it; the story of James False Face, an Amerind friend of the family and grandparent figure who describes Arilla's father as a "great wolf, hungered and wounded too many seasons";[3] and the story Old James tells Arilla of herself. She will keep his words and stories and will have a name so sacred for this storytelling role that it must always be kept secret.

On the way to her birthday party more stories come to light. She remembers the Fourth of July celebration a year ago when Sun lassoed several of the town bigots who generally accept Lilly Perry Adams, Arilla's light-skinned mother, a clever and beautiful dancing teacher, but call Arilla's Amerind father a "breed." The story shows that in the face of such a colorful family Arilla feels invisible—and colorless—failing to see what we soon notice: that she *does* have an important talent—remembering and telling family stories.

At the party Arilla tries to sort out the meaning of her mother's mime dance story, wondering aloud to her father as she watches, Is this a warning? Is it possible to get hurt even at your own birthday party? (And she does get hurt; the horse she receives is not what she wants for a birthday present since horses frighten her; she wants instead a name like Sun has—with power.) He answers, "Yes, at any moment. All you can imagine is possible" (*ASD*, 72), a statement signaling a large, encompassing theme for many of Hamilton's books. Imagination can involve risk and trouble. It can also rescue us from trouble, danger, and disaster. It can even "overcome" death, as we see later in this book.

Later in rememory time once more, Arilla as a baby has wandered off from home and enountered Old James and his wife, Suzanne Shy Woman. Shy Woman's embedded talk story, heard by Arilla at this point, tells more about the Amerind people, especially about the importance of women in the tribe, as well as about Suzanne's first meeting with James (called James Talking Story because he was the clan storyteller) and about her own childhood. There were many orphans Suzanne says; people starved and died. The word "die" spoken at this point triggers Arilla's memory of her mother's remark that Cliffville (their hometown at this time) is dying. When Arilla speaks the word "Cliffville" aloud, they then trace her to her family and return her to her home. (Words save us; language saves us. Language keeps us linked to time and place. Words—and stories—are the "goodness" of our kind or our cultural heritage.)

Rememory and Narrative Focus

Back in the present as she arrives home one evening after riding with Sun, it all suddenly comes back to her the way Old James taught her to see pictures in "bunches" (*ASD*, 21) of his words, that remembering (or rememory) works the way a flash works, like "heat lightning around the skating rink, outside but way off dead in the darkness. Do all kids lose whole times and most of years like I do, and then see a little bit of them all in a flash? . . . You watch it repeat itself, echo itself and give off then one image of itself in the dark. But watch out, you have to work fast. Heat lightning only flashes a second. . . . I let the flash echo in my brain again and again until I have grabbed every piece and particle that is in it" (*ASD*, 123).

Back downstairs in the kitchen this night, Arilla thinks about her feeling that she is ugly because of her light complexion and plumpness, especially in relation to Sun's "Red Indian" (*ASD*, 127) looks. Then she listens to Sun's story of why Indians are called "red" and her mother's story of their father's ethnic background (his mother was Indian, but how much is uncertain; she and Sun might be one-sixteenth Amerind or three quarters). This story initiates the argument of which is "right" in defining identity: appearance (Sun's view) or social customs about race (their mother's view). The two stories taken together form another important theme of the book: what it means to grow up in a biracial American home—and the ensuing question that arises for the child: Who am I culturally? Am I what I look like? Or what society says I am? As Arilla discovers, it is both—and neither.

Finally, up in her room, she wrestles with a school assignment ("Write a paragraph about your life"), eventually creating a story of Old James as her best friend in childhood. In the next chapter she is back in rememory time with him. The family, on horseback, is on the way to "see" James who has died. Sun and his mother are riding together on one horse;

Arilla is with her father. As they ride, Arilla begins "seeing" Old James in rememory the day he found her lost in the woods (chapter 5). Her father says that perhaps she will be "the one to talk stories again . . . to save the words in a memory pouch . . . and cause us to be strong and not afraid" (*ASD*, 184).

Arilla has the choice to go with James (because she is so closely connected to him as a kindred storyteller she could be drawn with him into the spirit world) or to stay, "following" him in his role of "clan" storyteller. She chooses to stay, understanding that in the "circle" of time he can still be with her. *"Then I thinking to stay here"* (*ASD*, 196), she says. The progressive verb tense reinforces the notion or rememory time encompassing past and future in present time. *"Stay, then,"* he answers. *"Live with honor. And Wordkeeper . . . Remember who you are"* (*ASD*, 196). Thus he reveals that in matters of racial or ethnic conflicts of identity, neither mirrors nor societal decrees can tell us who we are; only the cultural memories of our family past can define us. And if no one steps forward to serve as wordkeeper of ethnic stories, all our identities are lost.

The remainder of the book shows how Arilla comes to terms with her gift of imagination and how she assumes the responsibilities of it. When Sun and Arilla are riding their horses one day in November, an ice storm strikes and a duck crashes on Sun's head. Three times that day she says the words "Sun is down," as she speaks to herself about the accident saying, "Arilla, Sun Down" (*ASD*, 214). Words (poems or lines of poems) are forming subconsciously to tell her who she is and what she can be: she is the retiring, poetic one, but she is also the one who must now climb the steep hill with two frightened horses in order to save Sun's life.

Later Arilla takes a bus trip to Cliffville, to assume the role usually undertaken by Sun; their father often returns there to recover his culturally splintered past, and someone must always bring him back. She must be the son/Sun now—moon and sun combined—as she replaces her brother in rescuing their father, her final task before she is "entitled" to name—or rename—herself. (All of the characters exchange roles constantly, the way any family does to remain bonded successfully.)

Stories flow through Arilla's mind as she rides along: she resees the day of Sun's rescue, his injuries, his loss of memory, her father driving her home that day, the birds they saw frozen on a telephone wire. The framing effect this time serves to bring the reader up to date as the plot moves quickly along, since Arilla is both reflecting back and trying to reason out the past in this present eclipse of time. She remembers the first time she saw Sun after the accident, how he looked like the moon:

white headband, white cast, white light by the bed, white sheet. She is beginning to see him more realistically now, his vulnerability in this weakened state making him seem less godlike. He suggests that she rename herself, and she has thought of a name now but will not say it aloud. He guesses it will have the word "sun" in it, reminding us of the Jungian principle of anima and animus, male and female intertwined, or the mutual dependency of Moon and Sun in the universe—or here with Moonflower and Sun Run.

She discovers her father on a hill in Cliffville, sledding, and she comes full circle now, as he tells her the story of how as a child she came sledding with him in the nighttime (moontime). He tells why he gives the great wolf call (another story): "Long ago it must've been given to me, although I have no sure memory: a boy goes alone to a high place, a cliff. He stays there alone, looking for a spirit guardian. For the spirit that will protect him the rest of his life" (*ASD*, 258). Arilla sees why he must return to Cliffville: there he has what is his, the wolf howl that establishes his cultural identity. (*Arilla Sun Down*, takes up where *M. C. Higgins the Great* left off, considering what happens if a culturally rooted person were transplanted—or the fragmented life that might result.)

Her father explains how he collected the trunk items from Amerind people who had died, since these days, things are no longer buried with the corpse. They are given away to be used, and she sees a way to heal the fragmentation. They can take the trunk back with them, to be "used" by the family (celebrated, remembered, touched, understood, even worn) with its collection of silver bridle, stone hammer, leggings, belt, and moccasins that Sun himself has never seen.

She is the one with curiosity, her father notes. She is the one who opened the trunk. Sun plays with the idea of being an Indian as a defense against his fears, the same fears he externalizes by boasting. She internalizes her fears by feeling inferior to Sun and by imagining that he is trying to kill her. Yet her vivid imagination is what fuels her curiosity and eventually helps her to achieve something important in relation to the conflict the entire family faces (feeling fragmented culturally).

As the book ends, Arilla is telling herself the story she has been living through—her trip—and considering whether or not she can write it into her autobiography. As a "coda" for the story, she begins to sum up what writing is—a problem solving endeavor in which you can change things around and disguise the "for real . . . of what happens to you and what worries you. Or what you wish for" (*ASD*, 268).

She begins theorizing about writing at this point, that she could imagine her mother on a horse or as a dancer, if she added a new scene into her school assignment. She could create a name for herself more than Sun Down, she also decides. *Arilla Sun Down* grows out of Arilla's autobiography, we see; the title is the name that is more. She has already "written" her mother on a horse, in chapter 9, when Lilly mounts up behind Sun the day of Old James's funeral. And she has created her mother as a dancer from the beginning. As for her new name, it becomes the words she speaks in chapter 10, "Arilla, Sun. Down," as well as the title of Hamilton's book. *Arilla Sun Down* and Arilla's autobiography are becoming one at the same time that Arilla is becoming the "sun," or the sun and the moon are becoming one. Her real name (the one with real power), "Wordkeeper," remains in eclipse, a secret; but as Hamilton's book ends and Arilla's "book" begins, it is clear that she has accepted this gift of cultural wordkeeper as her role.

Thus the themes of how and why we create or tell stories, what it means to be a writer, and what it means to grow up in a biracial home, come together here in the action of storying cultural memories. Remembering who we are by reseeing our childhoods becomes one way we resolve tensions of cross-cultural allegiance. If our rememory time is strong and clear, we can become wordkeepers of the culture (those who tell or write to preserve memories, knowledge, and spiritual meaning through creative imagination—or rememory).

For the sheer beauty of the language, the integrity of the structural design, the thematic importance of the biracial conflict, and especially the way recurring images weave through the story to reveal family conflicts and their resolution (moon, sun, flower, moonflower, circle, tree, great wolf, white sun, plum moon, silver bridle, stone hammer/stone father, curving back roads, and darkness of trees), the book remains one of Hamilton's strongest artistic achievements.

It is also one of her strongest *cultural* achievements, filled as it is with so much learning about North American mythology, in terms of temporal constructs, and about nonhomocentric thinking. Old James's idea of death as traveling in a circle (he is here and now, then and there, in all things), his belief that if Arilla thinks of a time when they were together he will be with her (in rememory), and what we might otherwise consider Jungian concepts of anima and animus in the words "sun" and "moon" that are used so frequently here, all find analogs in John Bierhorst's explanation of North American indigenous cultures:

Each Indian culture, presumably, has its own outlook on the world. But there is a recurring theme that may be described as a sense of unity, or wholeness. People in tribal cultures, we are told, tend to identify the past with the present and to blur the distinctions between space and time, the real and the imagined, and, of course, the human and the nonhuman. We are given to understand that myths, though set in the past, are happening in the present. Even in trivial matters there are signs of unification that seem novel to outsiders. For example, many Indian languages have the same name for the sun and the moon and the same words for blue and green.[4]

During the ice storm Arilla sees—and *lives*—this sense of unity or "fundamental idea" of tribal cultures "that all things are related" (Bierhorst, 232). Nature is beautiful but dangerous, a force to be respected. And man is not necessarily the center—or the most important species—of the universe; all living creatures are entangled in the same web. The sleet blinds the birds (the geese and ducks); the birds stun Sun. He falls; Arilla (the moon) must then save him. But she does not merely save human life. She cares for the horses at the same time; she even runs the risk of losing human life to do so. She does not put Sun's life above the lives of the horses; she does not engage in homocentric thinking. All living creatures are equally important. The horses may in fact be what enable her to save Sun, since they provide the comfort of living creatures in her lonely mission.

Later she sees the birds have frozen and died on a man-made telephone wire—a wire, nevertheless, that will save human life when she uses it to call for help at the skating rink, once she struggles up the hill. It is all a circle, as she has learned from remembering Old James and his storytelling. Arilla accepts the gift of creative imagination and curiosity, of saving words and talking stories. And this theme—the responsibility of imaginative sensibility—Hamilton would continue to explore in her next three books, when another young female, Justice, would discover that her power to see inwardly was taking her not just miles and years but worlds beyond home.

The Justice Books

In Hamilton's 1981 trilogy called the "Justice Cycle" (*Justice and Her Brothers, Dustland*, and *The Gathering*), four children in a small midwestern town form a "unit" of time travel (to a mythic or psychic "space") when the youngest of these children, 11-year-old Justice, discovers she is the recipient of a special gift. The power of the Watcher, a force of precognition and extrasensory, genetic strength, is filling her with the imagination and curiosity to explore (or create) an unknown world of the future: "The Watcher was Justice developing on a higher plane."[5]

Language Patterns and Narrative Focus

Time fantasy is a particularly fortunate choice for the narrative framework here, since it gives Hamilton greater latitude to develop the thematic premise of *Arilla Sun Down*: all you can imagine is possible. In their hometown the children sit in a circle, their hands clasped, their backs against an ancient Buckeye tree that grows beside the water of the Quinella Trace. Here "time seemed suspended" (*JHB*, 88), as the Watcher power of concentration and purpose takes them to Dustland, or Earth, in the future. (The Dustlanders are an "original race" that Hamilton created for the story.) There they discover a timeless void, without water, sunlight, or plant life—a world devastated by nuclear disaster, drought, and deforestation, in which mutant survivors exist merely to search for an end to their suffering.

Later in Sona, a domed city or experiment to reclaim Earth as it was once known, the children discover a way out for the Dustlanders—or the way back to Sona, since many of those in Dustland are exiles of Sona. A synthetic world where machines and mutants have replaced humans, Sona is a place where conformity, sameness, and regulated life is the norm. Anyone rebelling against such a life is whisked off to Dustland for small group survival by a "force" of indifference and ill will, the "Mal."

In its "crossover" or time-travel to Sona the "Unit" has brought with it several nonconformists who had previously been ejected from Sona. One of these is a large canine creature, Miacis, who had earlier chosen to worship a "god" of nature in Sona (rather than a god machine), the sun. Miacis at times becomes a fifth member of the Unit, working with Justice to retrieve her brother Thomas when he breaks away from the others and jeopardizes their unit strength or their ability to mind-travel home.

Unity, or the fused energy of several individuals linked together for greater concentrations of purpose, is what Justice comes to know and act on as the best way her own species can survive, especially in the future. For then her species will have expanded or mutated to encompass multiple life forms that must each be treated equally or given freedom if any are to survive.

The children see a vision of the future filled with supernatural beings as descendents (rather than predecessors)—beings who embody a prophetic vision of the world. And their ability to create such a vision results from the disequilibrium of the emergent adolescent state in which they find themselves. Each child is isolated, either socially, emotionally, physically, or mentally, and each wishes for greater feelings of belonging.

Justice Douglass, the younger sister of twin brothers, is often excluded, ostracized, or physically threatened by the first born of the twins, Thomas, because he is jealous of her. Dorian, almost 13, their neighbor and the son of a sensitive (or psychic medium), is regarded with contempt by Thomas because of his ragged condition and his family's lower economic status. Thomas, at 13, is a clairvoyant with a stuttering problem that has plagued him since Justice's birth and the onset of his sibling jealousy. And Levi, his twin, although gifted with both sentience and strong but dormant analytical ability, is nevertheless physically weak because of asthma and vulnerable because he lacks Thomas's telepathic gift. Consequently Thomas can invade Levi's mind whenever he wishes, controlling his verbal and physical behavior in order to conceal his own stuttering problem.

The mutual desire among the children for "sameness" arises out of their collective—but interconnected—vulnerabilities. The fear that Thomas instills in Justice and Levi, the rage and jealousy that her birth and Levi's presence has instilled in Thomas, and the need of each sibling for the healing power of Dorian, the son of a clairvoyant, produces the need for Unit strength. Unity is forged through the ability of Justice to observe and know through her senses—or through the Watcher power, now embedded in her, that is transferred to the others as they fuse or link together in prescient thought. With their power of sentience, however, these "gifted" children become, at the same time, an endangered "species": they must leave the present and enter the future so that "authorities" in the present do not attempt to control their power or conduct experiments with them, to study their extrasensory gifts.

Place, then, in these books, fills a mythic space of mind; the children's minds both create a place and transcend it to create knowledge about the future. They have been given the gift of sight—the Watcher power—or the ability to envision or create an alternate reality, based on what humans *do* in the present to save animals and plant life, and to support human well being. The names of characters and places in these books resonate with historical, cultural, and ecological associations, producing layer upon layer of meaning.

The word "justice" denotes "right" (equity, honor, fairness); the name Justice or the character here, by extension, is therefore endowed with farsighted, observant abilities and clear-sightedness. The power of the Watcher, filling Justice in her growing "power," denotes knowledge, foresight, and wisdom. But the word "Watcher" also implies the "time" that watches or clocks "give." And because the destiny of Justice (and the Unit) is to bring the gift of the Watcher to the giant machine Colossus in Sona, where it will remain to watch over all time, the word "Watcher" indicates that the children of the Unit will bring the gift of time to those living in the future—or time for knowledge about saving the Earth to grow and develop.

Justice's twin brothers each have names with derivations that carry additional meanings. "Thomas" (from the Greek word "twin") uses his gift of extrasensory perception—in this case telepathy—to invade and control the mind of his twin, Levi, and to "control other minds with marvelous and terrible illusions."[6] Thus he is also called "Thomas the Magician."[7]

Levi, whose name in Hebrew means "joining" and who is described as "the caring, kind brother" (*Gathering*, 25), serves as conduit, connecting Thomas's thoughts to the world when Thomas's stuttering distances him from others and ameliorating Thomas's harsher words and actions with his own sympathetic treatment of Justice ("Levi suffered for them all" [*Dustland*, 9]).

The children begin their time travels at the Quinella Trace lands, the words "Quinella" and "Trace" producing an intriguing puzzle for Justice and revealing that inner stories foster critical thinking. Does "trace" mean "to follow lines . . .or to disappear—and leave barely a clue. . . .If you did leave a clue, you'd leave a 'trace.' . . .She began to puzzle it out" (*JHB*, 35). The word "trace," embedded within which is the word "race," also builds on the meaning of the Great Snake Race (a game Thomas has created for the neighborhood children) as a competition among snakes to determine which snake came in first. The word "race" is, however, in Thomas's plan, a contest among the children to see how many snakes they can collect. The cultural implications of the game therefore generate questions: Is there power in numbers—or in individual strength? Do we have the right to collect snakes—or to race them? Do animals have rights—or are they here to provide our pastimes and entertainment?

These questions, superimposed on another meaning of the word "race" as the color of a group of people, alert the reader to the part that race is playing in the cultural "mythmaking" of the fantasy, as well as to answer to the question of numbers versus individual strength. Socially isolated individuals grow stronger if they are functioning as members of a unit (a family, a community, or a small ethnic or cultural group within the larger community) working together in a "joined" condition or in a common mission—especially when those in power may use (or "toy" with) others for their own pleasure or self-indulgence.

In addition, the word "snake" in the Great Snake Race has the connotation of treachery (Thomas's usual stance toward Justice because of his sibling rivalry). Justice has created a vision of the cottonwood tree that stands beyond her bedroom window as a protector that she has named "Cottonwoman," for she sees it as ancient, "better than a hundred and fifty years old, I bet" (*JHB*, 29), and female, suggesting the female slaves in the cotton fields.

She is befriended by the female sensitive, Leona Jefferson (Dorian's mother), who guards her against Thomas's malevolence. This friendship, plus the inspiration and strength Justice gains from the cottonwood tree, provide the magical help she needs. Justice wins the race when the one large snake she collects (in her mistaken idea that size, rather than number, is the object of the game) gives birth during the "race," thus producing the greatest number of snakes anyone has collected. The female magic helper, a common folklore character, is seen here as righting the wrong of oppressed female. (The Douglass brothers are based to some extent on Hamilton's own family constellation. Says Hamilton, "My mother had very definite ideas in what a girl did. It was a very traditional household. I think I felt that I couldn't do what the boys did, and I resented that. So if you notice, I get even with the boys in the Justice books!")

The alternate fifth member of the Unit is Miacis, a female canine creature that the children encounter as they mind-travel to Dustland, the future (polluted) world of the Earth. (Miacis is a word alliterating with "miasma," from the Greek word *miainein*, to pollute.) Additionally, the dog's appearance in the second book, *Dustland*, coincides with a chemical smell emitted by the ashes the children find on the ground (probably poisonous, they decide). And they begin to infer a "chemical disaster" (*Dustland*, 16) when the dog imprints these very words in her thoughts to them. The thick, noxious atmosphere of Dustland is thus linked, in metonymical ways, to the dog that roams its murky setting.

Language Patterns and Cultural Learning

In speaking of the way language and ideas serve to evoke the human condition, Hamilton has said, "I want readers, children and adults, to care about who these black, white, and native American book characters are that I write. Even my fantasy characters I want you to empathize with. Miacis, the animal out of the future in the Justice trilogy, was a very sympathetic character, although described from the dog family."[8]

Hamilton evokes empathy for this creature by making her vulnerable (nearly blind), friendly, a female sensitive, and especially funny, since her language becomes often a jumbled mixture of colloquialisms that she has collected from "tracing" through these human minds. About Thomas she says, *"Talking about worlmas, Master, shoot. . . . Worlmas ain't no nevermind to nothing, man, lady. He hiding something?"* (*Dustland*, 26). She is also especially large and powerful; weighing over 200 pounds, she is larger than any of the humans, except for the Slakers, a Dustland people who in male form are called Jammers.

Jammers are so named because they have a mutant third leg, used as a weapon against enemies ("jam" denoting the wedging action these beings use to move forward by leaning on their leg). Female Slakers, in contrast to the males, have third legs that have mutated into an appendage used to hoist them up into the air for short-term flights. The male forelimb has evolved into a pouch, as well, for storing "kill." And because they share their kill with females only on threats from them, and because their "inability to fly also causes them occasionally to attack a female attempting a lift-off" (*Dustland*, 91), male Slakers take on associations of male oppressors, even enslavers.

The word "Slaker," taken alone, denotes one who is cooled by water, and the waterless setting of Dustland, causing thirst, hardship, and desperation, reinforces such a denotation. But the word also reverberates with associations of a cultural diaspora, when the Slakers, in the dilemma of crossing over Dustland or leaving it, are caused to rethink their own cultural mythmaking in the face of hope and curiosity about the unknown: "The unit actually went down into the dust. As it ran, as the others ran, they felt a cool, smooth surface underfoot. The dust was at the level of ankles and knees. . . . Slakers, whose myth was that they would never again go beneath the dust, were outraged at going under" (*Dustland*, 61).

Justice and her brothers also encounter in Dustland sets of identical or "duplicate" children. Duster is the leader of a Unit of his own, a "packen" of 15 other children, all age 15; Siv is his "leggens," or fast runner, a skillful hunter (the addition of a letter here brings to mind *siva*, the Sanscrit word for "successful"). Glass is a female companion who runs even faster than Siv, but who kills only on the command of Duster. This time the "beings" are somewhat smaller than human adolescents (but similar in their patterns of conformity), and the names, size, and talents of these characters as runners suggest horses (racers, or even ponies).

Duster's mind-pictures, or memories of tunnels in this setting, produce additional associations with runaway slaves and shelters of the Underground Railroad. "I be on the run myself" (*Gathering*, 13), says Duster to the Unit members at one point. The two meanings of running animal and runaway slave merge for a stronger picture of swiftness and steady purpose: "Inside [the mind of] Siv, Thomas felt he was looking down a dusty tunnel. . . . Lining the tunnel was a dark coating of fear, relieved only by sudden memory flashes of running and killing, eating and sleeping" (*Gathering*, 38).

The force of the "Mal," who comes sweeping over Dustland to check on outcasts and misfits and who ejects from Sona those who, like Duster, are freethinkers, suggests the malevolence (male violence) of both the slave hunters of American history and the totalitarian dictators of many cultures throughtout history who have suppressed nonconformists. Duster's name reflects his exile from Sona into Dustland. The various "crossings" or crossovers of the Dustlanders echo both the Middle Passage (slave trade route) and the passage out of slavery into freedom.

Sona, the city under domity that the Unit and the Dustlanders finally reach (despite the interference of Mal), has associations with the Latin word *sonare* (to sound), since all sounds in domity are in conformity. Matter in Sona is manipulated carefully in order to build life, and humans are controlled for "corporate" efficiency, there being no time for ordinary evolution or mistakes.

From words and names to associations and ideologies, ideas of race, culture, and gender intersect here with ideas of human, animal, and plant relationships, so many characters have become mutants and so few of the original life forms have survived in this future mythic place. Thus we see once more the interdependence of different species or the concept of nonhomocentric thinking that Hamilton emphasized in *M. C. Higgins the Great* and *Arilla Sun Down*. The snake character or figure intersects with the race, culture, gender triad most propitiously to reinforce the author's vision of nonhomocentricity. Justice's sympathy for this primal creature and for its primal habitat is highlighted throughout the Justice

Cycle. At the end of the Great Snake Race, when the snakes must be let loose, she remembers that they could die outside their water habitat at the Quinella Trace.

At the end of the three books it is the Trace that fills her with remorse when she returns from her time-travels having restored the power of the Watcher (the missing knowledge for saving Earth in the future) to the machine Colossus. She realizes with regret that when the Watcher power was with them, in their mythic future space, they did not use it for the good of the Earth in the present:

> Thomas looked at the river with no feeling for it whatsoever. It just smelled foul and he turned his back on it.
>
> Justice wished the river were clean, like the water pool they'd given to Dustland.
> Why didn't we ever set our minds to cleaning up this place? she wondered. With all the power we had, we could have done it easily. We didn't think of it because we take everything for granted—what's one small stream when we have so much? (*Gathering*, 129)

Thus Hamilton emphasizes the choices that humans have in the present—either to turn their backs on saving the Earth or to change the direction of global devastation (their responsibility to nature as a cultural ideal or a social ideology). Cultural values or options can also be seen in the way the children envision an alternative reality or reshape the present reality, as when they make or "see" illusions of themselves or of their culture (imagination as a way of testing, exploring, and entertaining themselves with their newly discovered powers). Justice creates a great "statue" of herself as she wrestles with the heavy burden of the Watcher power within her, and Thomas, the Magician, fashions clothing for the Unit members to wear as they travel through Dustland. He also creates a magic goblet to test the water they create for the Dustlanders, as well as a huge MacDonald's sign, with the aroma of Big Macs, to "feed" them when they return, tired and hungry, from their travels.

Imaginary power can also be seen in the questions they ask and the creative thinking the questions stimulate and in the visions they have— each according to an interest, talent, or need—for reshaping the world and transforming lives. (Dorian, the sensitive, sees the colossus machine of Sona as a great computer; Thomas, the trickster, sees it as a gigantic spaceship; Levi, the artist, as a sculpture; and Justice, the explorer, as a giant coil or spring.) But it is through stories that characters tell themselves and others as they puzzle out their predicament that ideas take strongest root to reveal how separate but intertwined life forms find ways to survive and thrive in an endangered world.

Inner Stories and Cultural Learning

In book 1 of the cycle, *Justice and Her Brothers*, Justice remembers the day that leeches at the Quinella covered Levi's body and Thomas felt the pain even before he saw Levi's body some distance away. Remembering (telling the story back to herself) causes her to understand that Thomas has clairvoyance. It also prepares her for the time (at the end of this book) when Thomas will intentionally cover his own body with leeches, causing Levi to feel the pain, and she will need to use her newly discovered Watcher power to intervene. Friends of Thomas and Levi tell a story about Thomas and his ability to cure a snake bite, demonstrating and therefore establishing the credibility of Thomas's magical gifts (later in the book the narrator will name him the Magician). We see through this story that Thomas is a figure of power and respect among his peers—flawed in his jealousy, cruelty, and selfishness but filled with mythic, charismatic strength.

In book 2, *Dustland*, Justice probes the memories and thought pictures of one female Slaker, the Bambnua, who protects the nonflying male infants by carrying them under her wing to safety when she "flies." And what she sees and learns as she traces (researches, follows the "lines" of) the Slaker heritage, history, lives, and quest provides a mature, female model for Justice in her own quest and in the intolerance she must face from Thomas. In the long struggle of the Bambnua for balance—or in the relentless pull of her independence or her desire to fly in the face of her cumbersome bulk and the burden of her many female roles, responsibilities, and abilities—Justice has a mirror image of her own potential.

As she attempts to sort out the female Slaker's plight, Justice's growing insight, curiosity, care, and concern for others begins to emerge: "They [male Slakers] disliked sharing, and they shared only after threats from the females. Sometime in the distant future, males more than likely would not share. Females would then die out; and so, too, the species. *Maybe the females who learned to fly could learn to do more than threaten. Why don't they try something else?* Justice traced, unsure of what she meant by that" (*Dustland*, 60).

The Bambnua's stories thus enable Justice to create a new mythology for the female Slakers, bold and courageous in its hypothetical reasoning. But these stories also pave the way for further communication with the Bambnua; soon Justice is "tracing" (sending thought pictures of her

own) to the Bambnua a story of her home and history and of the Unit as
a group of time-travelers. Thus she explains through pictures why she
and her "brothers" are a unit and she reveals the power with which she
has been entrusted and the care she feels for her fellow creatures. The
result is that the Bambnua's curiosity overcomes her fear (the same way
curiosity about the quest constantly overcomes Justice's own fears). In
turn, the Bambnua begins projecting her own thoughts within Justice's
picture scenes, stories within stories, so that a new question for Justice
arises: "Is it language we think in? Or is it pictures put into words?"
(*Dustland*, 102).

In Book 3, *The Gathering*, four important inner stories emerge: the
story the children see in Duster's dream memory about Sona when
Duster resided there; the stories the children make as they communicate
in dialogic conversation about what they are observing; the story of the
history of Dustland told through mental pictures that the Dustlanders
make; and the story of Celestor, a Cyborg (a "creature," part human,
part machine, with a human brain).

The first story shows how dreams originate or how the people of
dreams might be those of other space or time dimensions who have
inhabited human minds (as Justice and her brothers inhabit the dreams
of Duster to learn more about Dustland). The second reveals how critical thinking, as opposed to aggression, force, or violence, produces action
in the world to change it:

> *We'd better show ourselves*, Justice traced back.
>
> *Wait*, he traced. *What are they? Somebody knows how to make people just
> alike here.*
> *I don't think so. Not here in Dustland*, she traced.
> *Then there is an outside!*
> *We knew there had to be, else why would the Slaker being try to find an end to
> Dustland?* Levi traced.
> *When I saw them Slakers with their wings and three legs, I said this place had
> to be a zoo!*
> *And I said it was a prison*, Justice traced.
> Thomas nodded. *I think you're right. But who put the Slakers and Duster
> and them here? What have they done?*
> *We'll have to find that out*, she traced. *Come, we'd better get on with it.*
> Gradually the four became visible. (*Gathering*, 27)

The third story reveals how aspects of race and culture, slavery and
environmental blight intersect in the word "dust" (the thirst for free-

dom, life, quality of life, and greenness). Thus it tells Justice, as they undertake the crossover from Dustland to Sona, that the Unit and the Dustlanders are a movement for social justice, with "leaders and hunters, with killers and fools, and thinkers" (*Gathering*, 59–60). The last name of Justice and her brothers (Douglass) serves to underscore this notion, recalling as it does renowned black abolitionist Frederick Douglass.

The fourth story explains how Sona was created to provide reclamation of Earth, how Colossus was built to solve problems of survival, how Starters had made the crossover so that the one mind with the implanting (the Watcher of Justice) could eventually find its way to Colossus, how the gifted of the Earth, the "Starters," left it rather than stayed to save it, and how Colossus healed a mutant, starting the life process all over again.

At last, and through story, Justice learns the meaning of this quest: why she is there in this mythic place, why she and her "brothers" were sent, why they created their mythic "space" and how the green place will be theirs to reclaim in the present "now," if they accept the power. "'Why me?' she wondered. Why is power forever mine? Chance, she answered herself. A roll of the dice. Power is my destiny. And my destiny is wherever power leads me. . . . Accept it, she thought. And she began to walk in tune with her usual energy" (*Gathering*, 157).

The Justice Cycle presents cultural learning about dealing with being different, about how children shape meaning out of their experiences (creative or critical thinking "lessons" or how humans puzzle things out), and most especially about environmental issues and how children serve as change "agents" for the adult world.

The imaginative power of Justice and her brothers enables them to create a mythic story space of future time in which they act to change the world by entering the thoughts and dreams of "beings" in another imaginative sphere. Imagination, then, is what can save the Earth—or destroy it, Hamilton implies. The power of the Watcher is imagination allied with intelligence, care, and concern—all bringing about vision. Each member of the Unit brings something that another member may lack: Thomas has the power of magical invention without caring; Levi has the quality of caring without magical power; Dorian has the ability to heal and care (intuitive intelligence) without magical power; and Justice has creative intelligence or imagination without experience and confidence (like Arilla, she is the youngest and feels she knows "nothing").

Endowed with the Watcher power, Justice is able to keep things steady and balanced so that cultural learning can take place, with imagination as catalyst. And as Raymond Williams has asserted, perhaps *only* imagination can enable us to know in new ways "the structures of feeling that have directed and now hold us" and that cause us to find "in new ways the shape of an alternative, a future, that can be genuinely imagined and hopefully lived."[9]

The kind of literature Hamilton was writing here falls clearly into the realm of what Alex McLeod defines as literature of "social action" or writing that *matters*, considering as it does questions "about what's going on in the world, what's wrong with it, how it might be different and what the future could be like" (McLeod, 101). "I see imagination," says McLeod, "as a process by which people energetically engage with—and ask questions about—their lives and the circumstances that shape their lives" (McLeod, 102). Justice and her brothers are asking such questions and finding answers. So is the heroine of Hamilton's next novel of psychic realism.

Sweet Whispers, Brother Rush

In 1982 Hamilton produced a heroine, Teresa Pratt, who takes control of her life with strong imaginative power for cultural learning, as she struggles backward into the past to reclaim a family history. Here we find neither a cyborg nor a bird mutant helping the heroine; instead it the ghost of her uncle—Brother Rush.

Living alone with her retarded brother, Dab (their mother is a practical nurse, at home only occasionally), 14-year-old Teresa Pratt, nicknamed Tree, sees Brother Rush for the first time on a "dark Friday"[10] three weeks before she knew he was a ghost. "Leaning on a stoop of an apartment building . . . Tree saw him at once. It was the way you see something that has been there all of the time, but you never had eyes open wide enough to see. It was like the figure of him jumped right out of space at her. Brother Rush hit her in one never-to-be-forgotten impression. His suit was good enough for a funeral or a wedding" (*SWBR*, 10).

Actually Rush, who died some 15 years before at about the same age Dab is now, does appear to Tree just as he must have looked at his death, even wearing his funeral suit, it seems. And like M. C., Geeder, and Arilla before her, Tree draws hasty conclusions: Rush wears a belt with a silver buckle with an inscription of the word "Jazz," and Tree decides he is a musician—a piano player. Unaware that Rush is her uncle, she falls instantly in love with him, a fortunate mistake actually, for this is what

saves her from fearing or rejecting the ghost. Even after she learns who
(and what) Rush really is, she remains attracted to him—to the style,
even the "melancholy" of the "stone finest dude" she had ever seen.

Narrative Focus and Creative Process

Three weeks after this first "sighting" Rush draws Tree into the past
through the stories she sees in a small, oval mirror–shaped space of ghost
time that he holds before her. Again imagination is what enables a
Hamilton character to enter a mythic space—in this case a family space.
"It is through imagination," says Hamilton, "that often I can piece
together what might have been known at a particular time. Using all the
facts, the resources that I can bring to bear on a subject, I can speculate
and come up with reasonable explanations" ("KRI," 72). Hamilton's creative process—and that of Tree—or the way Tree reconstructs the story
of her own family past from Rush's mirror time, can be understood better if viewed alongside a description of Maxine Hong Kingston's process
in creating *The Woman Warrior*. As Joan Lidoff says,

> Kingston constructs a fiction of the self that questions the construction of
> the self. She tells her story in wide cultural context, understanding herself
> by understanding her mother and the other women of her family and
> understanding the family through its national culture. In ever-expanding
> circles, she perceives the self as part of a group system in which an indi-
> vidual's inner world is shaped by family mythology, which is formed by
> cultural systems of thought. At the outermost circumference, she creates
> an imaginative version of Chinese culture and the culture clash immi-
> grant Chinese families experience in America.[11]

If we substitute the name Hamilton for Kingston and the words
"African American" for "Chinese," we see that Hamilton is constructing
(for Tree) a self through the rings of growth and the ever expanding circle of family that she sees in this "mythic" space of her family "tree."

The book forms a companion piece to *Arilla Sun Down* in that each
character becomes a wordkeeper discovering and transmitting stories of
a cultural past, to attain for both individual enlightenment and cultural
identity. Cultural learning and internal stories (approximately 19 here)
are woven closely together to produce the fabric of the main story, with
the theme—all you can imagine is possible—surfacing once more in this
book. But the theme emerges with the protagonist drawing pictures this
time, rather than writing or time-traveling to the future.

Tree draws two to six pictures a day—of people, houses, trees, windows, curtains, and families. And what she draws is seen later in the oval-mirror space Rush holds wrapped in a sheet from her ream of paper, when he appears for the first time in a cold, haunting light, "smack through the hard wood of the round table of the little room" (*SWBR*, 23). Her drawing, in effect, has invoked him. (She brings the ghost.) She looks into the space (drawn so strikingly by Leo and Diane Dillon for the original edition of the book) and sees herself and a road, then a house, then a porch swing.

She is now inside a woman's mind (we later see it is that of her mother), where she will "see" the story of her family past. As a story within the story, she also sees the day the ivy fell—the day Brother Rush died and the family members fell down the stairs as ivy tore loose from the wall—nature reflecting the epic proportions of the tragedy.

In the ghost stories of the mirror (a total of four, in chapters 3, 6, 9, and 15) Tree finds the pattern of her family's past life, and she puzzles out the meaning of their story for herself. The pictures she draws are drawing her into her family's past; in creating the pictures she re-creates the past. The ghost is both a device to make this path to the past more visual and concrete (for both Tree and readers) and a thematic necessity because Dab is dying from the same disease that afflicted Brother Rush—porphyria—the hereditary ailment that killed all of Tree's mother's brothers. And his death can be accepted by her more easily if she knows he is being taken by a loved one and not simply left to "go" alone.

Chapter 4 brings Tree's memory story of Dab mixing up his words (humor used by Hamilton to lighten the tragic and melancholy aspects of the story), a girl calling Dab a Loony Tune, and Tree's anger, which reveals her strong love for him. We therefore see here many cultural "lessons" in caring for and understanding a retarded person. In chapter 5 we hear Tree's story of talking to M'Vy (her mother, Vy, or Viola) about Miss Pricherd, a friend who comes to clean each week; then in the main thread of story Miss Pricherd sees the ghost in the little room but later is convinced by Tree that she imagined the scene. In chapter 6 the second story of the oval space unfolds as Tree and Dab go together into ghost time to see more of their family past; this time it is M'Vy beating Dab (a family skeleton of child abuse in this little closet room).

In Chapter 7 Tree reads to Dab a chapter of their favorite book—*The Cool World* by Warren Miller, a 1959 novel about black, urban street life as well as about the rural southern life of the boy (Richard) during childhood. The naturalistic language of the setting is reflected in the dialect

Dust jacket illustration by Leo and Diane Dillon. From *Sweet Whispers, Brother Rush*, by
Virginia Hamilton (New York: Philomel Books, 1982). Reproduced by permission of
the Putnam Publishing Group.

that Hamilton utilizes for the speech patterns of the Pratt siblings. Thus they feel comfortable with what Dab calls the "true words" of the book (*SWBR*, 81).

Inner Stories and Cultural Learning

The reading experience here is especially important for the empathetic, or as Wayne Booth might say, "ethical" learning, that emerges naturally for Dab and Tree. This way of reading involves two stages that Booth describes as "surrendering [to the literature, emotionally] as fully as possible . . . but then deliberately supplementing, correcting, or refining our experience with the most powerful ethical or ideological criticism we can manage."[12] (Ethical reading in Booth's view means ultimately that the story has invited readers to care about a nurturing character.) Dab and Tree first find the pattern of meaning for the book after they read it together. "Say what it means, Tree," Dab says, and she retells the story after reading it aloud, interpreting or explaining as she goes ("Love is it . . . the love in the boy," Tree tells him. "The love the Grandpaw leave him. . . . The boy never, never forget" [*SWBR*, 84]).

Then Dab feels "sadness coming over him" (*SWBR*, 84) as Tree explains that the "enemies gone and kill the Grandpaw for nothing" (*SWBR*, 84). They are "peaceful, knowing for certain why the chapter . . . made them feel so close" (*SWBR*, 84). They are lost and lonely too, waiting for M'Vy to return, like the fictional child, Richard, who waits for his grandfather the day he is lost in the woods. And like Richard, they "could wait out the time" (*SWBR*, 84). In terms of Booth's theory, they care about Richard, and he nurtures them in return. (Literature serves as metaphorical "mirror," helping readers know themselves, others, and the world better for having entered the character's story time.)

Mirror time recurs in chapter 8, when M'Vy returns home and Tree tells her the story of how she has seen Brother's ghost. Her talk and story reveal that even with the knowledge she has gained of this forgotten or unknown child "place" of her mother's abuse of Dab, she still loves M'Vy and accepts her as human. It also reveals M'Vy's shame at her behavior as well as her acceptance of her human frailty (the cultural "lesson" of how humans learn to live with guilt, forgiving themselves in order to survive and keep going).

In chapter 9 Tree takes her third journey to ghost time when she and Dab see Brother Rush in the little room the night M'Vy returns (she enters the room too and senses the ghost, but she does not or cannot go into the "story" time with her children). This night in rememory time

Brother takes them for a car ride that they took as children. They wander off from him as he sleeps, and Dab becomes ill, foreshadowing his later ailment. When they return, Rush pulls off his gloves, revealing sores on his hands (he is ill with porphyria). Later in this ghost time they see Rush as he rides off to a ball game with their father and is killed—or, as Trees feels, commits suicide—when the car crashes and he leaps free of the pain in his life. M'Vy tells them that Rush came for the two of them (to bring them love and a family past). And Tree does come to know herself better for having seen her family roots; she also discovers what a family is like, having been on her own for so long.

In chapter 11 M'Vy explains to Silversmith, her male companion, how Tree can see a ghost; it is a gift to her from her African heritage that Vy describes as the "mystery":

> Oh, when I was a girl, they talk about it. Long time, in a place deep in country. New Jersey, where I come from . . . I never seen the *mystery*. . . . But I remember the talk. Like it happen this morning! Old womens, hanging around. They didn't belong to nobody no more, even they children had left the place or died off. There was one who'd look at me and say, "Afrique! Afrique!" And say some kind of words that rolled out of her like dancing on drums. And she told of *mysteries*, the way you learn them and see and feel *them*. I guess my Tree doing something right. For she seen without nobody telling her how. Say it's in the blood of centuries, comin down the line, just like health or sickness. Dab seen it. It in him too, down the line, blood and sickness! (*SWBR*, 130)

Tree then tells Silversmith her own story of seeing the ghost. They are each sorting out, in dialogic terms, these ghost appearances (why Rush came to Tree at the age of 18, rather than the age he was when he died, and how ghosts can appear to some people and not others). When M'Vy, with her logical, down-to-earth personality, accepts the "fact" that Tree has seen a ghost, Silversmith and Tree begin to accept the reality of it too.

Finally, M'Vy tells the story of her husband's car crash to fill in gaps of the ghost story Tree has "seen." Questions remain unanswered, however: Where is Ken (Tree's father) now? Where are Brother Rush's brothers? Why this strange ailment, porphyria, and what is it? At the hospital where they have taken Dab who is now dying, M'Vy tells the story of the inherited family illness that has afflicted Dab: porphyria strikes between the ages of 17 and 50; all of her brothers died of it. As M'Vy will later explain, "It comes from Africa . . . way long time ago. It was a white man's disease. Traced to South Africa and a Dutch settler.

Then, it became a *colored* porphyria and made its way to America probably through the slave trade" (*SWBR*, 183). (Hamilton had a great deal of
firsthand information about porphyria, since it appeared in her own family in the offspring of her mother's generation.) Chapter 14 tells a story
of Tree's dream of herself and Dab climbing a cable to a tower. She falls
off; Dab dances on up the cable (a prophetic dream, it foreshadows the
future for the reader and helps Tree to deal with what really happens
later).

In chapter 15 more gaps are filled when M'Vy tells the story of why
she was physically abusive to Dab. Ken, her husband, left her alone (and
he eventually abandoned the family entirely), and she took her loneliness
out on Dab. Children thus gain knowledge about child abuse or some of
the conditions that may motivate such behavior. "When you leave
women to raise children," says Hamilton, "you are oppressing them. I
think that black women have been very much oppressed. That's very
telling of my racial experience." Men bringing women down, not letting
them "fly," is a theme of *Dustland*; here Hamilton dramatizes the dire
effects for children when women are weighed down with as many roles
and responsibilities, as the Bambnua was.

In the fourth scene of ghost time Tree sees Rush and Dab laughing
and talking as they drive away, and this story of the mirror causes her to
understand her dream—that Dab danced up the cable to die and she fell
off to live. (He *chose* death just as Rush did.) The dream enables her to
accept the finality of Dab's death ("knowing Dab was dead for good"
[*SWBR*, 181]) and to understand the reason for Rush's return. He came
back for Dab, just as the grandfather came back for Richard in the Miller
novel—because family members take care of one another in death as
well as in life.

Sweet Whispers, Brother Rush is important in Hamilton's "canon" and
for the field of children's literature generally because it is one of the few
books of high artistic merit (many awards it has won) to confront such
serious issues as the death of a young person, problems of single-parent
families, especially black families, and child abuse, all in one book, and
in such surprising or unconventional ways. The book itself, with strong,
vivid characters and a straightforward plot, presents few obscurities for
readers. The difficulty for some readers may instead be in the major
premises—that a mother who physically abuses her child later can
exhibit understanding of self rather than self-recrimination and self-
destructive guilt, and that for these particular characters ghosts really do
exist—at least within the context of the fantasy here.

Hamilton succeeds in gaining reader acceptance of both premises again through techniques similar to those Kingston uses in *The Woman Warrior*. As Lidoff asserts about Kingston's book, "Using multiple points of view produces an irony . . . of compassion rather than judgment. Instead of measuring every action by its distance from a single moral standard, Kingston recognizes the legitimacy of more than one point of view, more than one set of standards" (Lidoff, 119). When Tree enters ghost time we see things from the perspective of Rush and Dab, but most especially from that of her mother, for we enter M'Vy's mind and field of vision, almost as if Tree were still in the womb taking mental nourishment from her mother's feelings and ideas.

Because of these multiple perspectives we begin to feel the pain of this woman who lacks Tree's deep caring nature and her strong imagination. It is Tree's ability to feel deeply about others that causes her to break through the wall of despair that Dab's condition imposes on M'Vy. And it is Tree's strong imagination that enables her to see the ghost and to travel back into the past more often and more intensely than anyone. Her imagination is stronger in fact than that of anyone else here who sees the ghost, because it is fueled by curiosity (she is the child figure with a growing need to know more about her family). M'Vy lacks imaginative feeling; life has hardened her to the extent that she is able to act and act intelligently and logically, but she denies her feelings. Dab lacks intelligence. He feels what is in the world, including the ghost, but he sees differently from Tree; his mirror time with Rush is not hers, and he cannot even communicate clearly enough to Tree to reveal much of what he sees. Miss Pricherd lacks the imaginative courage to enter very deeply into ghost time. Yet she *does* see the ghost for a brief moment. And having more than one person (and especially someone *outside* Tree's family) see the ghost was a daring step for Hamilton to take. Had Tree been the only one to see Rush, the reader could easily have accepted the premise that, in a dream, daydream, fantasy, or mirage, a ghost did seem to materialize for *her*.

Having Miss Pricherd see the ghost, however, placed Hamilton in the predicament of convincing the reader that a ghost was really there to be seen, at least by anyone who believed in ghosts. (A true believer, it is implied, *sees* what is there for others to miss.) In assuming such a risk Hamilton also achieved something important for cultural learning: an exploration of Old World beliefs about ghosts. Because a 1991 Gallup poll revealed that 45 percent of Americans believe in ghosts,[13] it is important for children to understand better those who may have such beliefs. According to Hamilton, the word "mystery" means something that is carried down through the centuries that is extra-ordinarily secret, something kept close to the African heritage. The term occurs again and again in the African-American culture. I'm not sure what it means. I have used it to convey the magic, fetishes, to bring across the Africanness I've described. It is a very African word. It is "conjure" but more than that. It is all of the dark secrets. It is a magic they brought with them. It is spells. It is everything that they believed that we now couldn't understand. . . . A long time ago I came across a black community in New Jersey. I found it very strange to see people who were black living so close to a large metropolitan area but who were living in a rural place, 10 houses in a hollow, just as in the mountains. So very different and so strange. I wanted to convey the place, the "ghostly" qualities of people living their superstitions and their superstitions coming to life. In my childhood there were people who believed these things and they always will. The other world and our world, ancestors, in a certain strata of people, their culture and their heritage (and their ancestors) come together in their belief.[14]

It is not surprising that Hamilton dramatizes Tree's discovery of ghost time through a metaphorical "mirror." Mirrors occur in African-American folk tales as one way for the ordinary person to see ghosts.[15] It is also not surprising that Tree's ghost appears in a wooden table. Traditionally ancestral ghosts in African culture were invoked through wooden objects or images,[16] and Hamilton adds that "here in America, descendents of Africans use carved wooden figures in graveyards." Hamilton's ghost in a table may even be rooted in the belief of the Baganda of Central Africa and the Calabar of West Africa that a child's afterbirth, if buried under a plantain or palm tree, would become a ghost in a tree, guarding as well as ensuring the growth of the plant and in turn the growth of the human child.[17]

What is surprising to M'Vy is that Tree, so long separated culturally from the African "mystery," can see and feel it without being taught. "Say it's in the blood of centuries" (*SWBR*, 130), says M'Vy. Like Hamilton's African-American females Arilla and Justice before her, Tree is filled with the gifts of sensitivity, curiosity, and imagination. Thus she is chosen to enter a mythic space of rememory time and to tell the stories she sees there so that others learn more about the various strands of culture that weave through American life.

Sweet Whispers, Brother Rush is the last novel of psychic realism that Hamilton has written, and in its accessible literary style it is perhaps the most accomplished of the five books explored here, although not the "happiest"—Brother's affliction and Dab's sad life linger in our minds long after the last page is read. "Be a damned ghost" (*SWBR*, 23), Tree says when she first sees Brother Rush through the wooden table, and we see ultimately that "damned" *is* the condition of the porphyria victim, for the disease becomes, in the context of the book, a symbolic damnation that the white slave trade helped to disperse globally.

Chapter Four

Fiction of Contemporary Realism for Young Adults

Between 1984 and 1987 Virginia Hamilton wrote three novels for adolescents: *A Little Love, Junius over Far*, and *A White Romance*. In the book she focused on issues with which teens are often faced: parental desertion or death, female role choices, interracial dating, the drug scene, depression and potential suicide, nuclear disaster and other hemispheric dangers, familial displacement, and the search for a lost home or heritage. In these books she also continued to use language as a realistic scene builder in order to emphasize the social and cultural background of the characters.

Junius over Far (1985) is a cross-cultural novel about a 15-year-old African American, Junius, whose father is of African Caribbean origin and whose grandfather has just returned to his home on Snake Island, off the coast of Puerto Rico, after spending years in America with Junius and his parents. The story has links to *M. C. Higgins the Great*, both books having adult characters who are very much in tune with nature and who serve as role models, helping the protagonists grow into greater understanding of a more natural way of life. Junius's dialect, emphasized throughout, serves to reinforce the dualism of cross-cultural identity, his father taking pride in having lost his island accent and Junius proud of having retained it (the result of his grandfather's influence). The pervasive use of dialect affected reader reception adversely at the time of publication, but fortunately the book is still in print now, when a Caribbean poet has won the Nobel Prize, nearly a million Caribbean people have settled in the city of New York, and the subject of African Caribbean studies at all levels is becoming increasing important for those who value multicultural learning.

A Little Love and *A White Romance*, on the other hand, have attained a significant degree of reader attention. Each speaks dialogically to the other on the subject of teen romance and female role choices, and each is especially thought provoking and important for the way it reverses traditional romance code thinking.

A Little Love

In John Rowe Townsend's words, *A Little Love* (1984) is both a teenage romance and a "considerable novel displaying some of its author's best qualities . . . a simple story . . . brilliantly characterized."[1] Townsend notes quickly the "profound depth of feeling [that] wells out the story. We move constantly into and out of her [Sheema's] mind, and when we are in it we hear her thoughts in the same black English as the dialogue" (Townsend, 277).

Social Stereotypes and Narrative Focus

Hamilton disputes the concept of a "black" English: "I don't know what black English is because black people, depending on where they live, talk a particular way." From one perspective "you're talking of city black people. *Sweet Whispers* is all city or recognizable town; it's based on a town the size of Springfield or Dayton, Ohio." From another perspective, she adds, there is the rural family of the Justice books.

In her own home there was a mixture of speech forms, Hamilton recalls, "It's a certain way that black people talk in the country, although it has a specific kind of colloquial speech and you cannot say it's black. It is Ohio country. It's flat. And so when they speak, it's flat. If anything they talk 'country.'" The members of her own family most often spoke as Justice does, although as she explains, "sometimes people would say, 'Don't you be doin' that,' which is equally a language form of rural white families. Then there were distinctly traditional ways of talking among black people that were in my home also. There were a lot of different influences."

Sheema's speech stands at some midway point between Justice and Tree, since she seems to live in a midwestern town larger than the one of the Justice books, or one that has grown larger during the time her grandparents have lived there. Because Sheema's grandparents are rearing her, her language is shaped by them, as well as by the larger community and culture in which she lives.

Says Hamilton, "I think of [*A Little Love*] as a working-class or proletarian novel. The people in the town . . . live there not because the locale suits them, but rather, because it is comfortably near the available work. When the jobs die out, the lives of the people go into a decline. Or the entrenched work force finds the courage to move to other places that are convenient to other jobs."[2] Of "ordinary intelligence," says Hamilton,

Sheema "is prone to non-verbal expression. Sex is a satisfying force in her life. So is music—she sings; her young man is a some-time musician. Sheema over-eats and is overweight. But food is deeply satisfying to her and she eats all the time. Yet, she is morbidly self-conscious about her weight and her size" ("Philomel").

A serious novel yet at the same time a teen romance, *A Little Love* is, like *M. C.* before it, on the surface a conventional, richly textured, well-told, accessible story (and has received ample awards as a result). Below the surface it is just as much an innovative, unconventional book, for Sheema is very different from traditional romance heroines. Overweight, fatherlesss and motherless since birth, and a vocational student, she enters the story with several strikes against her. Additionally, she is severely insecure and has a history of sleeping freely with anyone who asks her to do so.

Enter the romance hero, Forrest—tall, dark, handsome, undisturbed by Sheema's sexual past, patient, understanding, a prince among teen males. If he has any problems of his own, we do not hear about them. (Of course Sheema, so absorbed in her own problems, allows little room in her life to dwell on his.) So Forrest is also self-sacrificing—an ordinary person with sterling qualities. He needs Sheema more than she needs him, a situation that increases Sheema's power as a female, or gives her the confidence and independence finally to begin facing her crippling insecurities.

Hamilton may even be making the point that strong, dependable, and vulnerable black male role models are crucial for black female readers, or for readers generally who are immersed in mass media sterotypes of black culture. "What happens in America," says Hamilton, "is that most people don't relate to any other kind of black person except one kind—because they don't see them. They see the ones in the ghetto. They hear about them. And the others don't exist" for them. Here Forrest is presented, in no uncertain terms, as an idealized male who never at any time pressures the female for sexual favors and always behaves according to the romance "code" of the gentleman.

In providing Sheema with the allure of the romantic, serious, and caring male, Hamilton appears to be producing a conventional teen romance. From the book's beginning to end, Sheema is gaining the conventional goals that teen romance heroines strive for: the sense of belonging or peer recognition resulting from having a boyfriend, power in a sexual relationship, freedom from oppressive male behavior, fidelity of the male, even the marriage proposal. But she does not work for these goals in any determined, calculating, or even conscious way, as the heroine of teen romance usually does; her needs are elsewhere.

So the "message" of the book is somewhat less conventional than it at first appears: You do not have to be beautiful, thin, white, middle class, academically "quick," or obsessed with getting and keeping a man. You can be yourself, in other words, as Sheema is. You may, of course, have to make certain adaptations to society's expectations, such as keeping a schedule or maintaining sexual discretion, but you are not necessarily as bound by societal constraints as you think you are.

In analyzing the teen romance, Linda Christian-Smith discusses approximately 11 traits or conventions of the genre, all of which are eventually toppled here by Hamilton: peer recognition for the female resulting from a sexual relationship (social acceptance), female power through subterfuge, lessons in adapting to male needs, absence of sexual intercourse for the female, absence of sexual advances and sexual activity by the female, families in control of the female's sexuality, white standard of beauty for the heroine (blond, thin, cover-girl looks), boyfriend's approval as the first condition for the relationship (body over mind; the female's beauty is everything), idealized male behavior, good girl (innocent, non-assertive female) as dominant character, and no discussion among females concerning female role choices in life situations.[3]

Sheema's peer affiliations are so distanced (or her relationship with Forrest so all-consuming) that there is little social value for her in the relationship, at least none that she is actively seeking. As the idealized hero, Forrest has such complete adoration for Sheema (he adapts to *her* needs rather than the reverse) and such strong regard for her as an equal that no subterfuge on her part (nor any grand desire for his approval) is necessary. In her self-absorption, however, she becomes at times somewhat manipulative, or she toys with the manipulative female role as part of her passage to adulthood. At the same time she does not idealize Forrest; she sees him as long, tall, and "ugly"[4] at the same time that she sees herself as short and fat.

She is totally in control and at ease with her sexuality, and she is as sexually active in this situation as she would be in a marital relationship. When she leaves at night to meet Forrest, her grandparents never know, and they trust her so implicitly that they allow her to take a trip with Forrest without even discussing the overnight accommodations.

She is black and, in Forrest's and her grandparents' eyes, beautiful, even though she is overweight according to romance-code standards. She is also a reluctant reader (or in the "slow" category in her school achievement), but she applies herself assiduously to school assignments and completes them with more reflective thinking about societal issues than many high achievers. Finally, even though she does not discuss the romance code with female friends, her introspective tendencies are quite extensive; the book is filled to overflowing with Sheema's internal storying. And once again, as with *Sweet Whisphers, Brother Rush*, cultural learning and internal stories (approximately 22) are woven closely together to produce the main story fabric and the theme of finding one's place in the world, or the world of love—personal and familial.

Inner Stories and Cultural Learning

Internal storying begins for Sheema early in the book. Staring out the school bus window one day, she imagines a story about Forrest cutting off one of his friend's ears, after which Sheema sees herself saving Forrest from the police by saying something funny. The story establishes her as having a strong sense of humor and being aware of it, since she uses her comic talents to build the plot of her fantasy. It also reveals the confidence she has in herself and the ability she has to carve out a little position of power for herself (*she* saves Forrest). Thus, like other Hamilton characters, she puzzles out the world and herself through stories. This time, however, a new pattern in a character's story learning emerges: the story ends with a metaphorical coda that serves as a bridge of associative thinking to the next inner story. "Be something," she says, "if you could hurt somebody like Duane real bad once, and then in the next second they'd be all right again. Like in science fiction, somethin. *Nineteen Eight-four*" (*ALL*, 8).

Suddenly she is immersed in a memory-story of herself reading *Nineteen Eight-four* in the tenth grade. She was not allowed to finish the book; she was considered too slow. Now she sorts out her reading problem by telling the story of her reading (shaping her experience in order to see herself more clearly as a reader): "I *can* read it. It just takes me slow, some" (*ALL*, 8). Thus Hamilton provides cultural learning about how a remedial reader reads—and reads the picture of her classroom world through the "world" of the printed *word*.

Then metaphor again serves as a story bridge (and the heart of The Story): "Very still, in the back of Sheema's mind, curled up like a rag doll and a starving tomcat, were her dead mom and her missing dad" (*ALL*, 8–9). Stories continue as Sheema observes her mother in a photograph and attempts to sort out her own physical appearance. She also stories to herself about her grandparents and the senior citizens' leisuretime "store-front" they visit, as well as about Forrest, his car, and his job, her life with boys before Forrest, and herself and Forrest as a couple (prestories for the main story in order to bring readers up to date).

A important story for cultural learning occurs in chapter 5 when one day Sheema observes Granpop and Granmom dancing to the memory of a song they heard when they first met (lessons for Sheema in what it means to grow old and how memories contribute to life's meaning). She does not prolong or extend this "story" with questions or invitations for them to tell more. She simply observes it, and it heightens her awareness of time, change, and the way humans respond to the past; but, she sees, they should not go too deeply into the past because they must live in the present.

In the story coda Sheema indicates that she is both sad and content-ed, then anxious and worried, but she does not know why. This time the "bridge" is comparative; her grandparents notice that she is a lot like her father, Cruzey, in the way she uses her hands—an observation that leads them to tell a story of her father and his work as a sign painter.

Granmom later gives Sheema a book that Sheema's father has made of his paintings (Cruzey's "story" of his work). Sheema's story of the way she "reads" his book of pictures (a collection of his sign paintings with accompanying titles) reveals how we puzzle out language and how diffi-cult it may be for a reader (especially a remedial reader) to make sense of a text when there is so little narrative context:

> "Sign blank," she murmured, reading again, "cut and sewn by . . . " She stared at the next group of words, murmuring slowly, word for word, "Cruzé, signpainter, me." She stared. "Signpainter, me?" she said. "Cruzé?" She pronounced it Cruze. But then, it dawned. Such words and pictures were all so new-looking, so different. "Cruze . . . Cruze with a lit-tle slash line, an accent, behind it . . . Cruzé. Oh, my goodness! Cruzey, the signpainter, me! I mean, he means, him, Cruzey. My dad!" Sheema practically fell out on the bed. The book toppled from her hands. She came to, as if out of a faint, and grabbed it up again. "It's as plain as day!" she said, in a hushed voice. Sitting up again. "This, his book of signs he made. And he do that canvas sign. And this book tell all he do with painting and stuff." (ALL, 113)

Ultimately Cruzé's book of signs becomes his story (and her story of him) or her way to recognize him by the way he creates—his own way of doing things, like a hair style, she says, or her own handwriting. He has never written letters to her; he has sent only this collection of his signs. Thus pictures or signs become her only way to "find" him—or at least a way to begin looking for him. At this point Granmom tells another story of Cruzey (of the risks he took painting on high buildings), and as the coda of the story Sheema asks why did he have to leave her. Granmom then tells the story of Sheema's birth, and her mother's death, which in turn helps to explain why Cruzey has absented himself from her.

He and Sheema's mother did not get along; he distanced himself from her, just as he has done with Sheema by writing indirectly through pictures, or by assembling a collection of his signs. He does not share his life with her, nor the facts of his life, except for these "facts" about his work, revealing that perhaps the only pride he feels in himself, or the only identity he feels comfortable in sharing, is that of his work. As coda to the story Sheema says, "he blame it all on me" (*ALL*, 122), after which, in the following weeks, she lapses into a depression, the assumption that her father has never loved her taking its toll—and producing a great deal of cultural learning about teen depressions (the symptoms and how families deal with this condition).

Cultural Learning and the Outer Story

Sheema and Forrest later take to the road hoping to find Sheema's father in Tennessee. There they also visit the World's Fair, and cultural lessons emerge when they develop car trouble one night and are exposed to bigoted behavior. (We see the physical and emotional stress that such harassment imposes.) Discussing the motif of the road in fiction, Bakhtin says,

> The road is a particularly good place for random encounters. On the road . . . the spatial and temporal paths of the most varied people—representatives of all social classes, estates, religions, nationalities, ages—intersect at one spatial and temporal point. People who are normally kept separate by social and spatial distance can accidentally meet; any contrast may crop up, the most various fates may collide and interweave with one another. On the road the spatial and temporal series defining human fates and lives combine with one another in distinctive ways, even as they become more complex and more concrete by the collapse of *social distances*. (Bakhtin 1981, 243)

The road is the great equalizer as we see in chapter 10, when Hamilton creates a striking scene of "double-voiced discourse" (Bakhtin 1986, 110), and between the narrating and the narrated voices "mean-

ings thrive and multiply" (Lodge, 195). Before Sheema and Forrest take
to the road, so the narrator's story goes, they had not really known
themselves as Americans. Of course they knew they were teenage and
black; teenagers always think of themselves as another race, says the narrator. But they considered themselves Americans as a feeling that came
and went, since nothing up to this point had ever caused them to see
themselves like other Americans. Being black separated them from other
people. Being teenagers separated them also. But the road brought them
"in." They could be Americans on the road: "To go as fast as possible on
the road without hindrance or obstacle brought them calm, tranquility,
equality" (*ALL*, 142).

Sheema and Forrest, American tourists now, continue to search for
Sheema's father through billboards that might have been painted by
Cruzé. And just as the book he made of his signs signifies *him*, the signs
he paints are American markers for visitors—potential customers of
stores and restaurants, and sightseers. Such signs reveal, in Jonathan
Culler's words, a "systematized, value-laden knowledge of the world . . .
[and] our primary way of making sense of the world . . . [or] a network
of touristic destinations and possibilities which we ought in principle to
visit."[5]

"Signs everywhere," says Sheema, as they cruise along through a neon
blaze, even the Chattanooga Choo Choo signs advertising the train of
1880 linking North and South. "Everythin's a sign" (*ALL*, 165), she
says. And she pulls the small, hand-painted sign book of her father close
to her "for safety" (*ALL*, 165) from all this visual bombardment of culture. What is Hamilton saying about the American culture or social
order in all this focus on signs? What is there for Sheema to *read* as the
world beyond the "words" imprinted on these signs, or the "signs" that
imprint themselves on the traveler's psyche as *words*?

One answer, Culler explains, is the Marxist condemnation "for the
capitalist world system, a celebration of signification and differentiation
concealing the economic exploitation and homogenization that underlies
it (Culler, 167). But two signs that Sheema sees, at the same time, are
similar to those that Culler describes as "persistent and ubiquitous, central to any culture or social order" (Culler, 167), the road signs of I-75
South and the signs for the Chattahoochee and Oconee National Forests.
More than 800,000 acres "of the people's land . . . rich land, their
America" (*ALL*, 189).

Sheema finally meets her father at his workplace in an art studio in
Georgia. She asks him why he never called or wrote her in all these

years, and he tells his story, saying that he wrapped everything away so that he would not have to look at it. "If I didn't see you," he says, "I wouldn't have to care" (*ALL*, 198). The first picture of his book of signs comes to mind, the "Outdoor Close-Up" filled with red, blue, and yellow dots, dark places, and the shape of an eye through dots. Does Cruzey draw his innermost conflict in this "eye," the conflict he cannot voice and therefore cannot resolve?

Hamilton keeps Cruzey a shadowy and mysterious character—and rightly so. To Sheema, the important thing is not *why* this man is such a cold and distant person but simply that he is, and that she is strong enough to accept ultimately, as Granmom says, that "life have its hard edges" and she can "let it go." As Sheema and Forrest leave, Cruzey says he will write Sheema from time to time, and it seems that perhaps he will. But for Sheema it is too little and too late. As they drive home, she tells Forrest about the stories she made up of Cruzey. You think you love somebody, she says, but what you've loved is the *idea* of the person. You cannot really love a father unless he is *there*.

Back at home Sheema tells Granmom that Cruzey has a limp, and Granmom begins a story to explain. But Sheema does not pursue the subject. She does not want to know anything else about him; she cannot keep chasing a ghost, she knows. So the last story remains a blank space, an untold story, as Sheema moves on to a life with Forrest, her passage into adulthood ending as the trip and the book end. Sheema, one of Hamilton's most vivid, realistic, and memorable characters, has gained control of her life at last (and largely through stories).

A White Romance

The seed of *A White Romance* (1987) was actually planted in *A Little Love*, when Sheema and a white student, Peggy Ann, in an early scene appear to be discovering "what it was like being the other one. How the other one lived. Each holding to her own understanding of the other, true and false" (*ALL*, 28–29). Sheema's curiosity soon fades, however, and the book takes off in other directions.

In *A White Romance* this theme of biracial friendship sprouts full bloom when Talley Barbour's all black high school is suddenly integrated, and she finds herself becoming the friend of a white girl whose interest in running matches her own. Didi Adair is blond, beautiful, with movie-star looks; Talley is a small, dark kitten, but they become good friends. It is Didi's friendship, in fact, that sees Talley through the "darkest" moments of an ill-fated romance with David Emory, a white Prince Charming. Says Hamilton,

> I do hope that in this book I have given deeper meaning to the term *romance*. The romance genre is a form of writing that is suited to the young adult age with its moody instability and emotional growth. Traditionally, the love romance is associated with an ordeal, which is in turn overcome by a happy ending. In *A White Romance*, the form is turned around, from boy-meets-girl, boy-loses-girl, boy-gets-girl. It becomes *girl-meets-boy, girl-loses-boy, girl-gets-another boy*. The young man Talley "gets" is the character Victor. This turn-around form is made more complex by the fact that the "boy" Talley loses is white and the "boy" she gets is black, as she is.[6]

Narrative Strategies and the Romance Code

Hamilton does perhaps give the deepest meaning to the term "romance" that any teen writer has thus far given it, although she might have gone one step further and rejected the romance mode entirely, creating a plot of girl meets boy; girl sees boy is a lethal weapon; girl chooses another boy. Here we see instead girl meets the Prince; girl chooses lethal weapon instead; girl accepts the Prince—or is at last handed to him by lethal weapon.

Talley knows David is all wrong for her. (Older than the others in her school, he hangs around year after year, dealing drugs and manipulating the lives of people like Didi and her addict boyfriend, Roady Dean.) But she simply sighs, says so be it, and sits back passively to let him mistreat and manipulate her, right up to his last action: he turns Talley over to Victor, "assigning" her to the person *he* decides will be her new love.

Victor is the "victor"—of sorts. He wants Talley from the beginning, and finally he "gets" her—or she accepts him because he loves and wants her. It is the Cinderella story once more, except that here it is the real *Prince* who must appear. Victor does appear, and by the end of the book Talley has come a long way, saying that she does not want anyone touching her unless she tells them to do so, or anyone telling her "what to do or not to do."[7] But she is by no means at this time a ground breaking feminist. As she and Victor jog in tandem to the bus stop in the final scene, "no way was she going to pass him" (*AWR*, 191).

So we are still in teen romance country here. The question is, How will Hamilton topple conventions this time? She begins with the romance code heroine. Talley is Hamilton's most innocent female, "limited," Hamilton says, "by her city isolation in one neighborhood . . . self-conscious, lonely and overly romantic. She has a single father . . . strict and over-protective of her" ("Putnam"). And when she finds herself suddenly in an integrated world that is "no longer as safe and secure and predictable as it once was" ("Putnam"), she becomes a strong candidate for cultural initiation, largely because she has so many illusions and misunderstandings about the white world. At the same time, she becomes a strong candidate for sexual initiation.

Rule 1: To undercut the romance code in subtle ways, choose a character toward whom your audience of romance enthusiasts can feel generosity and sympathy. Here readers cannot help but revel in Talley's cuteness, her childlike lack of sophistication or her innocence. She is the universal child-woman, unthreatening to males and females both.

Rule 2: Once your romance character is established in readers' minds as adorable—and clueless—keep as many conventions of the romance code intact as you choose, since readers will begin questioning the code themselves when they see their beloved heroine so oppressed and dehumanized by it. (Sheema is not so innocent, so she rejects or ignores the romance code herself.)

There is social value for Talley in her relationship with David; he brings her the sense of belonging that she has not had before—an entry point into a new peer world. But the only power she has as a female in this relationship is what she attains through subterfuge, since David's approval is now everything to her, and she realizes that he likes "controlling her. Being the one pulling her strings" (*AWR*, 134–35). The book, presented as it is from Talley's point of view, provides romance code "lessons" she has learned from other girls concerning how to relate to men and adapt to their needs. "She was dressed. She got to her feet. You have to stay cool. They don't like you uncool. She'd heard that from other girls. But she was still nervous" (*AWR*, 128). There is no sexual intercourse for the heroine—or at least none until David arrives on the scene—and then of course it is only natural that she succumbs, since he has, as she decides, a body as "perfect as a god's" (*AWR*, 128). Even though they enter into a heavy sexual relationship, however, she is never the one who makes sexual advances. She is passive, always accommodating herself to him. Her family does not maintain control of her sexuality, yet her father's strictness—and his attitudes toward interracial dating—prevent her from discussing David or even allowing him near her home. The white standard of beauty here is given to Didi (assertive, poised, self-confident—everything Talley wishes to be), whereas the good girl as protagonist (meek, shy, naive) remains with Talley.

One convention of the code Hamilton appears to be rejecting from the beginning is the idealized male. That Talley sees David as the romantic hero for such a long time is a major irony of the book, especially when he is so blatantly oppressive. He seduces Talley on the first date. When she protests the swiftness of this matter, he orders her never to say the word "don't" again. He overpowers her, resists talk, taking no time for her feelings or for conversation. He calls her stupid repeatedly. He tells her that she is his property. He manipulates the physical relationship so that everything exists for his own convenience. He chooses her as his girlfriend at least partially because he can use or exploit what she has that he needs (she is a good cover for his drug dealing since she has a good reputation and she is black—and so is the assistant principal). When he tires of her, he tells her he likes her but also likes to date around and does not like sharing her with a black dude (his trumped-up charge). He is condescending about her father's work as a night watchman. Ultimately, he fixes her up with Victor, treating her as a puzzle piece, she notes, to be pushed around heedlessly.

As dark as this picture is, it pales considerably when placed beside his most offensive act. On their first date, he kisses Didi right after engaging in sex with Talley, even while he is still holding Talley: "Talley saw it all. She went dead cold inside. She couldn't believe it, but she saw his tongue part Didi's mouth" (*AWR*, 130). His need to control and hurt others is especially noticeable in this same passage: "He was kissing her. He wound his hand in Didi's blond blow-hair. Twisting it, pulling it hard enough to hurt her" (*AWR*, 130).

The one convention of the romance code that Hamilton does not leave intact at any time is absence of female introspection. Talley and Didi talk a great deal from the start, and Didi is very knowledgeable about the way reality deviates from Talley's romantic, escapist notions. Thus she manages to teach Talley a great deal. Of even equal or greater importance, Talley's internal storying is so extensive that the inner stories become the outer story for the most part, with Talley's thoughts, memories, narratives, conveying—or carrying—the main thread of the plot. Talley might even be considered Hamilton's most introspective character, her innocence providing fertile ground for her storying and consequently for her growth process, and the story becomes in many ways a female bildungsroman.

Inner Stories and Cultural Learning

The title of the book, *A White Romance*, is the name of the one big inner story that Talley is telling back to herself for a great deal of the book, as she moves through The Story. And this inner/outer story rays out into racial, parental, and sexual conflicts as the book proceeds. "A White Romance" is therefore the cultural picture she views through a rose-colored lens; at the same time it is, as Hamilton says, Talley's nickname for her new white friends, Didi and Roady,[8] and their relationship—or her illusions about it. Their "romance" takes on darker implications for Talley as the novel unfolds—from the first blush of their Hollywood sex life that she sees projected on the teen silver screen one day in the school corridor, to the more pathetic moments of Roady's drugged existence and Didi's dogged devotion in spite of it. Later the meaning of the phrase shifts to include the sex act of Talley and David, Talley's own white "knight," which occurs in chapter 11.

The book begins with Talley, on the way to Roady's apartment where she is meeting Didi, storying to herself about Didi, Didi's mother, her father, her school. Here the story memory of Didi and Roady's "white romance" also begins, but soon Talley begins thinking about issues of integration versus segregation in her school, and this stream of thought leads in turn to a bucolic idyll about white students and their dating patterns:

> A White Romance, AWR, like a part of her network, her screen of pretty pictures, a bloom of some kind. It sat there in the O's of figure-eights to smooth highways through spring-green hills and mountains. Pretty little cabins all in the flowering woods. Talley kept such pretties in clear pictures inside her. She kept AWR in manicured lawns—long skirts and pink parasols. And safely away from all the messes you could come across in these "sit-tay" streets. (*AWR*, 17)

At Roady's apartment she first encounters David Emory, who is "scoping" her (*AWR*, 23) and quickly insinuating himself into her life (sexual harassment, teen-romance style). Soon she is storying to herself the memory of an entire background of racial conflict in her school, as well as her father's attitude toward whites. The first lesson she is learning about whites is that all are not rich and a lot are not so bad.

As Didi and Talley leave Roady's apartment to go running, they talk about sex. Talley says that she imagines the sex act to be "wonderful" and the same for everyone in this "wonderful" quality. Didi explains that the individual couple will make each act different—and the real thing will not always be pretty. Her relationship with Roady definitely bears this out, Roady's condition becoming more and more hopeless as the book progresses. As the chapter ends, Talley remembers the "white romance" of Didi and Roady as something wonderful for everybody who saw it, revealing that a public display of sex will elicit a collective response that is different from the personal response of the participants themselves (similar to the Hollywood love scene that elicits generic box-office appeal).

The story of Didi's "white romance" finally unfolds in chapter 6. But first we hear about the dream Talley had the morning that this Hollywood "thriller" occurred. Above the bed she saw a mousehole (the female passage to maturity) and a bat looking at her. Her legs were bleeding; the bat had sucked a "bucket" (*AWR*, 59) of blood from her (the fear of sex, or fear of maturity in the female sexual passage). Then someone she could not see (a guy, a friend, she says) told her they would seal up the hole, after which he helped her out of this place. Here again, as in other Hamilton novels, dreams are used in a prophetic sense, portraying psychic images, in Jungian terms, that can be read by the character or the reader as a sign of the dreamer's wishes or fears working in tandem with nature. Since we know that Victor helped her the day she was pressed against a school locker during a hall fight (fascinated by the fight, as well as fearful of it), we see the dream also as foreshadowing: Victor is the friend who will help her through her own sexual "passage."

Then she tells the story of the day that this "white romance" was born: Roady, a "leather dude Prince Charming" in Talley's eyes, initiated the sex act with Didi, a storybook princess, at their school locker (actually a simulated scene says Hamilton: "They went only as far as they could go" before school authorities appeared on the scene):

> Didi was slanted half inside her own locker like she intended to lie in it. She'd backed away from the dude, who was now on her like snow on ice, melting. . . . He was lifting her up along the leather as high as his waist. She was up his body, no two ways about it. Talley saw it all . . . Dude, moving with Didi. Something so secret. Stunning, shocking, weren't *even* the words for it. . . . Going to get in some mess, too, she thought. But then she saw Didi's hands on the dude's hair. . . . Hands, like bright flowers; like white lily petals. . . . So romantic! Lilies. White and still. . . . It's a white romance, Talley found herself thinking. . . . "A white romance!" She yelled it, delighted by the beauty of lilies and love. (*AWR*, 64–66)

Chapter 7 is a memory story of Roady's dad when he is called to the school (Roady's punishment for the hall caper). Another lesson: money does not bring goodness or good sense; Roady is neglected, undisciplined, unloved. Later at home, writing a story for a school assignment (the scene speaks back, dialogically, to the scene of Arilla and her school writing), Talley creates a story in which a black girl falls in love with a black boy, but does not want to do so. The title "Say It Isn't So" implies the strong fear she has about an interracial relationship (in fiction—or life). The story of her writing process, of wrestling with how to create characters of color, provides interesting and important cultural lessons in the way that writers of color feel they must deal with issues of race in fiction. As Toni Morrison explains, white writers feel compelled to designate the race of their black characters, but the "white character is white, and we know he is because nobody says so."[9]

Talley always thinks of color as she writes (there is no way not to, she says), but now she realizes that Didi never has to wrestle with such problems. Thus friendship with Didi causes her to see better into herself and the deepening dilemmas of cultural identity she is facing. Ultimately, she sees that she does not really have to say anything about color; she just thinks that she does. She continues rewriting the story with no color references and discovers that color can emerge naturally and clearly on its own, indirectly, by what characters think, do, and say.

In chapter 11 Didi tries to warn Talley about David without really telling her the facts. (Didi had been David's girlfriend before he "passed" her on to Roady. At the same time he is Roady's dealer, so Didi must comply with whatever degrading tactics David uses on either of them.) There have been several clues in the text that David is a drug dealer, but Talley remains in a denial state because of her innocence and her attraction to him. Also, as Hamilton says, "David is slick. And that's the point about drug dealers; everyone knows them. They are your friends. Here everyone knew him but they didn't see him as the lethal person he was."

On their first date Talley has supper with David, after which they engage in sexual relations against a background of rock song lyrics that are as generic as Talley's emotions at this time—and as superficial as her perception of David are. Her adherence to the romance code is especially strong here, we see from her thoughts, as she becomes mesmerized by the lyrics ("Her body had a mind of its own" [*AWR*, 123] and "She was heat to this fire" [*AWR*, 124]). As the evening progresses her thoughts continue to be filled with romance-code thinking ("He kissed her and she went limp with her love" [*AWR*, 128]), especially ironic since David soon kisses Didi while still holding Talley.

Talley at last acknowledges that David is a dealer (the clues have registered one by one, as he constantly takes "something" out of his *silver* bookbag and passes it on to his classmates). She also sees that David likes controlling her; thus she begins to see this "white" romance as a "night" (evil) romance and to question the reality of it. She decides that she needs someone to confide in and Didi is not enough. She cannot confide in David, she also knows. He is not that kind of guy. So she is learning what real love means (and what Didi and Roady have beyond lilies and leather): having someone to talk to, trust, and love, without being manipulated, controlled, or used.

She remembers how she and Didi settled things after David kissed Didi. (Didi tells her only that it was a show of power, thus confirming her earlier suspicion about his dealing, and building her picture of David as having a pathological need for power.) Soon thereafter David tells Talley about his sister's involvement with drugs; at the same time Talley tells him that she has informed Victor about the drug dealing. David then tells his own story of why he deals; he says he knows what is best for people. He also offers Talley drugs at this point, saying he knows what is best for her too. Talley continues her relationship with David (when he takes her to the rock concert, she has a strong feeling of belonging in the world), but disapproval of his dealing eventually causes the relationship to wear thin, especially when he is caught and expelled from school.

Cultural Learning and Thematic Explorations

Victor gradually moves in on David's turf, and Talley ultimately accepts Victor as her new boyfriend, after lashing out at him for his conventional upbringing. Thus we see that a great deal of Talley's attraction to David has been the more exotic, liberated life he lives and the freedom from racial oppression and poverty that his race affords him. No matter how bad David is, he takes her away at least temporarily from this hated underclass condition. So we begin to see why Hamilton has created David as a drug dealer, the worst possible thing he could be (short of an overt killer). If conditions are so bad that a black teenager will accept—and crave—the attention of such a person, these conditions deserve closer examination.

Of course David is not simply a drug dealer; in fact, if we examine his character carefully we discover that his dealing is the top layer of a many-layered historical problem in America, one that alternately fascinates and repells Talley. Peeling off the layers, we see David as the drug-dealing male power figure that Talley slowly begins to see, as well as what David sees fueling his success: "How do you think I get away with dealing?" he asks Talley at one point: "Because I'm white and good-looking and act like I have some manners. Hey, Hollywood! And don't fit the stereotype of black and bad" (*AWR*, 142).

In historical terms, however, there are other layers of cultural meaning to be seen with these characters. Talley's first name is suggestive of an old southern city, Tallahassee, and David's last name is the name of an old southern institution (Emory University). Talley's romantic visions of long skirts and pink parasols are suggestive of plantation days. And David's "kissing" a white woman at the same time that he holds a black woman (plus Talley's notion that she is enchained, and David's attitude of racial superiority, coupled with the names of these two characters) suggests old southern places and memories of the days when female slaves were abused sexually by white owners and overseers.

In modern terms the layers go even deeper, with naked power as the great American pastime embodied in David Emory's constant need to control, his use and abuse of people, as well as his desire to assign sexual relationships rather than simply share his life with another human. The desire to play god, deal, make money, attain more and more property, speaks most powerfully here of a decadent white power structure. Roady and David escape the dehumanizing effects of upper-middle-class emptiness with drugs and drug dealing. Roady and Didi produce and star in their own R-rated "movie" (in reality the ostentatious display of sex: excessive, out of control, titillation for the classmates who watch, especially Talley with her childlike curiosity and fascination—and subtle ridicule).

A White Romance abounds in cultural learning, and especially important learning, since a black writer here is producing both white and black characters, thus revealing a perspective that white writers may not have, their own cultural blindfolds often held so tightly in place. Hamilton begins by examining how females can deal with the romance code more critically. ("Conditioning," says Hamilton, is what causes female oppression.) Some females are more adept at examining the code than others; thus Didi "teaches" Tally, and by extension any female reader, to become a more critical "reader" of the male-female world.

With Talley as her prime example, Hamilton reveals how females adapt so frequently to male needs for the sake of the "code," and why it is not to their benefit to be so passive and pliable. She also exposes readers to insights about what love can really mean, as revealed by Talley and Victor, in the last scene of the book: "When she walked faster, he walked faster. When she slowed down, he did the same. He wasn't so much watching her moves as he was feeling what she was feeling" (*AWR*, 190).

There is also important practical learning here such as "lessons" of living in a central city (the safe way for females to ride a bus in a dangerous place). Hamilton focuses particularly, however, on interracial school and dating conflicts, as well as on what a family is, and how, in the absence of traditional nuclear and extended families, friends can band together to create "families" of their own—small group-survival units such as that Talley, Roady, and Didi form in their lonely and dejected situation. And it is this notion of a created family, Hamilton says, that has tended to preoccupy those high school students, with whom she has conversed about the book, far more than the notion of interracial dating.

She also focuses quite clearly on what it is like to be black and searching for an identity in America. Talley is pulled in two cultural directions—African American and Anglo-European American. The cross-cultural cast reflects this tension. Didi is the all-American cover girl, blond and beautiful in Eurocentric terms. Vera Adair, her mother, is the European immigrant who produced this Daryl Hannah lookalike. Hale Barbour, Talley's father, is black American, conservative, and segregationist. Talley reflects both the obsequious posture of blacks enslaving themselves to white oppressors for greater opportunity, the result of too much innocence or unsturdy self-esteem and the hooray-for-Hollywood mentality of Americans generally. David Emory and Roady [James] Dean, weak, wealthy, and white, are two sides of the same devalued American coin. Victor Davis is the American black athlete, up-and-coming star, a "white" knight with the indigenous cultural strength to resist corruption. (Characters elude color stereotyping because of the way they have been placed in unconventional roles.)

Ultimately Talley chooses (or is chosen by, or absorbed back into) an African-American identity. The implication: white Americans, obsessed with power and replete with residual bigotry, continue to oppress and misuse black Americans. Black females—living with this power and identity vacuum, overprotected by black males—exploited by white males, are doubly oppressed. And they enchain themselves further by adherence to an archaic white romance code.

Hamilton leaves one intriguing question unanswered here. Is there an African-American romance code? If so, how does it differ from the white one? Sheema, as she maintains her own African-American sexual identity, reveals that a black romance code may be very different from a white one. Yet both Sheema and Talley (and, more recently, Buhlaire) are chosen by black males they eventually accept (rather than choosing these same males for themselves). So we might wonder which is more prevalent in teen romance codes of various parallel American cultures today: a propensity of males to choose females (and a propensity of females to perpetuate this condition) or a more equitable situation?

Another idea, untouched on here (in order not to undercut the "whiteness" of Didi's white romance and the notion of white upper-middle-class decadence in Roady's degenerative drug habit), involves what for black females today remains a troubling dynamic, as expressed recently by Bebe Moore Campbell: the white female/black male configuration of interracial sexual relationships.[10] Another book, another time perhaps. At any rate, with *A White Romance* Hamilton completed a small but strong collection of fiction for teen readers and began turning her attention to books for younger readers, her writing talents and interests equally at home in either camp, as we see in the next chapter.

Chapter Five

For Younger Readers: Fiction of Historic and Hometown Interest

Between 1983 and 1993 Hamilton published a cluster of six books in which either mystery, humor, a dialogue-driven plot, songs, or illustrations facilitate the story line: *The Mystery of Drear House, Willie Bea and the Time the Martians Landed, The Bells of Christmas, Cousins, Drylongso,* and *Plain City.*

These books are connected additionally through their focus on place—small midwestern towns not unlike Hamilton's hometown of Yellow Springs, Ohio. "Place establishes the multicultural and generational aspects of my work," says Hamilton.[1] For each book she has also conducted extensive research in the period dramatized, and she has integrated factual materials with fictional themes of the extended family, holidays, home, and hometown.

The Drear Books

The Mystery of Drear House is a sequel to *The House of Dies Drear*, a novel Hamilton had published in 1968 right after *Zeely*, and the two books speak dialogically to each other across a 20-year span. Each book has as its protagonist 13-year-old Thomas Small, who has just moved with his family from the South to a strange old house in Ohio, where his father has taken a position as a history professor in a small college not unlike Antioch, in Hamilton's hometown.

Once owned by an abolitionist, Dies Drear, the house was an important station of the Underground Railroad. (The house is not based on any one house of Underground Railroad days in Yellow Springs; Hamilton says; instead it grows out of a frightening childhood experience—a "haunted" house of a family named Dies that Hamilton passed each day.) The Dies Drear House of the story is now in the care of a man as strange as the house, or at least as haunted by history as it is. His name, Pluto, and his green eyes suggest a mythic underworld residence, as his home is actually an underground cave near the Drear House, where he guards a collection of domestic artifacts (tapestries, carved glass, Indian handiwork) buried deep within the hillside, a vast historical treasure accumulated by Drear for use in buying the freedom of runaway slaves. Pluto's neighbors, the Darrows, have for years searched in vain for this wealth, and it is his fear that they will discover and then squander it.

In the first book Thomas hears the legend of the house: two slaves were killed by bounty hunters the day that Dies Drear was murdered, but there were three slaves in the chase. So the mystery of the third slave becomes the focus of the book, since it seems that he may be an ancestor of either Pluto or the Darrows. Pluto tells the story of the Darrow grandfather, River Thames (named apparently for the Thames River in Connecticut where his Algonquian tribe had lived), who came down from the North with Dies Drear. Thames was a Mohegan, and he and his grandson, River Swift, had always hunted for the legacy as had Pluto. But they hunted, as boys together, for different reasons. Swift hunted out of simple greed; Pluto hunted for his identity, hoping or imagining that as the descendent of the last slave, the house would show him who he was. He hunted heritage and history as an answer to the puzzle of his own humanity; thus he grew to love the house and to walk the tunnels so often that he was able to walk them blindly.

In the second book the Darrow mother, Mattie, brings together these two strands of cultural heritage. (She is black, and there may be Indian ancestry in her background also.) The Indian searching for lost treasure and the black free slave searching for a lost identity therefore merge in her. She too is able to walk the tunnels blindly, but the burden of so much history and so many memories (and of two warring ancestral spirits or cultural strands within her) produces a schizoid mental splintering, and she becomes even more obsessed than Pluto about the house.

For Pluto (and Mattie) the past still exists in the present: Dies Drear *lives* in Pluto's thoughts and dreams; the historical orphan of slavery days lives *in* Mattie's mind. Years pass, and the next Darrow, River Lewis (Swift's grandson and Mattie's husband), becomes afraid of Pluto in his eccentricities and sees him as the devil. In the second Drear book fear also fills the townspeople, who think the Drear House is haunted (actually Mattie wanders all night through the rooms with her lantern glowing, producing the look of a haunted house).

Pluto's son, Mayhew, helps to unravel the slave mystery; in the first book he tells Thomas and Mr. Small about Dies Drear's decree that the cavern treasure would be "inherited" by the first son of slaves able to find it. (The one cut off from his past who found it would find *himself*, Drear said.) Pluto tells about stumbling onto the treasure because Dies Drear had built a wall of dyes over dirt. Walter Small speculates that Pluto was probably the great-great-grandson who heard the ancient tale but to whom it would, in each retelling, have become less clear and more mysterious (more openly interpretive). Mayhew explains that the third slave was not the only slave who ran free (the cavern still had one slave in the tunnel the day the others were caught). Pluto describes how the limestone bled through the paint to show him the secret opening in the cave wall and the way to the treasure. Thus the four of them—Pluto, Mayhew, Walter Small, and Thomas—construct a story, in dialogic format, of Dies Drear and the treasure, and Thomas is accepted as one of the adults (wise enough to contribute something with his questions).

A little later the adults are also young enough in spirit that they can "play" as children when they create a skit to frighten the Darrows as poetic justice for their earlier harassment of the Smalls. In the process they all learn valuable lessons of history through drama as another form of inner story. When Thomas and his father take on the role of runaway slaves, they begin to understand better the stories that Pluto has told, as well as to experience the feelings and attitudes of slave life. Dressed in tatters and rags, with chains clanging, Walter Small feels the loneliness, fear, and desperation that Thomas earlier imagined when lost in the tunnel.

Mayhew, playing the part of Dies Drear, understands better the man he has called a troublemaker. Pluto has the pleasure of really becoming the devil when he scares those who treated him as a devil. And Pesty, the Darrow child who has secretly befriended Pluto, has the fun of transforming her horse into a winged demon to accompany Pluto's act. "When drama is a group-sharing of a dramatic situation," says Gavin Bolton, "it is more powerful than any other medium in education for achieving . . . a deeper understanding of a fundamental human issue."[2]

In the second book historical puzzles are centered in the heroine of Mattie's stories—an Indian ghost maiden. Pluto tells the story of Mattie Bray and how history is "knotted up inside" her so that she is "ill in the mind."[3] Hamilton says she created Mattie as catatonic (a schizophrenic disorder characterized by immobility, negative behavior, and loss of speech) based on her observation of a neighbor with this illness.

Mattie can be compared to Junior Brown (her unstable mental condition, the comic lines she delivers at times, the way her mental state is used to reflect issues of race and society, and her large size). Here, however, Hamilton uses a mental disorder as a way to dramatize a thematic question: How should we deal with the past? Should we use it, as the Darrows would use the treasure, for ourselves? Or should we preserve it at all costs, even if the past is filling us up to the point of psychic bursting—or shattering? Mattie is a very large person: "She might have been five feet eleven inches or even over six feet tall, Thomas supposed. And she might have weighed two hundred, three hundred pounds, he couldn't be sure. But she didn't look fat. Just big" (*MDH*, 85). Metaphorically, she is very large also since she is filled with so many memories, and, as the narrator has said in speaking of Great-grandmother Jeffers, memories enlarge us.

Mattie carries so many memories, and so much history, so many conflicting ethnic strands that her mind is becoming unraveled with the burden, particularly with the story of Coyote Girl, which obsesses her yet cannot be put to rest because Coyote Girl herself cannot die. (In Indian trickster tales, Coyote is usually killed, but its death is not permanent. In the next story of the cycle Coyote is always much alive once more.)[4]

Mattie seems to see her daughter Pesty as both an orphan (in the first book her son, Mac, Thomas's schoolmate, has told Thomas the story of his little sister, Pesty, and her arrival in the family one night in a tin tub) and the Historical Orphan or runaway slave child (a role Pesty often takes in her play) who never ceases her running ("She stared at her orphan child, whom she kept safe in her house and hoped never to send along the underground road" [*MDH*, 173]). Such a dual identity explains why Hamilton keeps Pesty's origin a blank space in both books: like Mattie, she can then be seen as larger than life or, in mythic terms, as the historical slave child who never dies. Thus she keeps the myth and the mystery of Drear House alive.

The Drear books are among the strongest in matters of cultural history of all Hamilton's books. We learn how slaves navigated the Underground Railroad (how they read the slave cross, what crosses were made of, and where they were found, even where the last hiding place for slaves was—the black church). We see how members of a group culture help one another to help themselves by fighting ignorance, greed, and oppression with friendship rather than enmity and how a culture is made richer by the blending of races, ethnic groups, genders, experiences, educational backgrounds, and age levels. Dies Drear was a white abolitionist teaching slaves to read the cross and work the tunnels. Coyote Girl, the Indian Maiden, part black, part native, saved slave children with her courage. Pluto, with no formal education, and Walter

Small, a professor, are both black historians and keepers of history (caring about and preserving the past for others).

We learn how history and ecology intersect when Hamilton shows people interacting with the wilderness of Drear country in various ways. Great-grandmother Jeffers lives closely in tune with nature, in her cabin in the North Carolina mountains. When he whittles, Thomas reveals that he too is in tune with nature, since he never really thinks consciously about what he carves, his process is so natural. Not everyone has this feeling that nature and man can "fit" or work together, however. The Darrows rush about in hot pursuit of the treasure—to no avail—unlike Pluto, who waits out the time and finally sees the limestone "unveil" the treasure before him. Mayhew has no great love for the wilderness, for Dies Drear, or for the treasure. And Walter Small has not lived long enough in the wilderness to feel what Pluto knows—the living sense of the past—yet he brings rationality and balance to the question of the treasure when he meets it, in contrast to Pluto, who clings to the past rather than uses it to nurture life in the present.

Walter Small is really a very "big" man wrestling with a big dilemma: Do we preserve the wilderness or do we use it? If historical and ecological "treasures" are not saved from human use—and abuse—history and natural resources vanish from the earth. How do we protect and *preserve* history and nature yet find ways to *use* these resources when we need them? Small, in addition, is wrestling with a big responsibility—finding a way to keep black history alive in the present without its impeding or stifling life.

Ultimately Small decides to make a record of the cave treasure in order to create a museum (he accommodates himself to both the perspective of preservation and a larger social use than Pluto's hoarding had permitted). In addition he ensures that the Foundation will reward both Pluto and the Darrows. Soon Pesty has new clothes, and River Lewis, her father, is a more amiable and productive member of the community. Small also provides a home for Pluto with his own family in the Dies Drear house that he loves.

An extraordinary person, Walter Small *lives* the cultural principles he has studied as a historian. And when Thomas begins to complain that the Foundation is not paying him as much for all his work of cataloging the treasure as they are giving Mac's father, Small teaches his last history "lesson" of the book, one of the finest moments of adult perception in all of Hamilton's books: "'Thomas, Thomas!' Mr. Small sighed and put his arm around Thomas. 'Son I'm a historian. I'm happy to save a great discovery from its worst enemies—time and greed. I've held the "villain" in check. I've shown him I care about his welfare, and treat him like a friend. I've managed to help give him an even chance. Do you understand? And what you do with yours, Thomas, and Macky with his, is up to the both of you'" (*MDH*, 210–11).

Especially we learn here how families cope with economic hardship and changes in health and living patterns. We see the various roles women have played in families, as well as the roles families play in everyday life—or what the word "family" means when extended families and communities of families come together to create a "family." The Smalls are outsiders to the small Ohio community where they now live. There is no extended family for Thomas until in the second book Great-grandmother Jeffers comes to live with his family. Pluto and his son have a strained relationship. And the Darrow father has turned into a scheming prankster. Yet eventually all these people come together as one family because they see that the need for friendship is greater than the drive toward suspicion. "I think you'll find in all my books," says Hamilton, "that even though there may not be a total family, there is always the longing for one."

Willie Bea and the Time the Martians Landed

Of all Hamilton's novels there is none that focuses on family more so than *Willie Bea*. A long, old-fashioned, well-developed novel in which readers come to know the characters well and to enjoy them, this one is definitely her most humorous. It may also be her most heavily populated, this story of a large, loving, and definitely unique extended family. The comic turn to the plot here, the vivid characterization, the intriguing mixture of language patterns, the historical dimensions of the setting, and the realistic interplay of adult and child perspectives all work together to produce a dramatic and thought-provoking reading experience for children (or adults).

Willie Bea, age 12, has two grandparents (the Wings), her own parents (the Mills), two sisters (one older and married, the other around five or six), two brothers (one also older and married, and one still in a crib), as well as two uncles, three aunts, and three cousins. She also has a pesty friend, Toughy Clay, who makes himself part of the family. And the story we hear about this unusual group takes place in a small town in Ohio, not unlike Yellow Springs—all in a 24-hour period. It is October of 1938, the day, or the night, that Orson Welles presents his famous radio broadcast—his story of a Martian invasion heard by so many Americans. The program is also heard this night by Willie Bea and her family, just as she and the other children are preparing to collect Halloween treats from the neighbors. Before this, however, a family gathering has brought together aunts, uncles, cousins, and grandparents for dinner, and there have been squabbles enough for several days or weeks, each member of the family having different talents, personalities, and temperaments, as Willie Bea sees it.

Big is her favorite cousin. Awkward and overgrown, he is in several ways reminiscent of Junior Brown. They are both quite large, with comic lines of dialogue and preposterous actions, although Big is a slow learner, rather than emotionally disabled: "When he got hold of an idea," Willie Bea thinks to herself at one point, "it was like he was too big for the idea to get to his head. It would seem to simply sit well with him somewhere below his mind for a month of Sundays."[5] And he has the habit of using Bay Brother (Kingsley) as part of his archery target (he places pumpkins on the baby's head and then shoots them apart as the baby is kept occupied with a carton of ice cream).

In what might be the funniest passage in all these books, Willie Bea tells about this ludicrous practice, leading up to it quite carefully and quietly, in the same quiet and careful way that she and her mother are attempting to seize the moment—and the baby:

> It happened so fast. Willie Bea was aware of sound, like something gathering air to it and carrying it along at high speed. She had seen Big pull back the string of his great bow. Somehow, she had missed seeing the arrow that he pulled with the string. She saw Big's fingers move. . . . She heard that heavy-sounding rush of air. The sunlight and space of the clearing seemed to explode. The pumpkin atop Bay's head burst into pieces, dripping seeds. A few seeds fell on Bay Brother; most exploded behind him. Casually, he let the spoon drop, reached into the carton with his hands and came up with three fingers full of melted ice-cream. Which he managed to slurp into his mouth. Without moving his head a bit. Well trained! Willie Bea thought. (*WB*, 43)

Little is Willie Bea's least favorite cousin. "Mean" is the way she describes Big's younger sister, since she suspects that Little encourages Big in his foolish actions in order to cause trouble generally. Trouble does ensue, especially for Big, when Willie Bea's mother, Marva (pretty and kind but quick-tempered), sets out to punish Big severely for his thoughtless deed, and when Jason, her father (a well-read, quiet, hard-working man who dotes on his family and always provides the voice of reason), arrives home in time to ensure that Big's bow and arrows are confiscated.

Meanwhile, Willie Bea's Aunt Leah—beautiful, stylish, and daring, with a magical talent in telling fortunes—reads Willie Bea's palm and sees the Star of Venus there—meaning, she says, "fine, impossible good luck" (*WB*, 76). Willie Bea will know the strange and unknown and "win the world" (*WB*, 76), she says. That night when Willie Bea hears Uncle Jimmy telling that the Martians have landed at the nearby Kelly farm, she takes off on her stilts to save them all. What she gets for her trouble, however, is a concussion, and her mind inhabited for a time by giants of Venus (one-eyed shining lights that move and rumble around the cornfields of the Kelly farm this night—in reality the farm combines).

She does succeed at the end in setting things right. When Big visits her at her sickbed, she explains to him that even though he would never miss the pumpkin target (he is such a perfect shot), he must stop using Bay Brother in this way, since "grown folks only see what *could* happen" (*WB*, 183). Moreover, she thinks of a better solution for him than her parents' decree of no more shooting: she and Big will make a real bull's-eye from oilcloth and crayons. And she tricks her father on this trick-or-treat night into telling her where Big's bow and arrows have been hidden. She may be missing the Halloween fun, she sees, but she has something better—the knowledge that she can restore to Big the one thing he truly cares about—the fun he has in shooting.

Willie Bea is another interesting protagonist in Hamilton's gallery of childhood paintings. (No two are alike, and in the process of creating so many novels she has painted a great variety of children's portraits.) This time she presents a very down-to-earth, capable, and determined but imaginative child, or, as Willie Bea describes herself, "I hold the style, I got the nerve and the stubborn streak of a Wing" (*WB*, 21). But we come to know her best from the stories she tells and hears.

We find Willie Bea in chapter 1 hiding from Toughy Clay under the old wooden porch of her farmhouse. There she is telling herself memory stories to sort out things generally (and to acquaint the reader with this large family). We hear that her father is considered by her uncles as the worst farmer in the family (called by Uncle Jimmy a "city boy"), but Jason Mills is also a reader, and in these days of the late 1930s he is reading a great deal about Hitler. This story explains why Uncle Jimmy later will embroider a story he hears of the "Martians" in order to trick Jason

Mills (thus establishing himself in Jason's eyes as country but superior). It also introduces—subtly and naturally—the information that this family is black (Hitler hated Jews; Willie Bea reasons that he would hate blacks too).

In chapter 3 Willie Bea tells another memory story—this one about a game or talent she and her cousins have for walking the high cross-beam in Uncle Jimmy's barn. She knows Big would never take any chances with Bay Brother's life since he would never miss; he could shoot perfectly, just as they all can walk the high beams perfectly: "She and Little. It was their most favorite, dangerous game. They walked the three-inch-wide cross-beam *blindfolded*. Up there, she and Little were never at war. High up, where the sharp hay-mound odor stung their nostrils, they were not enemies, not brave, not even cousins. They were highly skilled. They did what they must. They kept the walk secret, knowing that grown-ups would not understand. But they could not stumble and fall. It never entered their minds they might" (*WB*, 48).

Chapter 5 involves Big's storying to himself (through Willie Bea's eyes) about the incident in the woods; and the passage shows how masterfully Hamilton can reveal one character's point of view through another character's internal storying. The purpose for this story "transference" here is to reveal how close Big and Willie Bea are, how sensitive she is, and how strong her empathy is for him in this particular situation: "They were still friends, she could tell. But Big was hurting. . . . He didn't know how it happened. . . . They had all been playing and talking. . . . And before Big realized what he was doing, he had snatched Bay Brother. . . . Big still didn't know how it could have happened that they bought a pint of ice-cream downtown. . . . Then they had peddled furiously to the edge of Big's daddy's wood. It sure was turning into the worst kind of begging time of Halloween, too, as far as Big could tell" (*WB*, 67–68).

She pieces together Big's point of view from any number of probable sources, as she stories his story in her mind (the *known*: Toughy or Hewitt may have reported or storied bits and pieces of these events; the *remembered*: she has experienced Big's actions before; the *imagined*: she visualizes what probably happened, in order to see his story in her own mind). She becomes, in effect, a fictionalist of her own life experiences—and we see more about how creativity works. In chapter 8 a different but equally intriguing example of how stories emerge from intersecting points of view is revealed for us. The Orson Welles broadcast has already occurred, and Aunt Leah suddenly appears on the scene to retell it to the rest of the family. Uncle Jimmy at this point embroiders the tale of the radio broadcast, announcing that Martians have been sighted at the nearby Kelly farm. All the while Jimmy watches Jason Mills, Willie Bea notices, to see how gullible her father might be. Jason, remembering the story of the Hindenburg that he heard on the radio the year before proves to be very gullible indeed, deciding soon that these "Martians" are really Nazis.

For her part, Willie Bea, in chapter 9, also embroiders the radio story, imagining that the supposed Martians are really creatures from the planet Venus, based on Aunt Leah saying she has the Star of Venus in her palm. (The male-female/Mars-Venus/aggressive-relational difference in responses here is worth noting.) She decides that with this "gift" the space people will not harm her. She might even be able to save the world, as Leah predicted, from a Martian-Venus takeover, blessed as she is with this good fortune. Toughy then tells a story of seeing something at the Kelly farm that he thinks is from Mars (in reality it is the giant farm combines). Soon in the wake of general chaos at the Wing compound (Leah screaming and fainting, Jimmy racing around with his shotgun, Jason anxious) Toughy and Willie Bea—followed secretly by Big—set off for the Kelly farm on their stilts to see these giant "aliens" for themselves ("They strode the world stilting" [*WB*, 153]).

In chapter 11 the reality of this night emerges for Willie Bea, now recovering from her concussion, as she remembers stories of the doctor's visit and hears Big and Little's story of her fall and of the moving giants, their one eye shining, their huge roaring noise. Big knows that the "giants" were really the combines, but he allows her to awaken from her fantasy slowly, in order to preserve her pride. The newspaper stories she sees help her to sort out further what happened.

The book is about storytelling in every way: famous people like Orson Welles telling stories as entertainment (or retelling a famous story—H. G. Wells's 1898 novel *The War of the Worlds*) and everyday people retelling and re-creating stories—and using story in many ways (to entertain others, characterize themselves, and make sense of and interpret the world). "There are scenes out of my childhood," says Hamilton,

> that are very surreal, very strange, and I think it has to do with the fact that my rural Ohio or my growing up there was very surreal. To me it was in a sense scary. There weren't a lot of people around. We lived on the edge of Yellow Springs at that time on a farm and my uncles' farms all around. But you were isolated and the nights were long and dark. My

father worked late, and I always had a sense of anxiety when he wasn't
there at night, plus the fact that all those big silos of farms reminded me
of spaceships. They took on a strange, eerie aura in the night. So I think
that's why in rural places the Orson Welles story took hold so completely,
because there is that feeling of surrealism in the countryside—of strange-
ness, isolation. You really can believe—on smokey, starry nights—that
the Martians are coming. All you need is somebody to tell you.

The collaborative or dialogic stories of chapters 8 and 9 also reveal
how we tell stories to sort out the world *with others* in many different
ways, according to our own special personalities or our engagement with
the world at a particular moment. Leah's belief in the supernatural causes her to become severely frightened; Jimmy is a trickster; Willie Bea is
filled with great confidence and imagination after hearing Leah's palm
reading; Jason Mills, the avid reader, misreads the world. "The whole
story of the Martians is the story of my family on that night," Hamilton
says. "My aunt was really going to jump in the well."

Important cultural learning about history, or what it was like to live
in the 1930s and 1940s, also emerges in this book. Hamilton has an
uncanny ability to remember details of her childhood. "I see colors,
smells, entire conversations of the past" ("LT"), she says. In fact she has
explained that she thinks that those who write for children do so because
they have so many clear memories of childhood that need to be shared
with an audience of children.[6]

Here we have details about radio shows, the coming of the combine
(how it worked, what it did, what this meant to the farmer accustomed
to manual labor), the ways doctors once practiced medicine (house calls,
extended personal conversation, extensive knowledge of the entire family), the ways children made Halloween costumes half a century ago
(lessons in creativity), clothing styles and nearly forgotten fabrics (tulle,
organdy, dotted swiss, chiffon), and the ways extended families of small-
town midwestern America at one time lived and worked together to
form a strong support system, each member having weaknesses and
strengths that balanced the others.

Children in extended families, Hamilton reveals here, based on her
own family experiences, were at times friends, at times enemies; in their
play, however, they acted and reacted like adults at work—with great
pride in their skill, as we see in Willie Bea's remembered story of walking the cross-beam with Little. Says Hamilton, "My cousins and I were
as agile as cats, risk-takers, just like the characters from my novels."[7]

Risk-taking in *Willie Bea*, however, goes beyond pride in skill. Willie Bea defends Big when her mother lashes out at him, and Big is there for her to fall back on when she needs him, because each understands the mutual support system not just of extended family members but of children in league with one another as survivors. Willie Bea does actually fall on Big the night of her stilting adventure (or they fall together) at the Kelly farm when the frightening combines throw her off balance—his "bigness" cushioning her fall, and probably saving her life. Stilting was part of Hamilton's childhood experiences too ("We made our own stilts," she says, "and we knew how to do it all. We stilted a lot; that's African tradition—making stilts and stilting and ceremonies or stilt dancing").

As an elongated support structure that either elevates a character physically or helps the character to walk or stand a great distance from the ground, the stilting image or action is an idea that reverberates, dialogically, through several of Hamilton's books. And each time we see a stiltlike structure (Zeely's height likened to an ebony pole, M. C.'s pole made of steel, Junius's grandfather's bamboo staff, and Willie Bea's wooden stilts), we see also that the empowering influence of the support system is linked to natural elements of the earth. The implication is that with all our illusions of power, we are not without need of the earth and its resources, or, in the case of Willie Bea, we are not without need of others.

Not only children of extended families playing on stilts but adults like Aunt Leah, with their stiltlike (supportive) personalities, provide important cultural learning here. They in fact extend the symbolic support system for children like Willie Bea who have chosen them as role models. Jason Mills finds Willie Bea's fascination with Leah (three times married) disturbing, however. In his eyes Leah is not dependable like his wife, Marva, who is "solid and rock steady" (*WB*, 87). And surely the side Leah shows us here is for the most part histrionic and self-absorbed. Yet as always in a Hamilton book, things and people are often not what they seem. It is Leah who treats Willie Bea to the richest "lesson" in the book, the theme that Hamilton has woven through so much of her work: all you can imagine is possible.

Leah arrives at Willie Bea's sickbed like the good fairy, to help exorcize the monster-ghosts of the combine that are still lurking in Willie Bea's mind, or to explain them in such a way that Willie Bea can bring closure to the experience in a positive, hopeful way. Not just good and bad, Leah goes on to say, but that "*anything* can happen. Anything under the sun. One night you look up, there's a monster, it's a combine, it's a monster. One time a space ship lands right there on the Kelly farm. And who's to say it can't! Who's to say it didn't? And why that radio play just then on this night in this world?" (*WB*, 204). "Don't ever say never" is Leah's creed.

And it is a generous, thoughtful, all-knowing Leah who brings Willie Bea a wonderful Halloween costume for the next year, a fairy princess dress of stars and sparkles, with a note that tells her to wave her magic wand and anything can happen. Willie Bea promises herself that she will be just like Aunt Leah when she grows up. Of course she will not. There could only be one Leah, and Willie Bea is probably already more "solid and rock steady" now than her own mother, despite her entanglements with monsters.

The Bells of Christmas

Hamilton's next book of historic and hometown interest was a picturebook published in 1989. Set in 1890 in Central Ohio, *The Bells of Christmas* is filled with information as it tells the story of 12-year-old Jason and his family a century ago. And because of the striking artwork of Lambert Davis (acrylic paintings in soft colors and sculpted images of photographic realism), we view, as if through a modern color lens, an old picture album filled with toys, gifts, and Christmas customs of the era, as well as details about the way people in this place, at this time, earned a living.

Jason's father is a carpenter, making cabinets, pantry cupboards, fine tracery for windows and panels, and he trains his sons to do this work too. Jason's Uncle Levi is a master carver and has made, for Papa's Christmas present, a fine mechanical leg to replace Papa's old peg leg. Jason's mother is a seamstress, making shirtwaists, knickerbockers, cushions, quilts, and robes, in her home. His aunt is a teacher, just like his brother Bob wants to be.

The illustrations reveal that this family is African American; at the same time, nothing in the text mentions anything about race or ethnic background. Thus readers are able to see better the members of this family as participants of a "parallel" rather than a minority American culture—equal yet diverse, and wholly *inside* the American mainstream. Concerning this term or concept, "parallel culture," that she generated several years ago, Hamilton says, "I write from a parallel American culture of African Americans, which culture was at one time in the past, in the Plantation Era, wholly outside the American mainstream. Presently, it weaves strongly in and out of other group cultures. Parallel culture best describes the polyethnic, culturally diverse communities of present-day America" ("Toiler").

In 1890, as we see here, the African-American parallel culture was alive and well and thriving, at least in the Midwest. The adults are seen working in traditional occupations or holding traditional American values such as belief in free enterprise. At the same time they hold traditional African values, such as pride in finely crafted products and in fostering close family ties and nurturing the needs—emotional and physical—of each family member (sociocentrism versus egocentrism).

Jason is part of a large, extended, African-American family. He has three older brothers and a younger sister, age seven, and he has four cousins, the children of Uncle Levi and Aunt Etta Bell, who live in a nearby town in Ohio, West Liberty. And the two Bell families are meeting for Christmas dinner this year of 1890, just as they trade Sunday visits regularly from town to town throughout the year. Inner stories are tightly encased within Jason's first-person narrative—stories that tell about this particular Christmas event, which is very similar to the holidays that her mother, Etta Belle, celebrated in Yellow Springs in this era, Hamilton says. All of the internal stories woven through the outer story are important for projecting the realism of this historic setting.

The book ends on a cheerful but poignant note with Jason wondering what it will be like for children a hundred years from now. Will they ride sleighs down this road on Christmas night? His father suggests that children will ride in horseless sleighs "for a new twentieth century is just up ahead."[8] And as the horses carry them along "toward the warm lantern light of home" where "patches of gold made the lane sparkle" (*BC*, 59), we see that these ghost children who come to life so clearly here have taken us as deeply into the past as the blue snow that is fast covering the National Road.

The Bells of Christmas is a rare achievement in a picturebook—except that it is not really a picturebook as we normally know it. Again Hamilton's ability to create or experiment with new genres produces an illustrated text of 50 to 60 pages, an innovative, hybrid form—more text than pictures, and more pictures than an illustrated story would have. "I write long," she explains. But there may be more to it than that.

Says Margaret Meek, "For me, the beauty and power of picture books lie in the fact that they break out of the moulds we would cast them in. They subvert the known genres. The artist-authors want curious, innocent readers eager to look, and adept since their first year of life at seeing. Then, artist and reader set about *discovering* making plain, what reading is good for, beyond established cultural boundaries. In picture books the. . . convention[s] of reality and imagination are constantly redrawn, redescribed in the playful dialogue of reader and book-maker."[9] As a bookmaker (a storyteller for the picturebook form), Hamilton takes a different path from the usual and the known here, producing an excitement for readers that is, as Meek says of openly interpretive forms in general, "like life itself, unpredictable, like art, exploratory" (Meek, 37).

Cousins

Another of Hamilton's innovative works appeared the year after *The Bells of Christmas*, in 1990. Longer even than a long picture book (125 pages) yet shorter than most of her novels (200–300 pages), *Cousins* is fashioned to match the reading interests and habits of contemporary children, with a less complicated plot and more action and dialogue than her earlier fiction. In some ways it is a chapter book with eight untitled chapters or short stories (combined as four parts, "The Care," "Long Sleek Rides," "The Bluety," and "I Get It"), all linked by the main character, 11-year-old Cammy, her conflict with her prissy, "perfect" cousin, Patty Ann, and her concern and need for her grandmother who is living now in a rest home.

In other words, *Cousins* is longer and more cohesive than most chapter books—and shorter with a less complicated plot than a traditional novel like *Willie Bea*. Thus it appeals to a wider segment of the same audience: contemporary readers of "middle-age" fiction (third to sixth grade children, or ages 8 through 11). Yet *Willie Bea* and *Cousins* can be read as companion pieces, since each extends the other.

Both books have similar settings, with links to Hamilton's hometown. Says Hamilton, "The blue hole [the bluety] really existed, and we were warned never, never to go in the water and we never did and nobody ever drowned." Both have the same rivalry between cousins. And similar cultural lessons arise in each book: the cross-generational family as rich resource for children's lives, peer jealousies as part of the ups and downs of growing up, and ways of dealing with the possibility of death. Also in each book inner stories provide a window on the heroine's shaping and reshaping of experience, and family and community storymaking feed into this meaning-making process to reveal the social "connections" of personal learning.

Early in *Cousins*, in the main story thread, we see Cammy at Patty Ann's house, their cousin rivalry strongly at work as they bicker about whether Gram Tut (a Grandmother Patty Ann never cares to visit) is dying. Cammy wishes her cousin would "vaporize the way people did on *Star Trek*. . . . Coo-el if little *her* beamed up to a big blue star or to the moon or somewhere."[10] She calls Patty Ann a pig who looks like death; Patty Ann accuses Cammy of being jealous of her ability to sit on her hair and to get all A's.

Chapter 5 produces five of Cammy's memory stories and introduces a third cousin, Elodie. On the bus to day camp (with both cousins) Cammy remembers a conversation she has had with her mother about Elodie's name, after which she produces a reiteration of what happens each day at camp during swimming time, a story of her morning so far, a story observation of Patty Ann and her boyfriend as they ride along on the bus, and a story of Elodie's background. All of these stories bring the camp day more clearly into focus and involve us more strongly in the action than a linear, bare-bones narrative would achieve. And this use of time-shift places greater reality into the main thread of narrative, since we do story our way along through the day by remembering and ruminating, and what we focus upon in our stories reveals what is important to us.

In Chapter 6 Cammy's story memories about the bluety emerge as a reflection and revelation of community sense-making: "The Little [River] swirled out toward this one place in the middle where the waters were still. Out there was an odd bluish color. Kind of sickly, and dark bluish-green. But mostly it was a blue mystery. Oh, so many stories about that blue place! Andrew called it the blue hole. Mama said it had been there forever and was bottomless. She called it the blue devil. All the kids Cammy's age called it the bluety" (*Cousins*, 85). This story serves to foreshadow the dramatic center of the book—Patty Ann's rescue of Elodie, and her own subsequent drowning.

Finally, there is the story of the drowning, seen through Cammy's eyes as the main thread of narrative, Hamilton's writing never better than it is here, every word producing gripping action and continuously strong unfolding of character:

> Cammy watched it all. She kept losing sight of it in a daze. It was as if her eyes were closed and she couldn't see. And yet, they were open the whole time. She felt she was actually using her own energy to help Patty Ann and Elodie. She could see Patty Ann's face now. That no-nonsense

look as Patty Ann tried to bring Elodie out of the current. Elodie kicked
her legs, helping.

And they were more than halfway back now

. . . All at once, the sure look left Patty Ann. Never strong to begin
with, now she seemed tired. . . . *I won't get an A this time*, her look seemed
to say. . . .

Cammy saw it all as her eyes closed, opened, she couldn't tell. But she
was seeing, and praying that she wasn't. Elodie, paddling for dear life. . . .

When Cammy remembered, or stopped making herself forget about
what could happen next, she looked. She couldn't see it.

But it happened. . . .

Beautiful Patricia Ann. All alone.

Her cousin.

The bluety.

Not a trace. (*Cousins*, 91–94)

Hamilton shows here how we may register a traumatic experience yet
not really comprehend it until hours, months, or even years later when
we allow ourselves to remember or to shape the experience through stories. In chapter 7 we see the nightmare that grips Cammy when Patty
Ann's ghost starts visiting her in her dreams, and the fantasy the other
children create—that the ghost of Patty Ann lives inside Elodie. They
begin storying to work out how the world is changed for them now,
their stories making a shape that explains their horror and reshapes it in
order to contain or circumscribe it. (Creating a ghost story is their only
way to bring Patty Ann back.)

In Chapter 8 Elodie tells Cammy about how, in sharing the memory
of the drowning with her mother, they exorcized the ghost from Elodie's
mind as they created a new story of the drowning: "She [Patty Ann] was
just looking at us all. I looked back and saw her. She knew all us was too
far away to help her. . . . Then she forgave us . . . Mama said so" (*Cousins*,
144). In the end Gram and Cammy's returning father complete the
healing that Elodie, in her frail and growing wisdom, has begun. Gram
teaches Cammy, with hard-telling words, that Patty Ann will not come
back; she must take what comes, put a "focus" on whatever comes
before her, one thing at a time, and "always be ready" (*Cousins*, 120) for
what comes. Cammy sees it then. "I get it now" (*Cousins*, 125), she says.

What she "gets" is that at times things go down deep, like Patty Ann
did, and they do not come back up for us to see. Yet with help from
those we love—and from those who love us—they can still rise in
unseen ways (Patty Ann could *really* beam up to a blue star from the

bluety) if all we can imagine is possible. Feelings that are deeply buried can and do rise, Gram implies, and we see also when Cammy's feelings for life rise at the end of the story. She watches Gram Tut breathing and knows what courage it will take to accept the moment when it will not be in-and-out for Gram's breathing. Yet when that time comes, she will be strong enough to face it because she will keep her eyes open and look (and love) while she can.

This, then, is *Cousins*, a nearly perfect children's book in contemporary terms: slim, swift, direct, layered yet accessible, the lines sure, the characters breathing and alive for us long after we close the book. It is also a book that continues to reward with each rereading, everything is so skillfully fused here: the people (the healthy mix of human good and "evil" in this triad of cousins), the place (the bluety in its mystery—and fate—replicating life itself), and the meaning (nature is beautiful but dangerous, and all the agility and courage of children cannot always win against the odds, yet, as Patty Ann shows us, sometimes children *do* prevail).

What produces such a strong book here is that, as always, Hamilton took the less-traveled road, and it made all the difference. Most authors, given this plot, would have had Cammy save Elodie, while perfect little Patty Ann held back and revealed herself to be the emotionally frozen, neurotic, mother-driven, overachiever that we see as the book begins. A few might have allowed Elodie to die, and Cammy almost to die trying to save her. A very few might have had Patty Ann save Elodie easily, to prove that a priggish overachiever can still have a heart of gold—and always is a winner. But Hamilton surprises everyone, most especially Cammy, by having the least obvious person try to do the job and succeed—yet fail at the last to save herself. In Hamilton's words, "The obvious villain is not a villain. The girl who drowns is really a good person—she's just too good for the rest of them, in a sense, and we don't know about her until it's over" (Rochman, 1020).

Children's authors often feel hesitant to kill off a familiar and well-developed, well-liked character, and it would have been easy enough for Hamilton to have chosen Elodie as the one to die, since Elodie was not introduced until later in the book, and we do not really ever get to know her well. Why make Patty Ann both villain and victim? Perhaps because it seems so right to us afterward. The overachiever *would* have seen her duty and would have done it, would have done it so thoroughly and competently, in fact, that she would have given up her life to do it right—if it took that. It is this quality of focus that Cammy needs to see when she is struggling to believe in herself and to accept her own weaknesses and strengths.

Patty Ann, Cammy realizes long afterward, wins her love, wins everyone's love, at that moment when she fights the bluety for Elodie's life—and wins. It is love that so frightens Cammy and her friends that they must turn Patty Ann into an ugly ghost (a way to fight off that love). Until Cammy is able to deal with the fact that she had earlier wished for the death of Patty Ann (and by leaving Patty Ann to save Elodie, she may also have contributed, in some strange and indirect way, to Patty Ann's death), she must live with this ghost on a daily basis. Love, we see by the end of the book, is just as difficult to live with as death, since loving someone means, ultimately, the possibility of losing the loved one (as Cammy has for a time lost her father), and it requires having the courage to love, despite that possibility. An important theme. An important and memorable book.

Drylongso

With *Drylongso* (1992) Hamilton created, out of American culture and African-American history, a unique blending of ethnicity and universality and also returned to the long picturebook—especially valuable for illuminating a rich cultural heritage. Set in the mid-1970s, the book tells the story of a midwestern African-American family struggling against climate, weather, and fate. It especially focuses on a mysterious fellow named Drylongso, who one day comes tumbling out of nowhere to befriend the family, especially the young daughter, Lindy, who adopts him for the short time he is there as her older brother. With his divining rod, Drylongso finds a hidden, underground spring to irrigate the parched earth and start plants growing again on the farm; then, as quickly as he appears, the boy and the drought disappear, leaving Lindy to puzzle out who he was and what his visit will mean to them in years to come.

Although *Drylongso* is by no means nonfiction nor an information book, readers sharing Lindy's experience will absorb a great deal of knowledge about duststorms (what they are, how to prevent them, how to survive in one, how often they occur), as well as about the history of drought. Also for the youngest child readers, there is a great deal of learning about how plants grow, as well as how figurative language extends narrative concepts.

There is no better lesson in what metaphor is and how it works than the way Hamilton uses it here, so that children see the "magical" connection of water and plant life, or water as one important "food" of plants. Water is like gravy, Lindy learns one day as she helps her father plant the garden, and she quickly grasps the connection, since gravy means her own "beans and gravy."[11] "Keep it straight and steady while I pour on the *gravy*" (*Drylongso*, 2), her father says about the baby plant Lindy holds. "Gravy! Funny," laughs Lindy in response to this surprising new use of the word. Her dad then pours "a skinny stream of water—gravy—down over the young tomato plant, careful not to spill a drop," showing Lindy how the water and gravy are alike: each is a skinny stream we pour over food, and to the child it would be "precious water."[12]

Lindy's parents continue to utilize metaphor to teach her about the natural world; it is their way of speaking, a creative use of language for playing on many different levels with many different ideas at once. When she asks what a cloudburst is like, her father says, "like the sky is opening up" and her mother adds, "like a river pouring down from above. Like buckets and buckets of just the longest rain-fella you ever saw in your life!" (*Drylongso*, 4). Soon Lindy is creating metaphors of her own. "Looking like pancakes, is the yard" (*Drylongso*, 6), she tells her mother, as they look at the dryly packed earth. Later she sees "jumping" and "dancing" dirt as she notices the grit bouncing along. Viewing the oncoming dust storm, she describes it as a "great big wall-a-cloud" with a "stick running against the wall" (*Drylongso*, 12).

Describing Drylongso's "shadowy, stick arms" that "moved like pinwheels," and his long legs that "scissored, in a hurry to cut out of there" (*Drylongso*, 13), Hamilton reveals her own talent for wordplay. Her creative fusion of sound and sense is also apparent in her choice of the word "drylongso" for the legendary character. The boy Drylongso is a personification of both drought (it was dry for so long that drought occurred) and rain, or the human longing for rain brought on by the drought. Thus he becomes, in the context of the story, the embodiment of fate, destiny, or fortune (both good and bad). He comes with the storm (the bad) but finds the rain (the good). As a folk spirit, he also grows out of the African-American folk tradition of slavery and especially of reconstruction days when many black Americans, set free to find their own livelihoods, suddenly found themselves facing man-made obstacles of bigotry and greed, as well as those of nature, such as drought.

Inspired by other legendary hope-bringers like John de Conquer, Hamilton's newly minted fantasy/folk hero appears and reappears at 20-year intervals, she says, because drought has been striking somewhere in America every 20 years since the dust storms of the 1930s—a situation she knows well, as a farmer's daughter:

> I am descended from black-dirt farmers who fared well through thick and thin. . . . Having been born in one of our bleaker states, Ohio, I suspect I evolved into a scribbler out of the desperate desire to create a less melancholy, *dryer* clime. Ohio has some of the hardest rains, the gentlest, sweetest fogs, and some of the richest soil in the country, which is the reason a "toilsome of laborers" such as my relatives are beholden to this verdant land. However, the state is also known for its harrowing droughts . . . [and] having experienced Ohio drought, I wrote *Drylongso* with a steady hand. ("Toiler")

The word "drylongso" was the Creolized Gullah word for drought during the plantation era, Hamilton further explains. Later it took on a more general meaning of "ordinary," or "something as regular as everyday." Even later, during the 1940s, the word was applied to an ordinary day or a plain-featured (ordinary-looking) person. A woman might describe herself as "drylongso." In this story the word, as a name, is applied metaphorically to a boy who wears ordinary gray, dusty, farm coveralls and a mist-green shirt, in Jerry Pinkney's magical pictures, a boy who is so plain (but paradoxically, so extraordinary) that he can break out of the dust "wall" that surrounds him.

It is difficult not to see adumbrations of the Celtic Green Man in Drylongso's mysterious background and his healing powers, both of which emerge when he shares his talents for divining water, when he teaches Lindy's family not to plow the grassland, and when he shares the mysterious story of his birth, beginning with his mother's dream: "Ma says she dreamed a hard dust time was coming. Another Dry-long-so. Then, I was born. Ma said, 'He comes into the world, and a time of no clouds will come after him. Where he goes,' she said, 'life will grow better'" (*Drylongso*, 22).

When Drylongso disappears one day, at the end of the story, Lindy becomes her own story, taking imaginative action to change the world—or to turn it green once more (and she is well named by Hamilton for her role, Lynn Dalia). She spends the day trying to use the dowser to bring the rain. When nothing happens, she imagines that she made it rain in

California and that someday this dowser will lead her to find Drylongso. Falling asleep this night, she sorts out further the mystery of her folk spirit brother—through story: "He's coming back," she says aloud. "But when? He'll come when it's cool again, she decided. She imagined him running before a cloudburst. A soaking-wet, shivering rain-fella! He was laughing, running to their house, bringing a downpour" (*Drylongso*, 54).

The Story that springs out of Lindy's bedtime story is the book itself—*Drylongso*, with its portrait of the boy Drylongso who comes to us 20 years after his visit to Lindy, as the next period of drought approaches. His lessons about how life can grow better above and below the soil stand encased within an implicit but unmistakable warning that if we keep ignoring the need to care for the earth, we could be left with the land of dust that Hamilton described earlier in the Justice Cycle. The book *Drylongso*, and Lindy's story blooming within it, reveal people learning to save the earth together and important possibilities of life, growth, cooperation, and communication while there is still time.

Plain City

If *Drylongso* is a summer book that we view through a dusty-misty lens, then Hamilton's next book, published a year later, is just the reverse—all winter whiteness and January thaw bringing hard rains. *Plain City* is about a town on a flood plain and the people of various colors and classes who live there. Most of all it is about a 12-year-old girl, Buhlaire, with "blond russet curls," as Hamilton explains, who is based, in appearance, on a member of her own family: "I have a little niece who is a carrot color. She has straw blondish hair, but her skin is brown. It's just the most beautiful combination. (She was adopted and she's an interracial child.) So I got this image of the girl and I developed a whole society of people [around her]. Her mother is Carman Bluzet Sims, called Bluezy Sims, and she's a nightclub singer and a fan dancer."

Bluezy is African American, nearly 30 years old, and divorced from Junior Sims, half-black and half-white, a man she married as a teen before giving birth to Buhlaire. As a roadhouse singer (who is usually on the road singing), Bluezy has through the years left her daughter to be cared for by Junior's half-sister, Digna, and half-brother, Sam, and her own sister, Babe, who live near one another as a large, extended family in a riverfront settlement of Plain City.

The story takes place one winter as Buhlaire is suddenly waking to the fact that she wants and needs a father and that until she finds him she does not really know who she is—especially when she looks in the mirror and sees that she does not look like anyone else in this family. The "problem" for the protagonist, in Hamilton's words, is that "nobody will talk to Buhlaire about the past—her mother, her relatives, everybody, protects her from knowing about it. So she's left hanging." And the story becomes the working out of this problem or the unfolding of Buhlaire's mysterious family past.

Plain City has clear ties to several of Hamilton's previous books with female protagonists. Like Willie Bea, Buhlaire has a large, extended African-American family. Like Sheema, she is searching for a missing father, and when she finds him she must accept that he can never be the father she has imagined. Like Tree, she has a mother whose work takes her away from home for long periods and who has kept hidden from her the knowledge of her family past. Like Lindy, she is an only child who forms a close friendship with a peer who also functions as a protective "big brother." Like Geeder, she makes up stories to try out new roles and she tells these stories to others, having convinced herself that they are true. Like Arilla, she is an unreliable narrator at times who feels different from others because of her mixed heritage. Like Justice, she is inexperienced and at times terribly insecure, yet she is also a courageous explorer. Like Talley, she is highly introspective—and sexually innocent—and she is wrestling with the sexual harassment of a boyfriend whom she finds both compelling and oppressive. Like Pearl, she is headstrong, impulsive, and tough-minded; therefore she is able to deal with misplaced aggressive tactics much more effectively than Talley.

What makes this book special and different, then, is not so much the issues, although they are certainly timely, and it is certainly time that Hamilton returned to a theme of biracial heritage, there being so few such books available for children these days. It is not necessarily the structure, nor even the character type (like so many of Hamilton's females, Buhlaire is spirited, sensitive, and wise beyond her years). It is instead the character herself, or the way all these "factors" come together in one person and the subtlety, economy, and facility with which Hamilton paints this portrait when she attempts a new narrative strategy: the narrator's story of the action and the heroine's reflection on the action are each told as one story or as one point of view.

Hamilton is thus not limited to a first-person perspective (as she used in *Arilla Sun Down*) because the heroine's thoughts have been set off in italics and set down or stitched seamlessly into the narrator's "quilt" of inner and outer stories. Inner stories flow simultaneously *between* narrator's and heroine's thoughts, rather than through one perspective or the other at different times. In this way the interpretive narrator and the interpreting heroine are subtly fused, and what the narrator says seems to be what is simultaneously filtering through the heroine's mind (or will occur to her at some future time):

> "Know who she is," said his [Grady's] dad. "Everybody knows Bluezy's daughter." . . . His saying that everybody knew her surprised and pleased her. *I didn't know that. Someday, everybody's gonna know me by my first name, too.*
>
> She would remember this day as the one when she made a friend out of an enemy. Grady. And the day her dad saved her. She would remember it as the day she felt she belonged somewhere. Funny that it would be the Shelter From storm that made her feel at home. *Not some home. Not even some cave.* "I'm Buhlaire," she told Grady's dad. "Buhlaire-Marie Sims is my full name."
>
> "Proud," Mr. Terrell said, and nodded at her. The word hung there on thin air, like some award he'd presented to her.
>
> *Means he's proud to meet me—man!*[13]

There is a nearly perfect dialogic meshing of the two narrative voices here, the authorial narrator and the heroine-as-narrator, each one speaking to the other in something of a rememory time, in the same way Old James and Arilla communicated to each other after his death (in italics) or the way Arilla's story for her school assignment is presented (in italics) and then interfaced with her reflections about story as she writes (shown in regular print). But *Plain City* has a much more suspenseful, fast-moving plot than *Arilla Sun Down*, the result of the book's three middle chapters that contain no inner stories (only straightforward, quick-paced action and copious instances of dialogue) and that are encased by 22 inner stories in the first half and 10 inner stories in the second half.

Each "portion" of inner stories serves a special and different function for the main thread of story. Those of the first half provide background information for the reader, and for Buhlaire they provide a way of sorting out who she is as she reflects on all of the relationships of her life (similar to the way stories function in *M. C. Higgins the Great*). Those of the second half present new information about her family. Thus there are as many inner stories here as in any Hamilton novel (32), but they are shorter in length for the intended younger audience, producing a more dramatic main story. Several scenes in chapters 2, 7, and 8 are highly charged with action and emotion, and several in chapters 5 and 6 are filled with a particularly striking degree of realism. The book has in addition an especially engaging heroine, the result of her vulnerable state and the inventive way she deals with it. No previous Hamilton protagonist has a mother with such an unconventional job or talent as fan dancing nor a father whom the family has rejected (and kept hidden completely) because he is mentally unstable—and a drug addict who steals to support his habit, according to Aunt Digna.

In *Plain City* Hamilton explores what happens when children are denied the stories of their family past or left sheltered for too long—and the strange ironies that can accumulate as a result. Buhlaire's mother thinks that Buhlaire is old enough to sing alongside her in a roadhouse but still not old enough to hear the stories of her father. Buhlaire discovers most of these facts for herself ("vanilla" is a word her family uses about her white grandmother to protect her from what they consider to be the disgrace of her mixed heritage, she finally discovers). And she surprises everyone, including herself by knowing—when the time comes—that giving her father $200 of her own hard-earned money is the *right* thing to do. It gives her the feeling of responsibility she needs in this "growing" time and a way to express the love she feels for him—the only way she has of doing so, since she also discovers that she is too young to run away from Plain City with him and that her real place is with those who have always been there for her—Aunt Babe, Aunt Digna, Uncle Sam, and, at odd moments, Bluezy. Like Buddy Clark, Buhlaire must assume the adult role in a world where her parents have for a long time abdicated it. Cultural learning is thus greatly in evidence for readers here, since the heroine is receiving her education about self, family, and world.

We see how a community institutes a facility to care for the homeless. Grady's father came to The Shelter from *Any* Storm years before and remained there as a manager. The shelter has since become a cottage industry for food service workers, office workers, guards, and volunteers, providing work for the unemployed as well as shelter at times for those who, like Buhlaire's father, are down on their luck.

We see how racial prejudice by those of either black or white background hurts those of mixed heritage, especially children. Buhlaire is striken emotionally by both the real and imagined negative treatment of adults and peers in her community who regard her as an outsider simply because her coloring is different from what they expect to see in an African American—an especially ironic situation since her coloring is what has produced her special beauty, as Floyd Cooper's cover picture so clearly reveals. Her father has also been strongly affected by racial prejudice. His mother abandoned him as a child because she could not get along with the black family into which she had married, and his mental condition stems from this rejection, Bluezy tells Buhlaire.

We see how helping others (whether it is the mentally ill, the homeless, the blind like Aunt Babe, or those afflicted by the flood that occurs at the end of the book) is the best "cure" for emergent adolescent self-absorption, as well as for peer and family conflicts. At the end of the book, when Buhlaire spends the day with her Uncle Sam, transporting the river people back and forth to the town, she discovers a sense of community and responsibility and a strong feeling of well being.

We see how knowing family stories is crucial to emotional health, self-esteem, and the creation of strong, intelligent, responsible citizens of the hometown—and the world. The book begins with Buhlaire's discovery, or lament, that she has no knowledge of her past, and it continues with more and more stories of this past unfolding as she searches for "back time" (*PC*, 7).

The book ends with Buhlaire storying to herself about her father's future, wondering if he will remain in his unbalanced mental state or get better. She decides that he will probably stay the way he is, which is not a happy thought. The book ends on a hopeful note, however. Buhlaire watches the frogs hopping up onto land in order to survive the flood, and she produces a lilting inner "song" about herself and her own future in response: "*Water running. You can't stop it. You can't stop rain, or fishes, running. Well. It was like I was asleep. Just hibernated, way down deep under. Still water runs deep. You can't stop running water. Brown, running water. It will seep away. I'll be out of the flood time, on dry land. Little frog, me. Hop. Blope. You can't stop, me*" (*PC*, 193).

From these flood scenes we see the way stories and writing are one for Hamilton—or that one is the reason for the other—and thus how and why she writes to tell stories, especially stories of historic and hometown interest. Recalling her mother's storytelling during storms and frightening weather and the way she told about something that was worse in order to calm the children or "diffuse scary things," Hamilton says, "I find in *Plain City* that I'm doing the same thing, only I'm making a more elaborate story. I've connected to the early spring floods of my part of Ohio and how my mother would talk about them . . . [so that for us] the unusual and the scary became ordinary." As the river rises in *Plain City*, telling its own "story" of visible danger to all, Buhlaire similarly finds her own troubles lessened, and the old refrain "it could always be worse" becomes one of the last cultural "lessons" of the book.

Finally, we see here more of what a female bildungsroman for children looks like. At this crucial time in her life when she is growing into adulthood, Buhlaire suddenly discovers that something in her life is missing—not just her father, Junior Sims, or even knowledge about him, but a feeling of being connected to others, which in turn produces connections to self (relational and individual learning fused). Hamilton has said that writing this book revealed to her that young females attain knowledge of self in ways not so different from those of the fugitive slaves she had studied and written about through the years in what she has described as her "liberation literature."

As Hamilton developed this story about Buhlaire she realized that she sees the female child or adolescent as one who seeks strength in the same way that the runaway slaves engaged in a journey into selfhood, or to what she calls the "ultimate freedom" ("EV," 376), for when they gained freedom they were also free to find a stronger sense of identity, just as the young girl reaching toward adulthood is questing for self. "In one sense," adds Hamilton, "there is no one quite so free as the one who is oppressed. For that one has developed such liberty of mind and imagination through suffering as to make all things possible by an act of will" ("EV," 376). We will turn now to this particular "genre" Hamilton has carved out in her work, her liberation literature, to see it in greater detail.

Chapter Six

Biographies and Folklore Collections: Liberation Literature

From the beginning Virginia Hamilton has had as a major interest the depiction of a "black social order that is characterized by tension, insecurity, and struggle" ("Hagi," 91). She has said that she sees the literature she creates as a "social action" since "black people are an oppressed people" ("Hagi," 91), and in her work she can liberate members of the black race from these struggles. Nowhere do we see more strongly her desire to show humans struggling out of oppressive conditions than in the biographical portraits she has painted of runaway slaves and in the folk tales she has retold or created in four impressive collections. She develops this literature, she says, as "a metaphor for present-day struggles and accomplishments of American blacks" ("Hagi," 90).

Anthony Burns and *Many Thousand Gone*

In 1988 Hamilton published one of her most important and highly regarded works. Here for child readers was structural integrity, a gripping story, a stirring human experience, and most especially historical and cultural learning. *Anthony Burns: The Defeat and Triumph of a Fugitive Slave* is, in Hamilton's words, "a narrative history of events surrounding Anthony's life as well as a biography,"[1] or what she has called a "historical reconstruction" ("EV," 374), a blending of biography and historical fiction that she created because so much of Burns's life had to be imagined from the little that was known of his slave childhood. Burns's young adult life was also very much an untold story. Hamilton discovered from her research that abolitionist advocates, witnesses, and lawyers had written themselves (rather than Burns) into the spotlight when they produced written documents and stories about Burns and fugitive slaves generally.

In the "accounts of the great abolitionist cause, the swirling intrigues surrounding Burns, and the battle between freedom and slavery," says Hamilton, "Burns seems to recede into the shadows. For once I wanted readers to have a book in which the oppressed slave, a common man, was at the center of his own struggle" (*AB*, 180). She achieves this goal through the delicate balance of inner and outer storytelling, but this time her use of framing or encasing stories, as a narrative device, works especially well for developing the picture of a common man who by the last words of the first chapter becomes uncommonly interesting for his strong love of his childhood and his remarkable tolerance of his oppressors.

Hamilton shows Anthony subduing the anguish he feels, imprisoned as he is for the majority of the book as a runaway slave with very little hope for release, by letting his mind drift back to himself as a boy again, "an innocent child" (*AB*, 23). She arranges the chapters so that Anthony's adult life in the present (the outer story) and his childhood memories (inner stories of this Story) are intertwined throughout the book in alternating chapters. The adult story is told over a 10-day period (Wednesday to the next Friday) in chapters 1, 3, 5, 6, 8, 9, 11, 12, and 13, and in chapters 16–20. The child's story—or Anthony's memories of his life previous to this time (at ages five, seven, 12, 13, and 19)—is told through his inner (flashback) stories in chapters 2, 4, 7, 10, 14, and 15.

As Anthony approaches the moment when it must be proved that he is a slave, he continues to take himself back to the time when he was a slave with no understanding of his condition. So in these memory times he is telling or remembering in order to learn more about himself, or what he has never really understood consciously: what the institution of slavery actually means. At the same time Hamilton is teaching children a great deal about slavery—and about freedom. As she says of Anthony, "By writing about him I found that he not only came to life for me but that he lives again for all of us. In gaining a sense of who he was we learn about ourselves. As long as we know he is free, we too are liberated" (*AB*, 180).

Hamilton has described *Anthony Burns* as a "docunovel" ("Hagi," 82). It could also be described as a docudrama as it is filled with so many courtroom and plantation "scenes," and Hamilton has even provided a well-detailed cast listing to set the stage for readers. In fact, she succeeds so completely in bringing to life a little-known and thinly documented historical character and in providing cultural learning for young readers that it is not surprising that she followed *Anthony Burns* with another biographical work five years later in 1993, *Many Thousand Gone: African Americans from Slavery to Freedom*.

A history or encyclopedia of slavery, *Many Thousand Gone*, illustrated by Leo and Diane Dillon, serves as a valuable companion piece to

Anthony Burns, since it illuminates so much about the plantation era. Here the genre is entirely nonfiction: biographical sketches of slaves and conductors of the Underground Railroad are presented as factual stories, encased within historical, nonfictional frame stories. The sketches begin with the exit of the slave ships from Africa and end with the emancipation period, similar to the format used by Julius Lester in *To Be a Slave*.[2]

Hamilton is at her best as she reveals the story of Sojourner Truth, who in her height and dark coloring might easily have provided inspiration for the character Zeely. Especially memorable also are the stories of Henry Brown, who "designed" his way out of slavery in a box two feet deep for a 26-hour trip on horse cart from Richmond to Philadelphia, and Margaret Garner, who slit her young daughter's throat and tried to drown herself and her young baby rather than be separated from her children sold into slavery.

Unsung heroes, the men and women brought to light in these sketches, provide valuable knowledge about the slavery experience as a human triumph of courage and determination. Of special importance, we hear them speak in their own voices. Hamilton maintains a plain, unadorned style so that as we hear such vivid—and often horrific—details, it is the people who survived slavery that we know better for their stories. The book ends, however, with Hamilton's own inspiring words about the conclusion of the Civil War and the fact that African Americans were then able to find the best in life after the war.

Education, jobs, family unity, ownership of land, and the freedom to read and write and to manage and defend their own homes were what black people now had and what they have continued to have, she says. And compared with what they did not have before, this is true. Yet *Many Thousand Gone* should be read alongside not only *Anthony Burns* but also Hamilton's two earlier biographies, *W. E. B. Du Bois* and *Paul Robeson*, so that it is clear how limited, at times, these newly found freedoms have continued to be for most black Americans, even though an amended Constitution had earlier set them free.

In these biographies Hamilton shows human beings striving to liberate themselves from societal constraints. In fact, she has called her work on the subject of slave life "liberation literature," since it "portray[s] the individual's and a people's suffering and growing awareness of self in the pursuit of freedom" ("PS," 676).

In this special type of literature, she says, "the reader travels with the character in the imagined world of the book and bears witness to the character's trials and suffering and triumphs. To the extent that the protagonist finds liberty, so too does the witness, the reader, recognize the struggle as a personal one and perceive a spiritual sense of freedom within" ("EV," 375). This created "genre" is seen clearly in Hamilton's biographical and historical nonfiction, but it can also be seen at various times and in various ways in four collections of folk, mythic, and fantasy tales that she produced between 1985 and 1991, *The People Could Fly, In the Beginning, The Dark Way*, and *The All Jahdu Storybook*. Each collection is similar in format to the others and each contains an extensive bibliography, but in thematic emphasis each is strikingly different.

The People Could Fly

1985 marked the year of Virginia Hamilton's foray into retelling folk tales and producing collections of such stories as an art form—a process she has said gives her great pleasure. She begins with existing stories toward which she feels an affinity so that she can improve on an established theme. The words then become a dialogic collaboration among many tellers—herself and all of those before her who told a particular tale.

The People Could Fly, illustrations by Leo and Diane Dillon, is the keystone of Hamilton's collections of retellings, fiction or nonfiction; it was the first of these books, and it set the tone and standard for the others. The subtitle, "American Black Folktales," emphasizes "black literature as American literature,"[3] as she has said. Black folklore is therefore seen not as separate from the American condition but as an important contributing force in the making of America, since these stories, set in the American plantation era, celebrate the human spirit that shone out of that time and place. Told first by members of the African diaspora, the stories were a creative way for an oppressed people to express their fears and hopes.

The source for several of the 24 stories in this book, similar to that of *Many Thousand Gone*, is the body of narratives complied by participants in the Works Progress Administration when they interviewed ex-slaves in the 1930s as part of the Federal Writers' Project. Told now by Hamilton in her own voice, the stories enable all Americans to listen and learn more about their history, and to see that, as Hamilton says, "storytelling is not merely a thing of the past, but a continuing cultural imperative. The tales illuminate the triumphs of talking and telling among the people in the present and reveal the connections of this ethnic group to its historical self" ("OB," 17).

They are retold in a language that Hamilton "felt echoed the language of early tellers," and "which would be understandable to today's readers" ("OB," 17): "I devised a 'voice' or an essayist/narrator for each tale. He or she would be unobtrusive, not a character in the true sense, but vaguely just a voice with a sense of personality to it that would set the mood of each story. In that way I was able to have the speech or the sound match the subject matter more closely,"[4] and match the speech patterns of the "original slave teller and later the free black storyteller."[5]

The book is organized around four groups of stories (animal fantasy, fanciful tale, supernatural tale, and slave tale). The first group includes seven animal tales, and the lead story, "He Lion, Bruh Bear, and Bruh Rabbit," is very likely the funniest rendition of the rabbit trickster figure that we have from American retellers these days. The humor arises from the informal, colloquial phrasing, the premise itself (that a powerful, erstwhile frightening creature—the king of the jungle—is behaving in a petulant way); the triad of major characters (a large, knowledgeable bear, a small, wily rabbit bent on teaching a lesson, and a grand but innocent lion); and the way Hamilton uses "signifying" as a signpost to meaning.

The second group of stories in *The People Could Fly* includes six fanciful tales (realistic stories with exaggerated motifs that stretch the imagination). There are tall tales, riddle stories, and even a cautionary Red Riding Hood story from the black tradition, "A Wolf and Little Daughter," filled with patter phrases (or patter song as a mysterious and intriguing inner story) that reflect the slave as storyteller to the slaveowner's children, as Hamilton explains in the story's postscript. "What child can resist this cumulatively cadenced retelling?" asks Betsy Hearne, who chose a passage of this story to exemplify what she felt to be Hamilton's distinguishing trait as a children's book writer: producing writing that always sounds "both deeply familiar and strikingly new."[6]

The third group of stories includes five tales of the supernatural (stories with characters like witches, devils, ghosts). The fourth group of stories includes six slave narratives (three realistic, three fanciful). Closing the book is the dramatic and memorable title story detailing a day in the life of a group of slaves when a person among them urged them to fly to escape the cruel overseer's treatment, and they rose into the sky, leaving captivity and cruelty behind. The people who flew, Hamilton explains in the story's postscript, are most likely the runaways utilizing the Underground Railroad, and the flying-slave story could be one that slaves created in order to explain why a group of slaves disappeared suddenly. Yet she also keeps the mystery alive, theorizing that the group might also have been composed of Angolan slaves, since Angolans were thought to have "exceptional powers" (*TPCF*, 172).

In the Beginning and *The Dark Way*

Hamilton's next two story collections, *In the Beginning: Creation Stories from around the World* (1988) and *The Dark Way: Stories from the Spirit World* (1990), reverse the emphasis of *The People Could Fly*, focusing as they do on the human spirit of liberation worldwide. Selections from African, African-American, and Native-American cultures stand alongside stories from all continents, not simply as political "tokens" to correct cultural imbalances but as parallel lines running, with equal strength and vibrancy, across the globe. With her ties to Eurocentric cultures through marriage, to African-American and Native-American cultures through birth (her mother was part Cherokee; her father was of black and Creole ancestry), and to East Asian philosophies through her wide reading, Hamilton brings to these collections a strong commitment to multicultural interests and extensive knowledge about a wide variety of ethnic communities. A great deal of cultural, as well as artistic, learning for children emerges as a result.

In the Beginning consists of four stories from North America (three American Indian, plus one Eskimo tale); one from South America (Mayan from Guatemala); three from the Pacific Islands; one from Australia; one from Northern Europe (Iceland); three from Greece or Southern Europe; three from Asia (India, China, Babylon); two from Israel; one from Russia; and six from Africa (Guinea, Dahomey, Togo, Zambia, Nigeria, and Egypt). *The Dark Way* consists of two Russian folk tales, three Asian (China and Japan), five British (England, Wales, and Ireland), one Norse, one African, one Jewish, one Greek, one Italian, one Indian, two Latino, two Native American, and two African American, one of which is Hamilton's own literary creation.

Both collections are matched in quality with *The People Could Fly*. As Ethel Heins notes of *In the Beginning*, "Text, design, typography, and illustrations are beautifully integrated. The eloquent paintings [by Barry Moser], one or more for each story, chiefly portray striking figures or concepts which, though realistically delineated, produce an effect of fantasy and symbolism."[7] And much the same can be said of *The Dark Way*, in which illustrations by Lambert Davis reflect the greater informality of the folk tales, in contrast to the myths or stories of supernatural gods that inhabit *In the Beginning*. The austere and luminous authority of the god Ra, who graces the dark and mysterious cover of *In the Beginning*, marks the spiritual, in contrast to the high-spirited, green, furry oni on the cover of *The Dark Way*, who roars with pain, his tongue having been pricked by a tiny trickster's needle-sword.

Hamilton's language reflects the difference in tone and mood in these two collections. *In the Beginning* reveals, as Heins notes, the mythic voice itself: "prophetic and authoritative; [thus] the effect is often strongly spiritual" (Heins, 83). "Let us think about when the earth was formed," says Hamilton in the book's Introduction. "Suppose there was a moment before time and space when the only things in existence were an object shaped like an egg and the darkness in which it was suspended. Suddenly, the egg cracks, and something slowly emerges from it. Imagine that the something from the egg is a great god who simply is all there is. That god makes the universe and humans and all things because that is the work of a god—to create."[8]

How different is the jaunty, mischievous, rhythmical introductory note of *The Dark Way*: "Between then and now is the channel where misty hoarfrost rises to the darkening shadows. And melting ice needles dribble down like glistening drool from a monster's fangs. Between thought and unthinking is this course of the shape-shifter, shrouded in gloom. Whether it be monster, gorgon, trickster, ghost, imp, fairy, elf, devil, phantom, or witch—all of these twitch, they change, nightmaring, slumbering there. In the Dark Way."[9]

It is clear that *In the Beginning* was the mightier task, presenting a definite challenge for the reteller: how to render the complex ideas understandable to a child reader yet still fill these mythic tales with the authority of the original voice and style of the particular culture. (In *The Dark Way* Hamilton had much greater freedom to play with language and have some fun with it.) In the Beginning is therefore the heavier and more demanding book, and it is especially important for revealing the ways members of various cultures have imagined themselves created by so many different kinds of gods.

Many common threads in the stories arise from dichotomies involving gods and men, as when in the Nigerian story "Olorun the Creator" Great God (a lesser god than Olerun) is jealous because he is not allowed to see how Olorun brings to life the human figures that Great God

makes. So he leaves marks on humans (thus human deformities or differences is explained). Good and evil are seen clearly in "Divine Woman the
Creator," the Huron Indian tale, when Divine Woman brings to life a
bad son who makes bad animals, including the greedy toad who drinks
up all the fresh water on the earth, and a good son who makes animals
of use to human beings.

Additional dichotomies include those of human/animal, black/white,
and male/female. In many of these stories common threads of homocentric, racist, and sexist views prevail, such as the notion that animals, people of color, and females, have been placed on earth to serve white males.
Concerning black and white, in "Death the Creator" from Guinea, we
see an early story revealing racism on the earth, as well as a story with
stronger plot than many in this collection. Here God Alatangana takes
Death's daughter from him; then Death (Sa) punishes Alatangana by
putting a curse on him: his children will speak different languages, and
he will not understand them. Also Death puts a racist scheme in motion:
white children will be literate (mental workers), black children will be
aliterate (physical workers), and blacks and whites will not intermarry.
The story thus reveals that racism existed very early in history, or
humans were attempting to explain the phenomenon of it from the
beginning.

Concerning male and female, sexist views predominate. In eight of
the stories women are either created after men are (and they are created
by male gods) or are blamed for something unfortunate happening in
the universe, such as the onset of mortality in the Blackfoot Indian tale.
In only two of these myths are women the creators themselves, and in
nine stories women play no part at all. The overall impression is that
women were created to serve men. In the Eskimo myth Raven makes a
clay woman for man (she is his helper and mate) in order to prevent
man's loneliness. In the Russian tale, as Maidere (the eighth man created by the god Ulgen) discovers, men do not grow or change without
women. Ulgen then gives Maidere the task of creating women to "serve"
men in this growth capacity. A story from India uses metaphor skillfully
to explore what happens to females when they shine too brightly in the
world or when they are too important or too wise: they are destroyed—
or diminished—by male power figures.

In the Beginning is a thought-provoking, one-of-a-kind book, and it
was followed three years later by another unique collection, this time
filled with Hamilton's own created fantasy stories rather than her
retellings.

The Jahdu Books

Also illustrated by Barry Moser, *The All Jahdu Storybook* (1991) consists of 15 stories of a character Hamilton had created 22 years earlier for the children's book *The Time-Ago Tales of Jahdu* (1969) and its sequel, *Time-Ago Lost: More Tales of Jahdu* (1973). In the latest collection are several newly written stories, but the original books have historical, cultural, and literary importance that should not be overlooked.

Hamilton had created for the earlier books a black female storyteller as narrator and a black child as listener, a welcome reversal of the black adult narrator and white child listener that Joel Chandler Harris had created for the Uncle Remus tales. In describing the Walt Disney film *Song of the South*, based on Harris's Remus collections, Alice Walker recalls that the movie caused her as a child to abhor the Remus character, who "saw fit largely to ignore his own children and grandchildren in order to pass on our heritage—indeed, our birthright—to patronizing white children."[10]

Hamilton's Mama Luca repairs this unfortunate picture, living as she does in Harlem and telling stories to the African-American child Lee Edward. Hamilton's child is also a more active character than he was in the Remus stories, for Mama Luca's stories are helping to fill him with pride and power (storytelling for social action). Jahdu in one story even transforms himself into Lee Edward (because Lee Edward is a very worthy person to be). The transformation is an effective way to dramatize that the black child is beautiful and important—a prominent slogan and literary theme when Hamilton was creating the book in the 1960s. Hearing the stories that Mama Luca tells, Edward imagines himself growing in magic power, just as Jahdu does; then in the second book he begins imagining his own Jahdu stories—or taking action, through storytelling, to change or reshape the world.

Hamilton's Mama Luca framework, from a literary perspective, makes a strong contribution to the integrity of the artistic design. Ironically, it works in a very similar way to that of Harris's framed Remus stories, where, while the stories themselves spoke of the trickster figure and his adventures, their framework "showed human kindness, patience, decency, and respect between the man and the boy. The framing device also helped to clarify many aspects of the tales, and because so many stories opened with, or included, the child's commentary on the previous story, it also served as a unifying device for interrelating the tales."[11]

The 1990s, however, are neither the 1960s nor the 1880s. In *The All Jahdu Storybook* Hamilton has dropped the frame entirely, choosing to focus more clearly, and completely, on Jahdu and his role of trickster. Says Hamilton as she closes the book, Jahdu is the "all-out trickster, magical and devilish, good and bad, imp and elf. He is the age-old transformer, the shapeshifter at liberty to become anything or anyone. Think of Jahdu as representing me, the author, having fun and playing tricks. Jahdu stories came directly from my attempt to do in words what members of my storytelling family did aloud: to make up and *give* a tale."[12]

The trickster figure is a favorite one for Hamilton in all of these collections. But nowhere has she produced trickster characters on the scale of the ones she created for her most ingenious and inspired example of liberation literature—the novel *The Magical Adventures of Pretty Pearl*, published two years before *The People Could Fly* and eight years before this latest collection of Jahdu tales. In the next chapter we examine these very accomplished and larger-than-life tricksters in some detail.

Chapter Seven

For All Ages: Historical Folk Fantasy

In 1983 Virginia Hamilton produced a novel very different from her other work, and also significantly different from the books of other authors. *The Magical Adventures of Pretty Pearl* is a fantasy rising on the scaffolding of black folk materials and the history of African-American experience. And, like her folklore collections, it exemplifies the sometimes invisible borders of adult and children's literature. According to the author, it was also her best:

> *Pretty Pearl* is a culmination of all the work I've done and all the things I have tried to do in each book. Each book was for me somewhat incomplete because I could never do everything that I loved in a single book. This time all my love for the mythology and the folklore of black culture and black history and my love for creating characters and plots seemed to come together to such an extent that I felt that it was a completely organic book. (Apseloff, 210)

The book tells the story of a god-child who travels from Africa to America in the eighteenth century to aid the African humans captured as slaves. Once immersed in human culture, however, Pearl succumbs to human predilections, forgets the rules laid down by her older brother (and "best" god), John de Conquer, and in the end loses her magical god power. The novel is essentially the story of Pearl's growth from childhood innocence to young adult experience.

How she grows is Hamilton's subject, and that she *does* grow—does not shrink in stature as she "falls" from god to human form—is Hamilton's challenge as author, perhaps her greatest challenge, for if she fails at her task the child reader will see despair rather than hope in any child taking action in the world.

Hamilton's desire to experiment (she never rests easy with pat formulas or with duplications of successful ventures of the past) and the degree to which she was willing to challenge herself in this book are what make it such a great achievement. As Lois Kuznets says, "Books are fascinating primarily because they are the product of *choices* that creative human beings make, choices that readers are persuaded to accept as natural and inevitable through the sheer power that the writer exerts."[1] The choices Hamilton made in writing *Pretty Pearl*, and the choices she revealed her characters making, produced a novel of special power for all ages.

Narrative Focus and Creative Process

Certainly the most obvious experiment or choice of the book is the genre itself—Hamilton's blending of history and folklore to produce historical folk fantasy and a quest adventure of African-American experience. Many fantasies for children rise on the scaffolding of traditional folklore. What seemed to be missing before Hamilton's work, however, was a fantasy of time-travel informed by African-American history and folk traditions. "You have to be steeped in the material," explains Hamilton, "before you realize this is a wonderful way to bring the African-American experience into literature with something other than historical facts. I always put history into my books, but this was a way to bring folk material and history together and create fiction at the same time."[2]

In order to create such a blending, Hamilton might have created African or African-American characters in some legendary time or place, or she might have exposed a modern-day African-American child to some ancient legendary character. But she took an entirely different path, introducing as her major characters mythic gods who, in their transformative abilities, could mingle with African-American humans in order to help them in one of the most turbulent periods of American history—the post–Civil War emancipation era. In addition, she introduced as two of her gods African-American folk heroes, High John (de Conquer) and John Henry, linking them as god-brothers and antithetical siblings (each is the exact reverse of the other, as their initials indicate) for the opposing tension of power that could be dramatized.

John Henry represents the postwar industrial hero confronting his adversary, whether man or machine, with open and direct physical power. Thus he was able to become a very familiar folk hero in African-American and American lore. John de Conquer represents the slave trickster hero, operating and surviving through mental power. And unlike his animal partner, Brer Rabbit, he has remained—at least for white audiences—a well-kept secret, since the dangers of publicizing slaves as tricksters prevented his stories from being told to whites well into the twentieth century. By juxtaposing these two figures, Hamilton could present contrasting avenues to power for the oppressed (open action as opposed to subterfuge). At the same time, because the two heroes were working together as actual and symbolic brothers in a common cause, she could show the greater strength that *unified* power brings to those seeking freedom.

Pearl, the god-sister of both heroes, is not based on a legendary character as the male gods are. "There are no famous black American women legends," explains Hamilton, "except for Harriet Tubman, none to the extent of John de Conquer or John Henry, and that's why I created her." Choosing to send Pearl forward into the world as a goddess, born of Mount Kenya, Hamilton has made Pretty Pearl a modern creation story, for Pearl is prototypical: she creates herself as she moves through time. This choice allows Hamilton great latitude for exploring many possibilities for childhood growth and self-creation, of motivation and desire, hope and potential.

In the beginning, however, what moves Pearl and the story into action is that, as a god-child, she yearns to "come down from on high,"[3] as the first sentence of the novel states. She is bored. Certainly a gifted and talented god-child, Pearl plays harder than the other god children and beats them in all the games. In her growing power she also sees a great deal. Looking down from the Mount, she sees the African humans captured, and she becomes curious and concerned. But she does not see enough; she is puzzled. And so High John explains: "What you see be subtractin . . . a taking away . . . for de sum of a human or a god be similar. It de life and freedom he born with. But subtract de life, you got no kind of freedom. Subtract de freedom, you got no life" (*MAPP*, 13).

Hamilton has drawn her gods as similar to humans, with distinct personalities rather than as impersonalized principles or forces of power (sun, moon, or thunder); this gives her the opportunity to comment on human foibles and strengths as she develops her theme of power and the wise use of power to produce the greatest human freedom. Gods at their best, she implies, are like the strongest, wisest, and most powerful humans, born with greater knowledge, thus having greater responsibility and finally fewer freedoms. But they are not perfect, and they are not always good.

In Pearl's strong pride and competitive spirit lie the seeds of potential weakness—or strength—mixed as they are with her deep, caring spirit. "Awful. Awful!" she whispers about the horrors of slavery (*MAPP*, 21). But all she can do is watch. She has no power to do anything else, and this makes her restless and discontent. She wants to follow the African humans to the New World and help them, and because John cares about her and sees she is ready to move on to the plane of god-woman, he gives her this chance.

Speaking of the legendary John de Conquer (a folk character who made his first appearance in print when Zora Neale Hurston published an essay in the *American Mercury* in the mid-1930s), Hamilton explained, in 1975, that "while individual black slaves may not have had the chance or spirit to run . . . [t]hey conjured a being who released power unto them. High John gave them strength and made them laugh; he freed their spirit if not their bodies."[4]

Eventually High John came to be a man in the legends and a "mighty man at that," says Hurston:

> But he was not a natural man in the beginning. First off, he was whisper, a will to hope, a wish to find something worthy of laughter and song. . . . The sign of this man was a laugh, and his singing symbol was a drum-beat. . . . He was treading the sweat-flavored clods of the plantation, crushing out his drum tunes, and giving out secret laughter. He walked on the winds of sound. Then he took on flesh after he got there. . . . John de Conquer was walking the very winds that filled the sails of the slave ship. He followed over them like the albatross.[5]

Hamilton adapts this same story framework in *Pretty Pearl* with two important changes. First, she makes Pearl the initial hope-bringer in order to dramatize the great potential or promise this child protagonist has for her mission. John from the beginning distances himself from humans—and by extension from the slavery condition. If you go too near humans, he tells Pearl, you begin acting human yourself. He accompanies Pearl to America because he knows she needs his help, not because of any quest of his own. Second, she uses Hurston's albatross image in characterizing High John. ("John de Conquer always had a giant black crow or raven," Hamilton explains, "and Hurston may have elaborated on this image to produce an albatross.") But she does not show John following the slaves *like* an albatross, a bird of luck or good omen for his people. Instead he is drawn as the great trickster he will become when he transforms himself and Pearl *into* albatrosses, birds that no superstitious white slaver would ever shoot. Thus these sibling gods have safe passage to America, and the human slaves standing under such large, protective wing spans *see* the African gods who will be their hope and power in the New World.

Once in America, John and Pearl shed their bird disguises and each helps the other take the next step toward higher god plane. At her insistence that he do something for the slaves, John sends two of his spirits onto the plantations to whisper words of freedom and thus encourage slaves to "run." So de Conquer at this point emerges equally as Con-*care*, instructing Pearl in the tests she must pass to become god-woman.

She must learn patience so that she will grow strong enough not to need him when she journeys on, he tells her. She must lie in the "blood-red southern soil" (*MAPP*, 17), just as he does, for several centuries of human time (50 years of human life being half a god day). She must learn to live with sorrow, sadness, and even evil before she will be ready to take action. And she must understand that even god power has its limits. "A shape of a thing," he explains, speaking of Hunger (which Pretty in her impatience has tried to beat to death), "will always be" (*MAPP*, 29). One can only act to change or diminish the shape of hunger.

Hamilton chooses to keep her mythology here complementary to West African beliefs of this historical period, when the universe was believed to be peopled with primary gods and secondary spirits, such as ghosts and witches, and when the gods were considered generally noninterfering and limited in the nature of their power, or fallible, as in Greek mythology (many lessons in cross-cultural mythology arise for readers here). No one god could do all things; expertise ran in certain lines of action.

By creating a family of gods, however, Hamilton can produce a *unit* of power (similar to the sibling unit of the Justice trilogy) working for a common goal. John de Conquer is spiritual power, first *seeing* what will unfold for humans and then, as he tests himself for the next plane of god-father, intervening to change the outcome. John Henry is physical power or action *causing* the future to unfold. Uniting them is Pearl, potential power or growing power, striving to be where the future unfolds, to see, to *act*, to intervene—to become, in short, emotionally involved. Each power, actually a balance of power, will be necessary or crucial for African-American survival and success as the years—and the story—unfold.

Narrative Strategies and Thematic Vision

Years pass; the Civil War ends. And where Pearl lies waiting on a Georgia hillside she sees a group of freed slaves called the Inside People hiding in a dark, secret part of a distant forest, and she knows where her quest will take her. John gives her two dresses, or shifts, to wear at this time as she prepares for the journey, thereby bringing to light a fourth member of this god family, Mother Pearl, a future self-within-a-self adult character or parent figure who materializes in Pearl's place when Pearl needs to become the adult yet is conceptually not ready to do so.[6] The shift of larger size will fit the "maw" woman part of her, god-children, he says, having no parents, only "parts" that they must "fit": part god-woman, part god-mother, part god-child.

Placing the parent figure or "role" *within* Pearl rather than outside her, as with a real parent, in order to enlarge her capabilities is perhaps Hamilton's most ingenious choice. To the extent that the child protagonist exercises power, the child reader will be able to conceptualize his or her own potential power in the world. Her power is further extended when, to her great joy, she discovers that John will allow her to choose four ancient, invisible African spirits of his own to take with her and bring to life whenever she chooses, as long as she maintains control of them. She has the power, he tells her. It is inside her already. And the knowledge of what power is, how to find it and use it, will also come— and come from *her*, as she learns to "fathom" it (*MAPP*, 39).

Pearl chooses a powerful six-foot-tall woodpecker (the Fool-la-fafa), a dog with a sharp, curved tail for cutting trees (the Hodag), and just for fun an ugly two-headed monster (the Hide Behind), with power to scare enemies, as well as a young man-spirit, Dwahro, who can feel, tell, and know better than most spirits and who becomes a fifth member of Pearl's created family (a protective older brother). All four spirits are kept inside a root necklace John makes for her from a bush growing on his chest. She must wear the necklace in her travels, he tells her, and she must follow certain rules: she must promise the necklace to no one, take it off for no one, frighten no one with it (unless for self-defense), and never use it to hurt human children out of spite or anger. Also she must keep the "spirit" of the de Conquer legend, related to the African belief in root magic. "High John de Conquer went back to Africa," says Hurston, "but he left his power here and placed his American dwelling in the root of a certain plant. Only possess that root, and he can be summoned at any time" (Hurston, 96).

Folklorists today credit the root of the Marsh St. Johnswort (a folk charm against everything from rattlenake bites to witches and nightmares) as being this "certain" plant, but Hurston does not name it directly, and Hamilton makes the same choice. Naming in folk tradition gives power, says Walter Ong, speaking of the "magical potency" of words for people of oral or preliterate cultures. And "names do give human beings power over what they name: without learning a vast store of names, one is simply powerless to understand . . . all intellectual knowledge."[7] In the context of African-American culture and experience, naming of the de Conquer root, believed to carry spiritual power and thus freedom from oppression, would release power to all people, a definite risk for the oppressed. As Pearl later tells the spirit Dwahro, "We goin where de secret is secret and will stay secret. The peoples is had enough of plantations and bosses and chains!" (*MAPP*, 66).

Hamilton's choice of setting—the African-American culture of Reconstruction days—brings with it the challenge of reproducing as many characteristics as possible of orally based thought. "Fully literate persons," according to Ong, "can only with great difficulty imagine what a primary oral culture is like" (Ong, 31). Hamilton investigates almost every possible means of oral expression: song, proverb, chant, historical African-American dialect, and carefully balanced formulaic saying: "High John de Con-*care*. Making get-up out of lie-down. And worth out of worthless. Making drumbeats of the soul. Making spirits grow" (*MAPP*, 43). Thus she manages to re-create a basically preliterate culture where everything was transmitted by sound. But because in this particular culture survival meant secrecy or whispered sound, she must also show that oral expression was the primary conduit for communicating survival strategies and that rhythmical pattern provided a primary aid for recall.

Hamilton therefore makes use of other patterned strategies such as "listing," as used in folk tradition—to weave idea rhythmically through the tapestry of story. In chapter 6, when he names trees and items made from trees, Dwahro teaches Pearl about the forest and why it is such a perfect place to life. Thus he helps her to understand how the Inside People survive so well there. Listing was a particular sort of "aggregative," or clustering device, says Ong, that, like the formulaic expression, relied on balance and pattern to aid recall. It also relied to some extent on another practice, that of "redundancy" or "repetition of the just said" (Ong, 40)—a device to keep both speaker and hearer together, and one Hamilton applies liberally throughout the book.

In chapter 3 Hamilton's repetition of the word "forest" and certain phrases about the forest seems at first glance to function as setting traditionally does in any novel: to establish the mood, introduce an important symbol for the story, and illuminate the theme: "The forest loomed closer. It was immense and darkly still. . . . The forest ahead was like a black night rolling over upland" (*MAPP*, 47). "The forest sparkled and was magical" (*MAPP*, 54). "It knew no hard times. It knew no wrong, no war. But it recognized the sound and frenzy of kinds, human, good and bad. . . . The forest was" (*MAPP*, 55–56).

All traditional literary objectives are met here. The reader perceives a mood of mystery and power. The forest is also established as the symbol of ultimate power or life force, beyond human, beyond even god power ("It knew no wrong")—the same symbolic use that Susan Cooper makes of water in *The Dark Is Rising*: "And the Book taught Will here the patterns of survival against malevolence . . . and showed him how water was the one element that could in some measure defy all magic; for moving water would tolerate no magic for evil or good, but would wash it away as if it had never been made."[8]

Whereas Cooper's water defies all magic, however, the forest here *is* magic, endowed as it is with human presence, based on West African animism, according to Newbell Niles Puckett, which often locates the soul or spirit in the "haunted tree" (Puckett, 115–16). Thus the primal power of the forest is beyond good and evil and immersed in both, for it holds them both, as gods and humans hold potential for either within themselves. That is the reason the forest power can be harnessed for the cause of human justice and freedom—or for injustice. In the case of the former, Mother Pearl in chapter 5 will harness the power of the poplar tree (a tree Pearl has seen, in chapter 2, holding the charred shape that she recognizes as a lynching) for both good and evil—to tie up the bandits who threaten their lives.

Hamilton's repeated phrase "the forest" and her repetition of the word "was" has thematic implications for the power of the forest as life force to reproduce, grow, or replenish itself, or to be, no matter what evil (or good) is visited on it (echoing the power and security that Sheema feels about the National Forest in *A Little Love*). But here repetition of words goes beyond traditional literary or "textual" meaning to serve an additional function, one especially related to oral people who could not backloop to reread or cause a teller to retell. Readers or listeners, especially child readers, exposed to a passage filled with such redundancy are allowed to move ahead in the telling of the story at the same time they internalize complex thematic patterns that spiral through the passage or, in this case, the entire book.

It is significant that chapter 16, the third chapter from the end of the book, begins with the narrator's words, "The great forest was" (*MAPP*,

266), reiterating the phrasing of chapter 3 (a cultural, ecological reminder of the condition of deforestation then and now). Hamilton thus indicates that power and freedom can be reconciled if power and resources are shared. Then no one is oppressed. Promise, a place where each toiled for the good of all, is modeled on the concept of African village life, as well as Cherokee values that Old Canoe, the Amerind leader, expresses when he says, "No land is owned by any one kind. No man on earth is owned by any other" (*MAPP*, 139). When the ideas of Promise were replicated by the Inside People in the outside world, the result was success. Promise did not thrive because of self-aggrandizement, selfish motives, or unwise use of power. Thus, as in the Drear books, we have more "lessons" in ways that members of two group cultures can work together for economic survival: the black people grow the ginseng plant, and the Cherokee people transport it to the marketplace outside the forest settlement.

Chapters 3 and 13, as Hamilton has placed them in perfectly balanced distance from the beginning and ending of the book, delineate her thematic vision of the forest as ultimate power and undergird the entire novel, composed as it is of 18 chapters in a four-part setting. Each part comprises one segment of Pearl's journey down from the mountain and over the long human "Trail Home." Each part also reveals a different "being" of Pearl or a different stage in the growth process as she travels through each of the four settings: Mount Kenya, the outer Georgian forest, the inside forest village of Promise, and the outside world of the American Midwest. And, as always, the internal stories Hamilton weaves through the book produce a great deal more story "meaning" and learning about storytelling itself.

Inner Stories and Cultural Learning

In the first "part" (chapters 1 and 2) Pearl, god-child of Mount Kenya, journeys to America where, on a Georgia hillside, she receives her instruction from High John in how she will carry out her mission of helping the slaves. Taken together, these two chapters serve to introduce the entire journey (the major characters and the motive for the quest), as well as to foreshadow the potential dangers of innocence that await the quester. In chapter 2 John tells Pearl about his part in the Noah's Ark story (he pulled the plug, he explains, in this comic rendition, and everyone went down the drain.) The story functions to help Pearl and the reader see John's role in things generally. He takes care of the really *big* troubles—world affairs rather than smaller domestic troubles like the slavery era and the Civil War. His use of humor also helps take Pearl's mind off their parting.

In the second "part" (chapters 3 through 6) High John releases Pearl to her mission, and she enters the forest (with her two shifts and her two parts of Pretty and Mother Pearl) to test her strength and fulfill her quest. In chapter 3 Dwahro "reads" a story in the "tea"/tree leaves of the forest, and he learns what is happening now in the places they have just left (a metaphor for hindsight). In chapter 5 Pearl falls asleep, and Mother Pearl enters the story—stepping, literally and figuratively, out of Pearl's dreaming, subconscious mind. Things will soon be getting very rough when the bandits appear, and only the adult part of Pretty (the trickster as African conjure-woman) will be able to cope with them.

Mother stands before a poplar, a tree she describes as a "woman and yellow" because "she's so old" (*MAPP*, 75), and she asks Dwahro to paint—on her apron—a picture of her, with dyes she helps him to make from bark, leaves, and roots. (Many cultural lessons in African-American folklore emerge in this section: folk remedies, voodoo practices, snake conjuring, poisons, and root antidotes.) The metaphor of woman as poplar tree (echoes of the "cottonwoman" tree of the Justice books) connects Mother Pearl to the tree that will later save them when the illusion of the apron picture hypnotizes the bandits. After Dwahro draws the first picture on Mother Pearl's apron, he must draw another (on the apron of the first picture) on and on, picture within picture, in this nesting box configuration—or conjure trick.

Hamilton has been teaching many cultural lessons through metaphor up to this point. Gods and slaves are both birds of passage in this "middle passage" from Africa to America. The earth is a book to be "read" by Dwahro—or any sensitive "spirit." Pearl and Mother Pearl are not one person but two, child and adult, signifying that humans do break "apart" constantly, or fail to meet their "adult" potential when they succumb to the "child" in themselves. Mother Pearl is a tree: old, real, and female (nature and human connected). The apron picture is a "vision" of unlimited imagination (again the theme of all you can imagine is possible), or of the unfathomable mind. Because imagination is linked to art and art is linked to action, the implication is also that art, or the creative imagination, can produce change in the world, since the reverberating images of the infinity picture quell the bandits. Picture as story becomes a way of acting to shape or reshape lives—or social action.

In chapter 6 Dwahro starts to tell Pearl the story of what he and
Mother Pearl experienced when she was asleep. But she does not let him
finish; thus she never hears the "evil" story or deed of Mother conjuring
the bandits. (Innocence is maintained.) Dwahro tells stories about the
trees and plants they see, the types and their uses, thus informing Pearl
before they arrive at the "inside" place of Promise that the ginseng plant
gives the Inside People their self-sufficiency. She learns how it grows and
where, what it does, how it is used in medicines and folk remedies, and
how this plant, the color of gold, is also the "gold" of the Inside people
(their economic survival) when sold in the outside world.

In the third "part" (chapters 7 through 14) Pearl and Mother, now
two separate god entities, reach the deepest part of the forest, the hidden
settlement of the Inside People or Promise, where Pearl forgets she is a
god-child with godly responsibilities and lets the Hide-Behind out of her
necklace to scare the human children and show her magical importance.
This "part" is especially important for storytelling: 15 of the total 28
inner stories of the book occur here. In chapter 7 Mother Pearl tells the
human children the story of John de Conquer coming to America as a
bird—a story that turns John's life into myth for those who would not
understand his god state (his appearance in this place would be, like hers
and Pearl's, so "real" and humanlike). Thus Hamilton produces a lesson
for children in what a myth is (a story to explain the unexplainable).

Then the children identify themselves, calling out their family histories for Mother and Pearl ("sorrow" stories that teach a great deal about
black history and the way that Native Americans and black people inter-
mingled to produce biracial families). Mother Pearl's reception of these
stories is especially important as a model of respect for the oppressed and
the powerless. She listens closely to the stories, exhibiting her pride in
these children and in their backgrounds, no matter how unfortunate—a
godlike model for human behavior. She sheds tears for their lives; she is
so overwhelmed by emotion that she becomes closed up, unable to say or
do more at this point.

In chapter 8 we hear Black Salt's talk story, a history of the Inside
People and a description of the way the Inside place of Promise operates
(and why). Old Canoe's story of the Cherokee Trail of Tears emerges
next, along with his announcement that the people of Promise must
leave the forest now because the white man is building a railroad. The
two stories and ways of storying (the black and the native), in dialogic
terms, bring the connection of these two group cultures to light for the
reader. In the context of the fantasy Hamilton is weaving, there are 150

red people and 150 black people living and working together successfully here, and they are supported in friendship by 800 "others" on the outside who have some knowledge of them. The two stories also speak to
each other in their contrasted speech styles: the rhythmical patterned,
call and response cadences of Black Salt and the formal, stilted English
of Old Canoe, a discourse pattern that appears strange and unrealistic
but is well-documented in speeches given by Cherokee leaders.[9]

In this chapter also Mother Pearl tells Dwahro the story of how she
and Pearl separated as they entered Promise—and why—thus filling a
gap of chapter 6 (how Pearl and Mother Pearl suddenly materialize as
two people). As Mother explains to Dwahro, Pearl was not ready to put
on the adult shift at this point. Her own growing child needs (to play
and work with friends her own age, such as Josiah) were greater than the
need to be a mother to the children of Promise and to see the Inside
People through this time of trial—or to fulfill her mission.

In chapter 12 Mother Pearl interrupts Dwahro's story when she hears
John de Conquer's special drum, or "hypocrite" (*MAPP*, 212), in the distance telling its own story. A particular type of drum that sings or
"tones" many different sounds, "hypocrite"—a word from the Greek
hypocrites (an actor) and *hupokrinein* (to play a part)—signifies at least in
part here the versatile, trickster-transformer role of High John.

In chapter 13 John Henry arrives in Promise to tell the story of himself (a tall tale of course) and the story of what it is like in the outside
world now for black people (what they are doing, how many there are—
five million—what opportunities there are to progress and to help others). His story teaches more about black history and riles up the
listeners, who respond to the risk—but also the challenge. They *must*
leave, they see; it is selfish not to do so. They cannot hide now; it is a
new era of change (time to face life in the open now and to experience
the world in all its possibilities, good and bad).

In the fourth and last "part" (chapters 15 through 18) Pearl and the
Inside People leave for the outside world. In chapter 15 John de Conquer
appears for a secret meeting of the god-family in the deepest part of the
forest. There he retells the story of Pearl's mission—a comprehensive
summary for the child reader who is traveling through this heavily textured plot. Pearl's failure to meet her godlike responsibilities is made just
a little worse when High John reminds her that in forgetting her god-
child status, she shrank the large Fool-la-fafa bird, who was dwelling
inside the de Conquer root. When the Hide-Behind escaped, the root
necklace withered in size and power; thus the huge bird has turned into

an ordinary woodpecker. So we have embedded in High John's story a lit-erary bonus: Hamilton's "why" tale of how the woodpecker came to be.

In chapter 17 the Inside People are on their journey North when one night Mother Pearl tells Pearl the story of "everything" (*MAPP*, 283): "It was as if Mother Pearl was giving her many, many lifetimes of talking and storytelling" (*MAPP*, 281). But the story she tells is left as a blank space of text. Pearl does not know if she is asleep or awake as she listens. It simply *seems* to her as if Mother Pearl is talking to her and that she is talking too (an interesting way Hamilton has of introducing the possi-bilities of dream, reality, or clairvoyance into the main story line). At this point Mother Pearl places the infinity apron over Dwahro, Pretty, and herself, and when Pearl "awakened, she had in her mind the shape of that great old she poplar that Dwahro had painted. It filled her up like a legend" (*MAPP*, 281–82). A new notion is thus introduced: the trans-mission of story through the ancestral unconscious. Pearl has not yet told any stories of her own. Up to this point the book has been an effort to fill her with stories from almost every character, foreshadowing her later role of wordkeeper of ethnic heritage for the Perry family that she adopts or joins (named for Hamilton's mother's family name).

Next John Henry tells Pearl and Josiah about his work as a steel dri-ving man at the Big Bend Tunnel, a story foretelling his own death, since it indicates that he knows what he has chosen to do and that he will do it, regardless of any advice or warnings. His story is followed by the talk and stories of Old Canoe and Black Salt, signifying the end of their union. Old Canoe says that the Shawnee people will be taking over now as guides for the Inside People, and Black Salt gives thanks to Old Canoe for his help.

Finally, Mother Pearl tells Pearl the story of John de Conquer coming down from on high as an albatross. Pearl asks how John became a bird. She listens and continues to question, until she understands the story that Mother Pearl is telling—and changing for Pearl—because in her fallen state she has already forgotten her own part in the story (or her life as a god-child). In the last chapter we see Pearl grown very tall, holding herself "most proud" (*MAPP*, 306), and the Inside People looking at her with new respect as she walks back and forth before them, as storyteller of her people: "'One long time,' she began, 'de god came down from on high.' . . . Came down from Mount Kenya on a clear day . . . Best start over . . . 'One long time, Pretty Pearl came down from on high.' . . . She didn't know how she could make up such tales. But she could and they made her laugh inside. 'Be a god chile, then'" (*MAPP*, 307).

If Pretty does not know how she knows this story, we at least do know, for we remember the story that Mother Pearl told—the story we did not hear but that Pearl did hear in her half-waking, half-sleeping state—and that she remembers now and tells as her own creation tale. She also remembers John Henry's talk and stories, and she goes on this day to tell his story, to tell about Dwahro as a spirit long ago, and about de Conquer the hope-bringer tricking the plantation owner. The Inside People do not believe that any of is this is real, but they take heart from it and enjoy Pretty as a fine teller. Thus Hamilton shows how the old myths are *true*.

We of course see differently. We know Pearl as a god, because we knew her at the beginning on Mount Kenya when she *was* a god, and we have watched her growing as a precocious and naughty god-child into a spirited young godlike adult. Thus Hamilton shows at the same time how the old myths are *real*. How does she produce such a literary somersault? How does she turn story into myth and back again so that *we* believe the story at the same time the story characters—even Pearl—see it always as myth? Very possibly by creating Pearl as a fantasy character who is so realistic, in psychological terms, that she is neither an "impossible" notion nor merely a "possible" idea, but a definite *probability*.

Historical Folk Fantasy and the Human Growth Process

Hamilton's four-part structure and characterization of Pearl—the precocious god-child, the god-child struggling to become human, the god-forsaken child, and, finally, the realistic young adult human—can be understood most clearly if viewed alongside Jean Piaget's analysis of adolescent thinking. His analysis, in turn, may help to explain how children develop interest—and belief—in this complex and multilayered character.

As one child, age 11, listening to chapter 1 said, "If you're an adult, it's so easy. But if you're a kid, you have to do something hard to get more power. Like they have to prove themselves good when they're young, so when they grow up, they'll be good rulers." Another child, age 13, said, as the book ended and he "saw" Mother Pearl flying away, "Pretty Pearl's soul is now going back to the mountain. The god part went up. The human stayed down. Only one part of her became god, the part that had already passed. Like your childhood is now a spirit, like a god. And your child part of you is somewhere else in a different time zone. It's the past. Cause you're not that anymore. You grow up."

In *The Growth of Logical Thinking from Childhood to Adolescence* Barbel Inhelder and Jean Piaget speak of the age of preadolescence, ages 11 to 13 (Pearl is said to be between 10 and 12), as the beginning of formal, hypothetical, thinking. This "indefinite extension of powers of thought," according to Piaget, "is conducive to a failure to distinguish between the ego's new and unpredicted capabilities and the social or cosmic universe to which they are applied. In other words, the adolescent goes through a phase in which he attributes an unlimited power to his own thoughts so that the dream of a glorious future or of transforming the world through Ideas . . . seems to be . . . an effective action which in itself modified the empirical world."[10]

Pearl begins her journey in part 1 expecting her brother to transform the world instantly. Why doesn't he free the slaves and take them back home? she asks John when they reach America, to which he replies, thinking of the wider cosmic universe, that it will be done, but it must "unfold some more" (*MAPP*, 19). She is not willing to accept his idea of limited god capability or his idea that "when you start something, you must know how to finish it" (*MAPP*, 29). If she had his power she would surely use it now. She does not have his power, he knows; she needs to grow into it. And growth, in Piaget's view, is not purely an "addition process . . . of one new learned piece of behavior or information on top of another." It is a "decentering or a continual refocusing of perspective" (Inhelder and Piaget, 345), and objectivity, the opposite of egocentricity, also demands the restructuring or accommodating of multiple perspectives to one's original point of view.

Pearl's perspective about power—her own, John's, that of the gods, that of the humans here—undergoes such a restructuring as the novel progresses. Through observing within her dream-time in chapter 5 what Mother Pearl does when bandits threaten their lives, she learns the many different forms of power for the oppressed: power of knowledge, action, subterfuge, and magic. Once severed from Mother Pearl in Promise with knowledge or power no longer within, she must begin learning and discovering the human way—from experience. Awareness comes more slowly now. What have I done? Pearl keeps asking after she has let out the Hide-Behind to scare the children and the Hodag leaps out next and begins slicing up the forest trees.

Later in the forest High John spells out hard words that conjure in their power what she has done, and she remembers at last what she has forgotten. But even though she finally realizes her mistake, and even though John admits that in his own limitations he too has erred—"I thought you was ready for you own self before you were, prob'ly" (*MAPP*, 256)—it is still too late to go back. John can, however, help her to forget she ever was a god child, thus erasing her grief. And he does. Soon Pretty is simply "pretty" and happily unaware that she has traded immortality for humanity.

Pearl forgets that she is superior because of her god power, and in forgetting it she loses it. For even if gods are not always good, as Mother Pearl says, they are always great. And great does not mean merely powerful in Hamilton's scheme. It means the wise use of power—or responsible action. Humans at their best work at being gods. Gods at their best work at helping humans. At their worst (or most foolish), gods play or waste power at human games, trying as John Henry to beat an unbeatable machine, or as Pearl, to scare those less powerful than they. This is the point of High John's rule that Pearl must not scare children with the root spirits or play with her power: scaring children is wasting power.

Having lost her god power, Pearl must now discover the human "will" power that is still within her—not magical, but still important for helping people as her caring spirit first led her to do. This human power can be seen best in Piaget's concept of "personality" or, as he defines it, the "decentered ego." Decentering, or the path from adolescence to the true beginning of adulthood, according to Piaget, "takes place simultaneously in thought processes and in social relationships. But the focal point of the decentering process is the entrance into the occupational world or the beginning of serious professional training. The adolescent becomes an adult when he undertakes a real job. It is then that he is transformed from an idealistic reformer into an achiever" (Inhelder and Piaget, 346).

Pearl finds her closest peer relationship in Promise with the boy Josias who teaches her that the ginseng plant is not as miraculous as the de Conquer root, just as humans are not as magical as gods. Still, it is important for its healing power. Her learning about the plant finally leads to choosing the job of sang gatherer when she becomes a decentered adult in the outside world. The sang plant is what draws her so strongly back to her own god-child roots, lost to her now in human life but found once again (remembered best) in another hidden inside place, deep in the forest of the American Midwest, where she feels closest to nature and her de Conquer family roots. She assumes the role of storyteller also at this time—a role that allows her to use her pride to its best advantage in order to bolster her caring spirit.

The greatest experiment of *Pretty Pearl* is the character of Pearl in all her changing lights—the so promising child protagonist who falls when she should have risen, plays when she should have worked, and who does work at last, playing out her own story as she tells it. The novel's great success is also Pearl, this paradoxical character with a four-part presence who struts playfully over the last pages to reveal at last what her quest became, as well as an important meaning of the book: that only for the child in a state of emergent adolescence (with her pride of confidence in unlimited god power) could such a quest be set in motion. And only by others working with her could it be completed—others Hamilton has linked together as members of a family.

The family unit becomes the spiritual human bond, the power that connects all forms and shapes here—god, spirit, human, even plant, as when the poplar tree bends its branches to the will of Mother Pearl's plan or the ginseng bends toward the de Conquer root, feeling or sensing its force and recognizing a kinship to the strength of it. Family is also the power that is necessary to complete Pearl's quest, for it takes each member of this family working together to bring about such a great goal.

High John brings knowledge, caution, a balanced cosmic view, an all-seeing ability to tell the future and make spirits grow. John Henry brings the ability to risk, to spur the people to leave Promise when they learn the railroad will soon destroy this garden-in-the-forest Paradise. Mother Pearl brings untiring work and knowledge of how things work. Dwahro brings playful spirit-lifting spirits. Old Canoe and Black Salt bring strong but caring leadership. Finally, and most important, Pearl brings herself, gives herself to the people, comes down from on high, falls into humanness, to complete the quest.

Thus Hamilton has produced here as her most inventive mixture of genres a fantasy of time-travel in which mythical heroes of African-American folklore journey from Africa to the New World, extending their powers to help liberate newly freed American slaves, exiled in the forests of Georgia. And the heroine, a young black god-child, becomes in the end an immigrant child, who crosses the ocean to take on human status and remain on earth to adapt, to become assimilated, to extend her cultural heritage, and, finally, to recognize herself as an African-American child in the American Midwest, who imagines (quite accurately) that she came down from on high—one long time ago.

This is the reason Pearl's "fall" is really success and not failure and why the novel is one of hope rather than despair. Pearl can help the people best, it turns out, if she becomes one of them and remains one, sharing the luck of the de Conquer root and handing down the stories of her god-family. Only then can African god power become African-American human spirit, for only a former god-child could form such a bridge between sky and earth.

The story comes full circle at the end. Transformed once again into albatrosses, John de Conquer and now Mother Pearl, in the place of Pretty, are last seen flying toward a ship that does not carry black slaves this time but free black seafaring men. De Conquer whispers to her as he goes, "Now you take the human and the life part and be happy" (*MAPP*, 294). Pearl is happy, for she sees only a small part of what John Henry, in his great adult awareness of this forsaken god state, knows. "*Remember me*," he says to Pearl. And she does, as she tells the story later of this character in all his boastful humor, his grandiose size, his tragic dilemma—his love of the human condition and his acceptance that he cannot ultimately change his nature in order to live: "*Say I wasn't good and I wasn't bad. Tell 'em a man ain't nothin' but a man*" (*MAPP*, 300).

The strong portrait of John Henry, the rich adult cast of characters here, the protagonist who takes the complete journey from childhood to adulthood, the vast array of folk traditions, and the panoramic historical background all work together here to produce a timeless book for all ages. "Don't miss *Pretty Pearl*!" says Geraldine Wilson. "The book will provide you with magical spiritual moments . . . [and] it will introduce you to some very serious African American ancestors and cultural archetypes who inhabit a great history we should all know better."[11] Thanks to Virginia Hamilton and *all* her work, from *Zeely* to *Pretty Pearl* and beyond, we all do know several parallel cultures of America better. Consequently, we know America in all its diversity better too.[12]

Chapter Eight

Virginia Hamilton as Writer

If an author produces a work as complex and stimulating yet as accessible for children as *The Magical Adventures of Pretty Pearl*, the next question becomes, How does she manage to do so? With *Pretty Pearl*, as with so much of Hamilton's work, we see a storyteller and cultural teacher coming together in one person who always shapes an original—and surprising—work of literature. What makes Hamilton one of a kind? Who are her "successors"? What is her authorial vision for children?

Distinguishing Traits

"I do believe that I think in terms of stories," says Hamilton. Above all else, she has also said, she wants to tell a "really good story."[1] But "people, even imaginary ones, live within a social order" ("WS," 617), so her work does admit political and social beliefs, as well as racial and economic issues: "Everything that goes on in me and around me that I perceive as fresh and new lends itself to story-making."[2] And it is this "basic storytelling nature" (Rochman, 1021) that Hamilton feels produces an organic creative process in her work, whereby she writes in order to see how the story will unfold. Thus she is only one step ahead of the reader in knowing just what a character will do—or what will turn out to be "right" for the story. Essentially it is the characters who create both the familiar and the new: "I make the characters come alive," continues Hamilton, "and they tell the stories. They define the world in which they live" (Rochman, 1021). Thus her books produce a wealth of inner or embedded stories, inner stories serving a mimetic function.

The passage of time in the outer story imitates more accurately than it otherwise might the passage of time in the real world when we are taken into the character's own "narratizing" of experience. At the same time, inner stories serve to *transcend* the real world or to convey with stronger realism the story world Hamilton is creating. "From necessity," she says, "I try to create a world outside of time that lives on its own, so when you open a book the time begins. If you notice, in any book when people start thinking, time stops." (And since quite often in a Hamilton book characters think in terms of stories, inner stories often have the effect of pushing an entire story through the space of a very short time span.)

This intricate and virtually seamless quilting of stories moves the plot along and provides a richer thematic texture for the entire book (a favorite narrative technique of William Faulkner, Hamilton's favorite author). Says Hamilton, "Each of us has a story we tell ourselves . . . about something of value that we respect" ("EV," 376). That "something of value" for her is ethnic heritage: "I descend out of an age-old tradition of using story as a means for keeping my heritage safe and to keep safe also the language usage in which that heritage is made symbolic through story. . . . The first generation of bond servants from Africa . . . were able to save some of their various histories and cultures by adding their African languages, which they were forbidden to speak, to their newly acquired American English."[3]

So Hamilton tells stories to keep her culture and heritage intact. "I began my literature from the omission and not from a flash of a concept," she says. "I took what had been neglected or absent form the canon, which would be the black child, and ran with it . . . while searching the heart of the child within myself" ("EV," 369). At the beginning of her career, in 1968, Hamilton said that she became a writer—and a children's writer—because she *had* to do so. She had to give back to children what her own society had taken from her—her cultural birthright: "You have no idea what it meant to be young and black in America in my generation. It took its toll also on the image we held of our parents and grandparents. A dichotomy bordering on the schizophrenic must arise in a child who, to feel himself a part of society, learns to ignore his own folkways as well as his historical past" ("FN," 3–4).

Tradition and Influence

Hamilton was the first black writer to win the Newbery Award, in 1975; Mildred Taylor became her successor just two years later, and Walter Dean Myers followed in 1989 and 1993, twice becoming a Newbery Honor Medalist, just as Sharon Bell Mathis had been in 1976 and Patricia McKissack would also be in 1993.

If black writers benefitted from Hamilton's achievement, they and other American writers of parallel cultures might also benefit from Hamilton having won the Hans Christian Andersen Award. We might expect that Laurence Yep, having many traits in common with Hamilton (artistic integrity, challenging themes, complex and multifaceted characters, multicultural emphases, experimentation with a variety of genres, interest in ethnic storytelling and in family and extended families as his narrative subject), could stand as a successor to Hamilton, winning the Andersen Award at some future time.

Artistically, Hamilton works in the tradition of innovative writers everywhere—one filled with those whom M. M. Bakhtin might describe as "centrifugal" in that they reject the limiting "unification and centralization" (Bakhtin 1981, 270) of authoritative discourse (prescribed conventions, fixed rules, and rigid notions about genre) for the play of "creating a life for language" (Bakhtin 1981, 270). It is difficult if not impossible to separate realism and fantasy in Hamilton's books, so many surrealistic scenes and psychic experiences occur in them.

For Eva Glistrup of Denmark, the Hans Christian Andersen Jury president, it was this "felicitous blend of realism and fantasy"[4] that influenced her response to Hamilton's books. "Sitting there—reading and reading and reading—for many long Danish winter evenings," says Glistrup, "I was overwhelmed, moved to tears, and visionally impressed. I was not present in my home any longer. I was in Yellow Springs, Ohio. And there was not only one real world, there was something more. And I—a very rational thinking person, I believed in ghosts and other phenomena from what is called superstition" (Glistrup, 5).

Culturally, Hamilton works in the tradition of such highly talented, multifaceted black female writers as Rita Dove, Joyce Carol Thomas, Paule Marshall, Buchi Emecheta, and Toni Morrison—her ideas centered on extended and created families (often these families are cross-cultural and cross-generational) as small pockets of survival in an often large and unfriendly world. Hamilton's ties to Morrison, however, appear strongest.

Both Hamilton and Morrison were born in small Ohio towns and into storytelling families; both exhibit a strong sense of place and "rememory" time; and both often create elaborate designs of inner and outer stories in their books. Perhaps because of this early immersion in rural landscape, both produce novels of psychic realism and surrealistic setting, filled with eccentric characters having supernatural perception and sensitivity. Both have been fascinated with the flying-slave legends, and both have produced highly acclaimed fiction based on these stories. Both have explored in novels the effects of the Fugitive Slave Bill on the lives of actual slaves, and both have evoked strong reader response as a result. Both have focused on the ancestral female as a culture-bearer and the restless black male as cultural pathfinder. Both also create ambiguous endings for their books in order to draw readers into the ancient, participatory experience of communal storytelling.

In addition, both Hamilton and Morrison reveal an extraordinary love of language and language play, and both feel that this ability to use language imaginatively—particularly to invoke the language of African-American ancestors—is what distinguishes their writing. Both have also achieved the highest honor of their fields (Morrison the Nobel Prize, Hamilton the Hans Christian Andersen Award), perhaps in no small part because they reveal black experience fused with a larger, more far-reaching human condition. The characters of their books are often storytellers who ask such questions as "Who am I?" and "Where am I going?" Says Hamilton, "I write about children who struggle to define their own selves" ("EV," 375). And her characters, like those of Morrison, create their own far-reaching myths to impose order on a chaotic world, to make sense of a particular experience, or to perform miracles of survival in an increasingly precarious universe.

Artistically and culturally, Hamilton works most often in the tradition of inventive multicultural literature, generally creating (similar to writers like Maxine Hong Kingston and Amy Tan) genre blendings focusing on diverse enthnicities and on the need for maintaining one's heritage through storytelling. Her recent attention to innovative "bookmaking" (folk tale collections and retellings and the longer picturebook) attests to her desire to expand her canvas of rich cultural and historical pictures.

Writers like Patricia McKissack, Hamilton notes, stand as successors in the retelling of black folk tales. "I developed the short entry with commentary," says Hamilton, speaking of the authorial commentary with which she frames her folk tales. "Children could read the story; parents or other adults could read the background information. And it has had an important influence in the field. Books like *The Dark-Thirty* [1992] wouldn't have happened before *The People Could Fly*." Writers like Jane Yolen, herself a wordkeeper of ethnic heritage and an explorer of many genres and parallel cultures, might at some point stand as a successor in the creation of longer picturebooks. Yolen recently expressed interest in the form invented for *Drylongso*, Hamilton says.

Hamilton's introduction of the term "parallel cultures" into the current literary vernacular has been a strong influence for opening the doors of children's literature to children of various ethnic groups. The *Horn Book Magazine* has now instituted a column entitled "Books of Parallel

Cultures," edited by Rudine Sims Bishop—evidence of the growing trend in the field to give stronger visibility and critical attention to books about many ethnicities, especially those books of both high artistic merit *and* strong cultural authenticity. And the concept of parallel cultures promises to displace dichotomous thinking about "mainstream" and "nonmainstream" children in the future.

In the production of artistic language and thought-provoking themes, certainly all writers who wish to produce literature of the highest quality for children are Hamilton's successors. As Betsy Hearne has said, "Virginia Hamilton has heightened the standards of children's literature as few other authors have."[5] The importance of Hamilton's work, Hearne adds, "lies in taking artistic integrity as far as it will go, beyond thought of popular reading, but with much thought to communicating. This is a tradition which is accepted in adult literature and which must be accepted in children's literature if it is to be considered a true art form. With plenty of books that fit easily, there must be that occasional book that grows the mind one size larger" (Hearne, 354).

Hamilton in return praises Hearne, as well as Paul Heins and Zena Sutherland, for the teaching they have provided her in their critical reading and reviewing of her work. Editors have also been influential (Richard Jackson and Susan Hirschman of Macmillan in the beginning, Robert Warren of Harper later, and, most recently, Stephanie Spinner of Knopf and Bonnie Verberg of Scholastic), as have writers: "There is and was a stream of Carson McCullers, Eudora Welty, Ralph Ellison, William Faulkner, William Du Bois, and Robert Louis Stevenson in my work" ("EV," 372), Hamilton says.

Hamilton's continuous production of award-winning books, especially her dedication to the illumination of parallel cultures in America and around the world, frees other talented writers such as Sook Nyul Choi to become successors in relation to artistic innovation and cultural learning for readers. *Year of Impossible Goodbyes* (1991)—with its gripping story, its strong female characters, its quilting of inner and outer stories, and its bright threads of cultural heritage woven throughout—is as exciting for its vision of the world for children today as Hamilton's vision was some 25 years ago when she produced *Zeely*.

Authorial Vision

"I wrote *Zeely* to say to you that black is beautiful" ("FN," 7), Hamilton said the year after her first book was published. She also wrote

Zeely, as she later explained, because of a deep need to stay in touch with her own historical past at a time when she was, in her college years, separated from it. The subject of historical connections seen in *Zeely* gradually became "the progress of a people across the hopescape of America" ("ASR," 635). At the time she was creating her trilogy about Justice, she said she found herself curious about "survivors of all kinds" (Townsend 1979, 109). Some would survive the "cataclysm," she noted, but most would perish. "Is it chance or fate," she wondered, "that the few survive, or do they survive because of an inherent difference from the victims who go under? Who are survivors? Are they you and I, or something we hold within us, such as our grace, our courage or our luck? And could they be our genes?" (Townsend 1979, 109).

On the eve of the publication of *Drylongso*, over 12 years later in 1992, Hamilton returned to her notion of survival, although in many different ways through the years she had never left it, having so often dramatized themes of historical links, racial continuities, the human longing for connections and the human ability to imagine the impossible as a way of coping with an imperfect world. Perhaps it is her story of how she came to write this book that helps us to see best her vision. "I had the word ["drylongso"] in my mind for years before I wrote the book" ("LT"), she says, "drylongso" being the Gullah word for "drought." As she explains,

> I've always been interested in drought from the beginning of the Justice books. I think it comes from growing up on a farm, the kind of storms we had. I started thinking about drought and the duststorms of the 1930s. I thought it was going to be a book like that. But when I started researching, I found out that there have been very severe droughts every 20 years, somewhere in this country, and not too long ago. As long ago as 1975 or 1978 there was what they call a black duststorm in Colorado, and cars and the highway, everything, had to stop; nobody could see. After the depression and the dustbowl of the 1930s, conservative measures were taken, and certain areas were not to be farmed. A certain way of farming was outlawed, and it has been forgotten, so all of the grasslands are being planted again. You cannot plant those lands and keep the soil. And all that's forgotten. The soil we're losing—tons—thousands of tons a year of topsoil. And this was very interesting to me. There's only so much you can do for the age level of this book, so I do this story of a family on a drought-stricken farm, and it's a very nice story of a black family—the mother, father, a little girl.

Who would guess that the little girl, Lindy, is in many ways Hamilton herself, as this story-behind-the-story tells us: "K. J. Hamilton made the long rows with his hoe, and I'd drop the seeds in the row and I with my hands, we would cover the seeds with the sweet-scented ground. And look to the sky to let it rain" ("PS," 675).

Hamilton's vision of the world is a place where all colors shade into *green*. For some time now, she has been producing the very literature for children that Peter Hollindale says has been "missing"[6] in a world in danger of destroying itself. Says Hollindale,

> I would like to see a scaled-down, touchable literature of the almost here-and- now, in which the commonplace predations of humankind, the ones familiar to us, are seen to confront the life of the natural world and force us to choose; we can have nature, or our present human nature, but not both. . . . We need stories with events and settings which are inches away from the everyday, and near enough to shock. They might compel us . . . to recognize the choices and our own complicity in choosing. . . . Although a "dark green" literature cannot but pass a hostile verdict on the collective human performance of recent times, there is often a quite different and more challenging attitude in its presentation to children. . . . Paradoxically a literature of warning is written out of hope. (Hollindale, 18)

If we look closely at Hamilton's work we see clearly what a "dark green" literature looks like, exemplifying as it does four major qualities that Hollindale implies may form the ideological undergirding of such a literature: the picture of humanity "dangerously at the mercy of its political and technological artifacts" (Hollindale, 17); a "few rebellious individuals (often children)" at odds with the conformities of society, or "small group survival in remote and uninvaded places" (Hollindale, 16); the child as symbol or agent of potential change, or children untainted by the adult world who are caused "to think radically about their own species and the global habitat which it should but does not care for" (Hollindale, 127); and "non-intrusiveness" as a "unifying moral principle" (Hollindale, 15), or responsibility for other life forms replacing greed and self-aggrandizement.

M. C. Higgins the Great dramatizes well the first quality. *The Planet of Junior Brown* illustrates well the second. The Justice Cycle exemplifies the third. But it is in the fourth area—that of "non-intrusiveness" or concern for the interdependence of all life forms—that Hamilton's work in its entirety becomes especially intriguing and inventive.

Respect for the intersecting lives or biological "space" of all inhabitants of the universe (nonintrusiveness) emerges continuously in Hamilton's authorial vision, with story as a way of action for the characters to shape and reshape their worlds, and with action as a way for children to "story" their own lives (the life-giving power of story in either case). Thus storytelling becomes the experience Hamilton sets forth or brings to life in her work, in order to communicate ideas of how separate but intertwined life forms must find ways of surviving and thriving in an endangered world.

Characters tell stories to one another as "inner" story embeddings in order to transmit this cultural learning or to generate it. Sometimes an adult, an older child, or a more experienced peer tells stories to a younger or less experienced character—as in *Zeely, M. C. Higgins the Great, Pretty Pearl, Sweet Whispers, Brother Rush, The Mystery of Drear House, Drylongso,* and *Plain City*—to awaken the listener to his or her potential as a "player" on the life stage or to reveal for children their place in the cultural and familial life force (Pesty's story of the Indian Maiden and Brother Rush's story of his family past). Often characters create "rememory" times of childhood, as do Arilla, Buddy, Justice, Tree, and Anthony; or they create stories of their own (or "story" through their lives), as do Geeder, Cammy, Sheema, Willie Bea, Talley, Buhlaire, M. C., and Junior Brown, in order to puzzle out the life conflicts they are facing.

In the main thread of story characters act to produce the major story line of the book, which in turn presents for the reader alternatives to the global peril facing the characters. M. C. Higgins begins to build a wall to hold back the strip-mining disaster his family faces. Thomas of the Drear books learns from his father to fight ignorance and greed through friendship (nonintrusiveness generates caring and kindness). Zeely asserts herself against her father's homocentric cruelty to animals. And Justice accepts the mission of returning the Watcher to its place in Sona, as well as the power that lies ahead for her because of the extrasensory gift of her genetic heritage.

Storytelling, in all these forms, permeates the style, structure, and thematic focus of *The Magical Adventures of Pretty Pearl* to reveal the natural world not as a plaything for human enjoyment but as a grand space filled with others with whom we must learn to coexist if we are to survive. In this novel Hamilton reveals that learning to understand ourselves, others, and the entire planet will result from listening to the wisdom of elders and absorbing knowledge about the interconnectedness of human and spirit worlds, as well as about the natural world as a revered and powerful mystery (the ecological and medicinal properties of plants, the balance of the ecosystem, the power of those in the spirit world helping to make order out of chaos for those in the human world), and about the vital chain of story as it educates children about the past.

Hamilton's folklore collections all speak about the future being jeopardized if knowledge is not kept alive through story. And such novels as *M. C. Higgins the Great, Sweet Whispers, Brother Rush, The Mystery of Drear House, Cousins,* and *Arilla Sun Down* dramatize quite powerfully for child readers the influence in children's lives of adult wisdom, and of storytelling as a way of preserving the links between human and spirit world. The image of ghosts, of embedded ghost stories, and of characters as historical ghosts who slow the slide into oblivion of ethnic wisdom is prevalent in each of these books.

All of the children of Hamilton's books—as they listen to stories told by others, as they learn about the cultures from which they spring, and as they story their own way through the larger story—serve to urge, warn, and reveal to us, in subtle and artistic ways, that something needs to be done if our lives are not to be destroyed by environmental carelessness, universal greed, prejudice, ethnic quarrels, misuse of the earth's resources, and loss of ethnic heritage.

We can have nature, or our present human nature, as Hollindale reminds us, but not both. Hamilton's literature of cultural learning causes us to recognize that there is a clear choice. Definitely a literature of warning, with so many of its warnings coming to pass in greater numbers every year that her books remain in print, it is also, with all the young apprentices stepping forth from these pages as gifted "starters," a literature of very strong hope.

Notes and References

Chapter One

1. All quotations of Virginia Hamilton's statements throughout this book that are not attributed to a specific published source originate from my correspondence with her, phone conversations with her, or interview with her at Kent State University, Kent, Ohio, 3–4 April 1992.

2. "Ah, Sweet Rememory!" *Horn Book*, December 1981; 637; hereafter cited in text as "ASR."

3. Keynote lecture, "Let's Talk: Books for Children and Youth," Thirteenth Annual Book Discussion Day, Carnegie Library of Pittsburgh and the University of Pittsburgh, 18 April 1993; hereafter cited in text as "LT."

4. "The Knowledge," in *Paul Robeson: The Life and Times of a Free Black Man* (New York: Harper, 1974), xv; hereafter cited in text as *PR*.

5. "Further Notes on a Progeny's Progress," speech delivered at the Children's and Young People's Meeting of the New Jersey Library Association, 4 May 1968; hereafter cited in text as "FN."

6. Quoted by Hazel Rochman, Booklist, 1 February 1992, 1021; hereafter cited in text.

7. "Planting Seeds," *Horn Book*, November 1992, 576; hereafter cited in text as "PS."

8. In Harcourt, Brace, Jovanovich publicity brochure, HBJ Profiles, n.d.; hereafter cited in text as "HBJ."

9. "Portrait of the Author as a Working Writer," *Elementary English*, April 1971, 238; hereafter cited in text as "PA."

10. Telephone conversation with Arnold Adoff, 30 July 1992, at the Adoff home in Yellow Springs, Ohio.

11. Quoted by Jean Ross in *Contemporary Authors*, n.s., vol. 20, ed. Linda Metzger and Deborah Straub (Detroit: Gale Research, 1986), 209; hereafter cited in text.

12. "The Mind of a Novel: The Heart of the Book," *Children's Literature Association Quarterly* 8 (Winter 1983): 11; hereafter cited in text as "MN."

13. Paul Heins, "Virginia Hamilton," *Horn Book*, August 1975, 346–47.

14. Quoted by Marilyn Apseloff, in "A Conversation with Virginia Hamilton," *Children's Literature in Education* 14 (Winter 1983): 205; hereafter cited in text.

Chapter Two

1. Nina Mikkelsen, "Dilemmas of Censorship and the Black Child," *The Leaflet* 83 (Winter 1984): 17; hereafter cited in text.

2. *Zeely* (New York: Aladdin Books, 1986).

3. *Zeely* (New York: Macmillan, 1967); hereafter cited in text.

4. Barbara Hardy, "Towards A Poetics of Fiction: An Approach through Narrative," in *The Cool Web: The Pattern of Children's Reading*, ed. Margaret Meek, Aidan Warlow, and Griselda Barton (London: Bodley Head, 1977), 13; hereafter cited in text.

5. David Lodge, *Write On* (London: Penguin Books, 1988), 199; hereafter cited in text.

6. James Britton, *Prospect and Retrospect*, ed. Gordon M. Pradl (Montclair, N.J.: Boynton Cook, 1982), 105; hereafter cited in text.

7. Zora Neale Hurston, *Their Eyes Were Watching God* (1937; New York: Harper, 1990), 14.

8. Harold Rosen, *Stories and Meanings* (Sheffield, England: National Association of Teachers of English, 1984), 10; hereafter cited in text.

9. Myles McDowell, "Fiction for Children and Adults: Some Essential Differences," in *Writers, Critics, and Children*, ed. Geoff Fox (London: Heinemann Educational Books, 1976), 143; hereafter cited in text.

10. M. M. Bakhtin, *Speech Genres and Other Late Essays*, trans. Vern W. McGee., ed. Caryl Emerson and Michael Holquist (Austin: University of Texas Press, 1986), 91; hereafter cited in text.

11. Harold Rosen, "The Irrepressible Genre," in *Oracy Matters*, ed. Margaret Maclure, Terry Phillips, and Andrew Wilkinson (Philadelphia: Open University Press, 1988), 16.

12. Introduction to *The Newbery Award Reader*, ed. Charles Waugh and Martin Greenburg (New York: Harcourt, Brace, Jovanovich, 1984), xii.

13. Louise Rosenblatt, "The Transactional Theory of the Literary Work: Implications for Research," in *Researching Response to Literature and the Teaching of Literature*, ed. Charles R. Cooper (Norwood, N.J.: Ablex, 1985), 40; hereafter cited in text.

14. Quoted by George Nicholson, "The Trumpet Club Authors on Tape" (Holmes, Pa.: Trumpet Club, 1989); hereafter cited in text.

15. "Thoughts on Children's Books, Reading, and Ethnic America," in *Reading, Children's Books, and Our Pluralistic Society*, ed. Harold Tanyzer and Jean Karl (Newark, Dela.: International Reading Association, 1972), 61–62; hereafter cited in text as "TCB."

16. *The Planet of Junior Brown* (New York: Macmillan, 1971), 16; hereafter cited in text as *PJB*.

17. Wolfgang Iser, *The Act of Reading: A Theory of Aesthetic Response* (Baltimore: Johns Hopkins University Press, 1978), 169.

18. David Rees, *Painted Desert, Green Shade* (Boston: Horn Book, 1984), 168; hereafter cited in text.

19. *M. C. Higgins the Great* (New York: Macmillan, 1974), 36; hereafter cited in text as *M. C.*

20. Terry Davis, *Vision Quest* (New York: Doubleday, 1979), 55.

21. Eugene Linden, "The Last Eden," *Time Magazine*, 13 July 1992, 67.

22. "Newbery Award Acceptance," *Horn Book*, August 1975, 342; hereafter cited in text as "NAA."

23. Paulo Friere, *Education for Critical Consciousness* (New York: Continuum, 1973), 4; hereafter cited in text.

Chapter Three

1. Patricia Waugh, *Metafiction: The Theory and Practice of Self-Conscious Fiction* (London: Methuen, 1985), 2; hereafter cited in text.

2. M. M. Bakhtin, *The Dialogic Imagination*, trans. Caryl Emerson and Michael Holquist, ed. Michael Holquist (Austin: University of Texas Press, 1981), 314; hereafter cited in text.

3. *Arilla Sun Down* (New York: William Morrow, 1976), 12; hereafter cited in text as *ASD*.

4. John Bierhorst, *The Mythology of North America* (New York: William Morrow, 1985), 232; hereafter cited in text.

5. *Justice and Her Brothers* (New York: Greenwillow, 1981), 193; hereafter cited in text as *JHB*.

6. *The Gathering* (New York: Greenwillow, 1981), 25; hereafter cited in text.

7. *Dustland* (New York: Greenwillow, 1981), 9; hereafter cited in text.

8. "Reflections," speech delivered for the Eighth Annual Virginia Hamilton Conference on Multicultural Literary Experiences for Youth, Kent State University, 3 April 1992; hereafter cited in text as "Reflections."

9. Raymond Williams, Tressall Memorial Lecture in Writing in Society, 1982, quoted by Alex McLeod in "Critical Literacy and Critical Imagination: Writing That Works for a Change," in *New Readings: Contributions to an Understanding of Literacy*, ed. Keith Kimberley, Margaret Meek, and Jane Miller (London: A & C Black, 1992), 103; hereafter cited in text.

10. *Sweet Whispers, Brother Rush* (New York: Philomel Books, 1982), 9; hereafter cited in text as *SWBR*.

11. Joan Lidoff, "Autobiography in a Different Voice: The Woman Warrior and the Quest of Genre," in *Approaches to Teaching Kingston's "The Woman Warrior,"* ed. Shirley Geok-lin Lim (New York: Modern Language Association of America, 1991), 118; hereafter cited in text.

12. Wayne Booth, *The Company We Keep: An Ethics of Fiction* (Berkeley: University of California Press, 1988), 281.

13. Anne Cronin, "A Statistical Portrait of the 'Typical' American: This Is Your Life, Generally Speaking," *New York Times*, 26 July 1992, E 5.

14. Telephone interview with Virginia Hamilton, 2 December 1984, at the author's home in Yellow Springs, Ohio.

15. Newbell Niles Puckett, *Folk Beliefs of the Southern Negro* (Chapel Hill: University of North Carolina Press, 1926), 139. Puckett's source is F. D. Bergen, *Animal and Plant Lore: Memoirs of the American Folk Society* 7 (1899): 130.

16. Puckett, *Folk Beliefs of the Southern Negro*, 170. Puckett's source is A. S. Gatschet, "African Masks and Secret Societies," *Journal of American Folklore* 12 (1899): 208; hereafter cited in text.

17. *Dictionary of Folklore, Myth, and Legend*, vol. 1, ed. Maria Leach (Chicago: Funk & Wagnalls, 1949), 24–25.

Chapter Four

1. John Rowe Townsend, *Written for Children* (New York: Harper Collins, 1992), 276–77; hereafter cited in text.

2. Philomel publicity brochure (New York: Philomel, 1983), n.p.; hereafter cited as "Philomel."

3. Linda K. Christian-Smith, *Becoming a Woman through Romance* (New York: Routledge, 1990), 16–106; hereafter cited in text.

4. *A Little Love* (New York: Philomel, 1984), 7; hereafter cited in text as *ALL*.

5. Jonathan Culler, *Framing the Sign* (Oxford: Basil Blackwell, 1988), 166; hereafter cited in text.

6. Philomel publicity brochure (New York: Putnam & Grosset Group, Philomel Books, 1987), n.p.; hereafter cited in text as "Putnam."

7. *A White Romance* (New York: Philomel, 1987), 191; hereafter cited in text as *AWR*.

8. "Hagi, Mose, and Drylongso," in *The Zena Sutherland Lectures, 1983–1992*, ed. Betsy Hearne (New York: Clarion Books, 1992), 79; hereafter cited in text as "Hagi."

9. Toni Morrison, *Playing in the Dark: Whiteness and the Literary Imagination* (Cambridge: Harvard University Press, 1992), 72.

10. Bebe Moore Campbell, "Brothers and Sisters," *New York Times Magazine*, 23 August 1992, 18.

Chapter Five

1. "Everything of Value: Moral Realism in the Literature for Children," *Journal of Youth Services for Libraries* 6 (Summer 1993): 375; hereafter cited in text as "EV."

2. Gavin Bolton, *Selected Writings on Drama in Education* (London: Longman, 1986), 8–9.

3. *The Mystery of Drear House* (New York: Macmillan, 1987), 141–42; hereafter cited in text as *MDH*.

4. *Dictionary of Folklore, Myth, and Legend*, vol. 2, ed. Maria Leach (Chicago: Funk & Wagnalls, 1950), 1124.

5. *Willie Bea and the Time the Martians Landed* (New York: Greenwillow, 1983), 39; hereafter cited in text as *WB*.

6. John Rowe Townsend, *A Sounding of Storytellers* (New York: Lippincott, 1979), 109.

7. "A Toiler, a Teller," in *Many Faces, Many Voices: Multicultural Literary Experiences for Youth: The Virginia Hamilton Conference*, ed. Anthony Manna and Carolyn Brodie (Fort Atkinson, Wis.: Highsmith Press, 1992); read in manuscript; hereafter cited in text as "Toiler."

8. *The Bells of Christmas* (New York: Harcourt, Brace, Jovanovich, 1989), 59; hereafter cited in text as *BC*.

9. Margaret Meek, "Books for Teachers," *English & Media Magazine* 25 (Summer 1991): 37; hereafter cited in text.

10. *Cousins* (New York: Philomel, 1990), 27; hereafter cited in text.

11. *Drylongso* (New York: Harcourt, Brace, Jovanovich, 1992), 6; hereafter cited in text.

12. Kermit Frazier, review of *Drylongso, New York Times Book Review*, 22 November 1992, 34.

13. *Plain City* (New York: Scholastic, 1993), 140; hereafter cited in text as *PC*.

Chapter Six

1. *Anthony Burns: The Defeat and Triumph of a Fugitive Slave* (New York: Knopf, 1988), 177; hereafter cited in text as *AB*.

2. Julius Lester, *To Be a Slave* (New York: Scholastic, 1968).

3. "On Being a Black Writer in America," *Lion and the Unicorn* 10 (1986): 16; hereafter cited in text as "OB."

4. "The Known, the Remembered, and the Imagined: Celebrating Afro-American Folktales," *Children's Literature in Education* 18 (1987): 74; hereafter cited in text as "KRI."

5. *The People Could Fly* (New York: Knopf, 1985), 5; hereafter cited in text as *TPCF*.

6. Betsy Hearne, "Introduction to Virginia Hamilton," in *The Zena Sutherland Lectures, 1983–1992,* ed. Betsy Hearne (New York: Clarion Books, 1992), 73.

7. Ethel Heins, review of *In the Beginning, Horn Book*, January– February, 1989, 84; hereafter cited in text.

8. *In the Beginning* (New York: Harcourt, Brace, Jovanovich, 1988), ix; hereafter cited in text as *IB*.

9. *The Dark Way* (New York: Harcourt, Brace, Jovanovich, 1990), xi: hereafter cited in text as *DW*.

10. Alice Walker, *Living by the Word* (New York: Harcourt, Brace, Jovanovich, 1989), 31.

11. Nina Mikkelsen, "When the Animals Talked—a Hundred Years of Uncle Remus," *Children's Literature Association Quarterly* 8 (Spring 1983): 4.

12. *The All Jahdu Storybook* (New York: Harcourt, Brace, Jovanovich, 1991), 108; hereafter cited in text as *AJS*.

Chapter Seven

1. Lois Kuznets, "Susan Cooper: A Reply," *Signposts to Criticism of Children's Literature*, ed. Robert Bator (Chicago: American Library Association, 1983), 112.

2. Telephone interview with Virginia Hamilton, 2 December 1984, at the author's home in Yellow Springs, Ohio; unless otherwise indicated, additional comments by Virginia Hamilton in this chapter refer to this interview.

3. *The Magical Adventures of Pretty Pearl* (New York: Harper, 1983), 5; hereafter cited in text as *MAPP*.

4. "High John Is Risen Again," *Horn Book*, April 1975, 114.

5. Zora Neale Hurston, "High John de Conquer," in *Book of Negro Folklore*, ed. Langston Hughes and Arna Bontemps (New York: Dodd, 1958), 93–94; hereafter cited in text.

6. For an extensive discussion of Mother Pearl as adhering to the Great Mother archetype of African tradition and black female literature, see Margaret Bristow, "An Analysis of Myth in Selected Novels of Virginia Hamilton," Ph.D. diss., University of Virginia, 1991.

7. Walter Ong, *Orality and Literacy* (New York: Methuen, 1982), 33; hereafter cited in text.

8. Susan Cooper, *The Dark Is Rising* (New York: Atheneum, 1973), 92.

9. See John Ehle's recorded speeches of Cherokee leader, Major Ridge, in *Trail of Tears: The Rise and Fall of the Cherokee Nation* (New York: Doubleday, 1988).

10. Barbel Inhelder and Jean Piaget, *The Growth of Logical Thinking from Childhood to Adolescence* (New York: Basic Books, 1958), 345–46; hereafter cited in text.

11. Geraldine Wilson, review of *The Magical Adventures of Pretty Pearl*, *Interracial Books for Children Bulletin* 15 (1984): 17–18.

12. This chapter is a revised and expanded version of the article "But Is It a Children's Book? A Second Look at Virginia Hamilton's *The Magical Adventures of Pretty Pearl*," *Children's Literature Association Quarterly* 11 (Fall 1986): 134–42.

Chapter Eight

1. "Writing the Source: In Other Words," *Horn Book*, December 1978, 617; hereafter cited in text as "WS."

2. "*Boston Globe–Horn Book* Award Acceptance," *Horn Book*, February 1984, 27; hereafter cited in text as "BG."

3. "Hans Christian Andersen Award Acceptance," *USBBY Newsletter*, Fall 1992, 8; hereafter cited in text as "HCA."

4. Eva Glistrup, "Awarding the Hans Christian Andersen Medals," *USBBY Newsletter*, Fall 1992, 5; hereafter cited in text.

5. Betsy Hearne, "Virginia Hamilton," in *Twentieth-Century Children's Writers*, 2d ed., ed. D. L. Kirkpatrick (Chicago: St. James Press, 1985), 353; hereafter cited in text.

6. Peter Hollindale, "The Darkening of the Green," *Signal* 61 (January 1990): 18; hereafter cited in text.

Selected Bibliography

PRIMARY WORKS

Fiction, Biography and Folklore Collection

Zeely. Illustrated by Symeon Shimin. New York: Macmillan, 1967.

The House of Dies Drear. New York: Macmillan, 1968.

The Time-Ago Tales of Jahdu. Illustrated by Nonny Hogrogian. New York: Macmillan, 1969.

The Planet of Junior Brown. New York: Macmillan, 1971.

W. E. B. Du Bois. New York: T. Y. Crowell, 1972.

Time-Ago Lost: More Tales of Jahdu. Illustrated by Ray Prather. New York: Macmillan, 1973.

M. C. Higgins the Great. New York: Macmillan, 1974.

Paul Robeson: The Life and Times of a Free Black Man. New York: Harper & Row, 1974.

Arilla Sun Down. New York: William Morrow, 1976.

Jahdu. Illustrated by Jerry Pinkney. New York: Greenwillow Books, 1980.

Dustland. New York: Greenwillow Books, 1980.

The Gathering. New York: Greenwillow Books, 1981.

Justice and Her Brothers. New York: Greenwillow Books, 1981.

Sweet Whispers, Brother Rush. New York: Philomel, 1982.

The Magical Adventures of Pretty Pearl. New York: Harper, 1983.

Willie Bea and the Time the Martians Landed. New York: Greenwillow Books, 1983.

A Little Love. New York: Philomel, 1984.

Junius over Far. New York: Harper, 1985.

The People Could Fly. Illustrated by Leo and Diane Dillon. New York: Knopf, 1985.

The Mystery of Drear House. New York: Macmillan, 1987.

A White Romance. New York: Philomel, 1987.

Anthony Burns: The Defeat and Triumph of a Fugitive Slave. New York: Knopf, 1988.

In the Beginning. Illustrated by Barry Moser. New York: Harcourt, Brace, Jovanovich, 1988.

The Bells of Christmas. Illustrated by Lambert Davis. New York: Harcourt, Brace, Jovanovich, 1989.

Cousins. New York: Philomel, 1990.

The Dark Way. Illustrated by Lambert Davis. New York: Harcourt, Brace, Jovanovich, 1990.

The All Jahdu Storybook. Illustrated by Barry Moser. New York: Harcourt, Brace, Jovanovich, 1991.

Drylongso. Illustrated by Jerry Pinkney. New York: Harcourt, Brace, Jovanovich, 1992.

Many Thousand Gone: African Americans from Slavery to Freedom. Illustrated by Leo and Diane Dillon. New York: Knopf, 1993.

Plain City. New York: Scholastic, 1993.

Essays, Articles, and Speeches

"Ah, Sweet Rememory!" *Horn Book*, December 1981, 633–40.

" Anthony Burns." *Horn Book*, March–April 1989, 183–85.

"*Boston Globe–Horn Book* Award Acceptance." *Horn Book*, February 1984, 24–28.

"Changing Woman, Working." In *Celebrating Children's Books: Essays on Children's Literature in Honor of Zena Sutherland*, edited by Betsy Hearne and Marilyn Kaye. New York: Lothrop, Lee & Shepard Books, 1981.

"Everything of Value: Moral Realism in the Literature for Children." May Hill Arbuthnot Honor Lecture, Richmond, Virginia, 4 May 1993. *Journal of Youth Services in Libraries* 6 (Summer 1993): 363–77.

"Further Notes on a Progeny's Progress." Speech delivered at the Children's and Young People's Meeting of the New Jersey Library Association, 4 May 1968.

"Hagi, Mose, and Drylongso." In *The Zena Sutherland Lectures, 1983–1992*, edited by Betsy Hearne. New York: Clarion Books, 1992.

"Hans Christian Andersen Award Acceptance." *USBBY Newsletter* 18 (Fall 1992): 6–8.

"HBJ Profiles." Harcourt, Brace, Jovanovich publicity brochure, n.d.

"High John Is Risen Again." *Horn Book*, April 1975, 113–21.

"Introduction." *The Newbery Award Reader*, edited by Charles Waugh and Martin Greenburg, xi–xiii. New York: Harcourt, Brace, Jovanovich, 1984.

"The Knowledge." In *Paul Robeson: The Life and Times of a Free Black Man*, x–xvi. New York: Harper, 1974.

"The Known, the Remembered, and the Imagined: Celebrating Afro-American Folktales." *Children's Literature in Education* 18 (1987): 67–75.

"Let's Talk: Books for Children and Youth." Thirteenth Annual Book Discussion Day, Carnegie Library of Pittsburgh and the University of Pittsburgh, Pittsburgh, Pennsylvania, 18 April 1993.

"The Mind of a Novel: The Heart of the Book." *Children's Literature Association Quarterly* 8 (Winter 1983): 10–14.

"Newbery Award Acceptance." *Horn Book*, August 1975, 337–43.

"On Being a Black Writer in America." *Lion and the Unicorn* 10 (1986): 15–17.

Philomel publicity brochure. New York: Philomel, 1983.

Philomel publicity brochure. New York: Putnam & Grosset Group; Philomel
    Books, 1987.
"Planting Seeds." *Horn Book*, November 1992, 674–80.
"Portrait of the Author as a Working Writer." *Elementary English*, April 1971,
    237–40.
"Reflections." Speech delivered at the Eighth Annual Virginia Hamilton
    Conference on Multicultural Literary Experiences for Youth, Kent State
    University, Kent, Ohio, 3 April 1992.
"Thoughts on Children's Books, Reading, and Ethnic America." In *Reading,
    Children's Books, and Our Pluralistic Society*, edited by Harold Tanyzer and
    Jean Karl, 61–64. Newark, Dela.: International Reading Association,
    1972.
"A Toiler, a Teller." In *Many Faces, Many Voices: Multicultural Literary Experiences
    for Youth: The Virginia Hamilton Conference*, edited by Anthony Manna and
    Carolyn Brodie. Fort Atkinson, Wis.: Highsmith Press, 1992; read in
    manuscript.
"Writing the Source: In Other Words." *Horn Book*, December 1978, 609–19.

SECONDARY WORKS

Interviews

Apseloff, Marilyn. "A Conversation with Virginia Hamilton." *Children's
    Literature in Education* 14 (Winter 1983): 204–13. Perceptive questions
    and richly textured answers about the fiction through *Junius over Far*.
Mikkelsen, Nina. "A Conversation with Virginia Hamilton." *Journal of Youth
    Services in Libraries*, (Spring, 1994). Focuses on Hamilton's work through
    Plain City and on her creative process.
Nicholson, George. "The Trumpet Club Authors on Tape." Holmes, Pa.:
    Trumpet Club, 1989. Insights into *The Planet of Junior Brown* and other
    books.
Rochman, Hazel. "The Booklist Interview." *Booklist*, 1 February 1992,
    1020–21. Insights into Hamilton as storyteller and about black authors
    writing outside the black experience.
Ross, Jean. "CA Interview." *Contemporary Authors*, n.s., vol. 20, edited by Linda
    Metzger and Deborah Straub, 208–12. Detroit: Gale Research, 1986.
    Information about *The People Could Fly* and other books before it.

Books

Townsend, John Rowe. *Written for Children*. New York: HarperCollins, 1992.
    Sections about Hamilton throughout the book offer enlightening com-
    mentary on the fiction through *A Little Love*.

Articles and Parts of Books

Apseloff, Marilyn. "Creative Geography in the Ohio Novels of Virginia Hamilton." *Children's Literature Association Quarterly* 8 (Spring 1983): 17–20. Investigates the way setting reveals character and mood in the fiction from *Zeely* to *Sweet Whispers, Brother Rush*.

Bishop, Rudine Sims. "Books from Parallel Cultures: Celebrating a Silver Anniversary." *Horn Book*, March–April 1993, 175–81. Discussion of the journey from *Zeely* to the Hans Christian Andersen Award Ceremony.

Glistrup, Eva. "Awarding the Hans Christian Andersen Medal." *USBBY Newsletter* 18 (Fall 1992): 4–6. On Hamilton's significant contribution to the field of children's literature worldwide.

Hearne, Betsy. "Introduction to Virginia Hamilton." *The Zena Sutherland Lectures, 1983–1992,* edited by Betsy Hearne, 71–74. New York: Clarion Books, 1992. On what makes Hamilton's works different and special.

———. "Virginia Hamilton." In *Twentieth-Century Children's Writers*, 2d ed., edited by D. L. Kirkpatrick, 353–354. Chicago: St. James Press, 1985. On the artistic integrity of the fiction from *Zeely* through *Sweet Whispers, Brother Rush*.

Heins, Paul. "Virginia Hamilton." *Horn Book*, August 1975, 344–48. Details about Hamilton's life and literary influences at the time of the Newbery Award.

Mikkelsen, Nina. "But Is It a Children's Book? A Second Look at Virginia Hamilton's *The Magical Adventures of Pretty Pearl*." *Children's Literature Association Quarterly* 11 (Fall 1986): 134–42. Discussion of what makes a children's book good in terms of Hamilton's work.

———. "Dilemmas of Censorship and the Black Child." *The Leaflet* 83 (Winter 1984): 15–28. History of the black child in children's books that includes a comparison of an E. L. Konigsburg novel of 1967 with Hamilton's *Zeely*.

———. "A Place to Go To: International Fiction for Children." *Canadian Children's Literature* 35–36 (1984): 64–68. Three fictional patterns of adjustment for immigrant children; discussion of Pretty Pearl as immigrant child.

Moore, Opal, and Donnarae MacCann. "The Uncle Remus Travesty, Part II: Julius Lester and Virginia Hamilton." *Children's Literature Association Quarterly* 11 (Winter 1986–87): 205–10. Informative discussion of the Jahdu books.

Moss, Anita. "Frontiers of Gender in Children's Literature." *Children's Literature Association Quarterly* 8 (Winter 1983): 25–28. Intersections of race and gender in *Arilla Sun Down* in terms of feminist theories of androgyny.

———. "Mythical Narrative: Virginia Hamilton's *The Magical Adventures of Pretty Pearl*." *Lion and the Unicorn* 9 (1985): 50–57. Sees the novel as reversing the traditional pattern of African myth: God is a female child rather than the all-powerful male.

Nodelman, Perry. "Balancing Acts: Noteworthy American Fiction." In *Touchstones: Reflections on the Best in Children's Literature*, vol. 3, edited by Perry Nodelman, 164–71. West Lafayette, Ind.: Children's Literature Association, 1989. Describes Hamilton as America's foremost modern children's writer, with any one of her works deserving of "touchstone" or classic status.

———. "Children's Literature as Women's Writing." *Children's Literature Association Quarterly* 13 (Spring 1988): 31–34. Argues that M. C.'s masculinity is "dissipated" rather than "integrated" and does not produce an androgynous state.

———. "The Limits of Structure." *Children's Literature Association Quarterly* 7 (Fall 1982): 45–48. Compares Toni Morrison's *Song of Solomon* and Hamilton's *M. C. Higgins the Great* in terms of reader expectations about form and structure.

Rees, David. "Long Ride through a Painted Desert." In *Painted Desert, Green Shade*, 168–84. Boston: Horn Book, 1984. Offers provocative reactions to the fiction from *Zeely* to *Sweet Whispers, Brother Rush*.

Russell, David. "Virginia Hamilton's Symbolic Presentation of Afro-American Sensibility." *Cross-Culturalism in Children's Literature*, edited by Susan Gannon and Ruth Anne Thompson, 71–75. Pleasantville, N.Y.: Pace University, 1988. Discussion of *M. C. Higgins the Great* in terms of communal heritage and family bonds.

Sims [Bishop], Rudine. "The Image Makers." In *Shadow and Substance*, 86–90. Urbana, Ill.: National Council of Teachers of English, 1984. Discusses the early fiction and Hamilton's ability to emphasize the positive aspects of growing up black in America. Discussion continues in *Teaching Multicultural Literature*, edited by Violet Harris. Norwood, Mass.: Christopher Gordon, 1993.

Townsend, John Rowe. "Virginia Hamilton." In *A Sounding of Storytellers*, 97–110. New York: Lippincott, 1979. Perceptive commentary on the fiction from *Zeely* to *Arilla Sun Down*, with an end note by Hamilton.

White, Mary Lou. "The 1992 Hans Christian Andersen Awards Ceremony: A Personal Reminiscence." *USBBY Newsletter* 18 (Fall 1992): 9. Detailed report of the Hans Christian Andersen Award Ceremony and White's reflections about prizing. See also Jeff Garret, "Reflection of a Jurist," *USBBY Newsletter*, 17 (Spring 1992): 3

Index

Adoff, Arnold, 7–8

Bakhtin, M. M., 18, 75, 145
Bell, Sharon, 10, 144
Bierhorst, John, 47–48
Bishop, Rudine Sims, 147
Bolton, Gavin, 90
Bontemps, Arna, 10
Booth, Wayne, 63
Britton, James, 14, 18
Brown, Henry, 117

Campbell, Bebe Moore, 87
Choi, Sook Nyul, 147
Christian-Smith, Linda, 72
Clifton, Lucille, 10
Cooper, Susan, 132
Culler, Jonathan, 76

Davis, Lambert, 100, 121
Dillon, Leo and Diane, 61, 116, 118
Douglass, Frederick, 58
Dove, Rita, 145
Doyle, Arthur Conan, 3
Du Bois, W. E. B., 3

Emecheta, Buchi, 145

Faulkner, William, 144, 147
Feelings, Tom and Muriel, 10
Friere, Paulo, 38

Garner, Margaret, 117
Glistrup, Eva, 145
Greenfield, Eloise, 10

Hamilton, Etta Belle (mother), 3, 9, 101
Hamilton, Kenneth (father), 2–4
Hamilton, Virginia: African-Americans as
    subjects in the works of, 10–11, 65,
    71, 77–78, 100–101, 106, 115,
    123–24; African-American folk
    imagery in the works of, 107–8,
118–22, 124, 125, 126–29, 130–31,
150–51; African-American speech
patterns, 70; child abuse as theme in
the works of, 65; childhood of, 1–6;
development as writer of, 6–8; ecology as theme in the works of, 38–39,
92–93, 148–51; editors of, 7–8, 147;
family life of, 7–9; homelessness as
theme in the works of, 19–20, 112; as
influence, 146–47; inspirations of,
147–50; international folk tales in the
works of, 120–22; inventive language
use of by, 28–29, 47, 49–54, 70, 119,
121, 131–33, 147; liberation literature of, 114, 115, 117–18; literary
influences of, 3, 144, 147; major
themes in the works of, 40, 149–51;
metafiction in the works of, 42; narrative abilities of, 143–44; parallel cultures, concept of for, 40, 100–101,
146–47; psychic power in the works
of, 41, 48–49, 59; recognition of,
145; rememory, concept of for, 1, 8,
42–45, 61–64, 145; slavery as subject
in the works of, 91–92, 118–20,
127–29; storytelling in the life of,
1–2, 4–5, 144; storytelling in the
works of, 143–44, 150–51

WORKS
Anthony Burns, 115–16
Arilla Sun Down, rememory in,
    44–48; story framing in, 42–44;
    themes of, 31, 47–48; use of sto-
    ries in, 44–47
Bells of Christmas, The, African-
    American theme of, 100–101; as
    picture book, 100–102; setting in,
    88, 101
Cousins, characterization in, 31; inspi-
    ration for, 9; setting in, 88, 102;
    unusual plot of, 105–6; use of sto-
    ries in, 102–5
Dark Way, The, 120–22

Drear Books (*The House of Dies Drear*; *The Mystery of Drear House*), cultural history in, 91–93; ecology as theme in, 92–93; inspiration for, 3; plots of, 88–91; setting of, 88; slavery as theme in, 91–93; use of stories in, 89–90, 150

Drylongso, African-American folk tradition in, 107–8; plot of, 106; setting of, 88, 108; themes of, 109, 148; use of metaphor in, 107; use of stories in, 108-109

Du Bois, W. E. B., 117

In the Beginning, 120–22

Jahdu Books (*The Time-Ago Tales of Jahdu*; *Time-Ago Lost: More Tales of Jahdu*; *The All Jahdu Storybook*), 123–24

Junius over Far, 69

Justice Cycle (*Justice and Her Brothers*; *Dustland*; *The Gathering*), cultural learning in, 56–58; narrative framework of, 49–53; use of language in, 50–54; use of stories in, 56–58

Little Love, A, cultural learning in, 74–77; narrative framework of, 73–77; romance code in, 69, 71–73; use of black English in, 70; use of stories in, 73–76

Magical Adventures of Pretty Pearl, The, African-American folk imagery in, 125, 126–29, 130–31; characterization in, 31, 138–42; cultural learning in, 134–38, 150–51; as fantasy, 125, 126; narrative structure of, 129–38; setting of, 131; themes of, 127–29, 132–33, 137, 139–40; use of stories in, 133–38, 140–41

M. C. Higgins the Great, creative process in, 27–31; cultural learning in, 38–40; indeterminacies in, 35–38; inspiration for, 4, 5, 7; narrative framework of, 30–37; role of stories in, 31–38; themes of, 27, 28, 38–40, 46, 69

Many Thousand Gone, 116–17

People Could Fly, The, 9, 118–20

Plain City, as female bildungsroman, 114; characterization in, 31, 109–10; homelessness as subject in, 19, 112; inspiration for, 7; narrative framework of, 110–12; racial prejudice as theme in, 112–13; setting of, 88; use of story in, 113–14

Planet of Junior Brown, The, cultural learning in, 21; homelessness as subject in, 19–20, 21; narrative framework of, 22–27, 28, 29; role of stories in, 24–27; themes of, 20–24

Robeson, Paul, 117

Sweet Whispers, Brother Rush, Afro-centrism in, 66–68; cultural learning in, 63–68; ghosts as subjects in, 66–67; narrative framework of, 60–65; themes of, 60, 65; use of stories in, 60–61, 67

White Romance, A, biracial theme in, 77–78; cultural learning in, 84–87; romance code in, 69, 78–84, 85–86; use of stories in, 81–84

Wille Bea and the Time the Martians Landed, cultural learning in, 98–100; inspiration for, 2; plot of, 93–97; role of family in, 93, 98, 100; setting in, 88, 97–98, 102; use of stories in, 95–98

Zeely, African-American heritage in, 10–11, 15; cultural learning in, 18; female roles in, 15, 19; inspiration for, 3; narrative framework of, 13–14, 16–19; plot of, 14–17; themes of, 10, 15–16; use of stories in, 13–19

Hans Christian Andersen Award, 144–45

Hardy, Barbara, 13

Harris, Joel Chandler, 123

Haydn, Hiram, 7

Hearne, Betsy, 147

Heins, Ethel, 120, 121

Heins, Paul, 147

Hollindale, Peter, 149, 151
Horn Book Magazine, 146–47
Hurston, Zora Neale, 15, 128, 130

Inhelder, Barbel, 139
Iser, Wolfgang, 25, 29, 38

Jackson, Richard, 7, 147
Jordan, June, 10

Kingston, Maxine Hong, 60, 66, 146
Kuznets, Lois, 125–26

Lester, Julius: *To Be a Slave*, 117
Lidoff, Joan, 60, 66
Lodge, David, 14, 75–76

McDowell, Myles, 17
McKissack, Patricia, 144, 146
McLeod, Alex, 59
Marshall, Paule, 145
Mathis, Sharon Bell, 10, 144
Meek, Margaret, 101–2
Miller, Warren: *The Cool World*, 61
Morrison, Toni, 83, 145–46
Moser, Barry, 120, 123
Myers, Walter Dean, 144

Newbery Award, 144
Newbery Award Reader, The, 34

Ong, Walter, 130–31

Perry, Levi, 4–5, 9
Piaget, Jean, 139, 140
Pinkney, Jerry, 11, 108
Porphyria, 61, 64–65, 68
Puckett, Newbell Niles, 132

Rees, David, 27
Rosen, Harold, 17, 18
Rosenblatt, Louise, 19

Shimin, Symeon, 11
Steptoe, John, 10
Sutherland, Zena, 147

Taylor, Mildred, 10, 144
Thomas, Joyce Carol, 145
Townsend, John Rowe, 70

Walker, Alice, 123
Waugh, Patricia, 42
Welles, Orson, 93–94
Wells, H. G.: *The War of the Worlds*, 97
Williams, Raymond, 59
Wilson, Geraldine, 142
Works Progress Administration, 118

Yellow Springs, Ohio, 1–2, 8–9, 97–98, 101
Yep, Laurence, 144–45
Yolen, Jane, 146

The Author

Nina Mikkelsen received her Ph.D. in English from Florida State University and has completed postdoctoral work in children's literature at Ohio State University and the Columbia University School of Library Science. She has taught at universities in Florida, North Carolina, and Pennsylvania. Her research interests have focused on children's responses to literature, the storymaking processes of children, literature-based reading programs and holistic learning, cross-cultural literature for children, American folk literature, and the black child in children's literature. Her articles have appeared in *Language Arts, Children's Literature Association Quarterly, Reading Teacher, Canadian Children's Literature, The Leaflet,* and *Journal of Youth Services in Libraries.* She lives in Indiana, Pennsylvania.

The Editor

Ruth K. MacDonald is associate dean of Bay Path College. She received her B.A. and M.A. in English from the University of Connecticut, her Ph.D. in English from Rutgers University, and her M.B.A. from the University of Texas at El Paso. She is author of the volumes on Louisa May Alcott, Beatrix Potter, and Dr. Seuss in Twayne's United States and English Authors Series and of the book *Literature for Children in England and America, 1646–1774* (1982).